# The curriculum in the middle years

SCHOOLS COUNCIL **WORKING PAPER 55**

# The curriculum in the middle years

the second report from the Schools Council
Middle Years of Schooling Project
Department of Educational Research
University of Lancaster

## A. M. Ross, A. G. Razzell and E. H. Badcock

Evans/Methuen Educational

*First published 1975 for the Schools Council*
*by Evans Brothers Limited*
*Montague House, Russell Square, London WC1B 5BX*
*and Methuen Educational Limited*
*11 New Fetter Lane, London EC4P 4EE*

*Distributed in the US by Citation Press*
*Scholastic Magazines Inc., 50 West 44th Street*
*New York, NY 10036*
*and in Canada by Scholastic–NAB Publications Ltd*
*123 Newkirk Road*
*Richmond Hill, Ontario*

ISBN 0 423 50250 6

*Printed in Great Britain by*
*Richard Clay (The Chaucer Press) Ltd*
*Bungay, Suffolk*

# Contents

... the reason why some of the useful subjects ought
to be taught to children – for example, reading and writing –
is not only the fact of their being useful:
it is also the fact that they make it possible
to acquire many other branches of knowledge.

ARISTOTLE, *Politics*, viii, 3, 37–40

# Preface

This report marks the conclusion of the Middle Years of Schooling Project, based at the University of Lancaster, 1968–72, and as project director I wish to thank the many individuals who have helped to shape the ideas expressed in this and our earlier report published as Schools Council Working Paper 42, *Education in the Middle Years* (Evans/Methuen Educational, 1972). Many hundreds of teachers gave up countless hours to discuss and criticize our early papers, and the leaders of these groups provided reports which we found very helpful. At the hundreds of conferences and meetings we have addressed, teachers have helped us to refine our ideas and have described to us the variations which exist in different parts of the country. Many teachers have extended to us the privilege of being allowed to visit them in their schools to observe for ourselves something of the rich variety of professional skill embraced by the term 'learning in the middle years of schooling'. We have made demands upon many people – inspectors, organizers, education officers and the officers of other projects. We owe a particular debt to the members of the Schools Council subject committees who prepared papers for us, though in fairness to them and to the Schools Council itself we have to point out that we alone are responsible for the views put forward in the pages which follow. Such a statement is, perhaps, particularly necessary in a document which inevitably deals with judgements for many of which there is no objective scale of assessment. Our colleagues in Lancaster have made their own distinctive contribution and we have been assisted greatly by our colleagues in the Schools Council. The members of our consultative committee, under the chairmanship of Sir Lincoln Ralphs, provided us with a well-judged balance of caution, encouragement, supervision, discipline and, above all, support. At least we cannot say, unlike the Hollywood actress, that our best work is on the cutting-room floor, and we are grateful to a hard-reading committee which, whatever the infelicities which remain (and for which we alone accept responsibility), did manage to eliminate most of our extravagances.

Finally I wish to record my thanks to those who were members of the team. Mr Arthur Razzell as Senior Project Officer in charge of the day-to-day work made that unique contribution which was to be expected from such an abundant personality as his – which has found its next outlet in the headship of a middle school. The other project officers, some of whom stayed briefly and others much longer, were, in order of appointment, Miss Irene Farmer, Mr Ernie Badcock, Mr Brian Daniels and Mr John Islip. To them and to the several secretaries who served us I extend my personal thanks and appreciation.

ALEC ROSS
*University of Lancaster*

7

# Introduction

The argument in this report builds on that presented in the project's first report *Education in the Middle Years* (Evans/Methuen Educational, 1972). For this reason there is some overlap. The first report focused on the broad educational issues which lie behind any view taken of schooling in the middle years. It underlined the professional responsibility of the teacher in making judgements about what should be learned. As a way into the decision-making process, it recommended a rational, systematic approach through an examination and clarification of aims and the formulation, wherever possible, of educational objectives across and within the curriculum. There was a plea for continuity in curriculum content and method in schools catering for the middle years, a stress on the process rather than the content of education, a claim that premature specialization should be avoided and that in consequence educational options should be kept open.

This second report is concerned more specifically with the content of the curriculum. Clearly different types of question can be raised about curriculum decisions in any school and some are more pertinent to the work of schools educating children between the ages of 8 and 13 than others. There are, for example, questions concerning the relative distribution of power, status, and authority in different schools and the extent to which these are shared – that is to say, questions concerning the procedures which result in the making of curricular decisions. There are related questions about the different levels of significance of decisions, from the executive, relatively long-term decisions of the headteacher or head of department, down to the day-to-day minutiae of decisions taken by individual teachers working alone or in a team. A discussion of power, status, and authority in schools would be out of place in this present report but it is clear that curricular decisions are influenced by the process from which they emerge.

For the individual teacher the greater part of the day is taken up with the immediate problem of providing for his group or class of children. At any one moment he may be coping with the overturned paint-pot, giving guidance on where to find more information about space travel and noting another child's progress in reading or mathematics. However the class is organized, formally or informally, teaching is still an activity which demands all of the attention most of the time. Behind these immediate pressures of day-to-day teaching there are, however, deferred issues and questions, some of which are concerned with forward planning. Should there be a project on 'the sea' next month? If so, where can the relevant material be obtained? Are there films which could be ordered? Can a visit be arranged? What are the stories, poems and pictures that could be used? The teacher may also be concerned about what the children are likely to gain from the work and what the scale of operation is to be in relation to the rest of the curriculum. Beyond these immediate and forward-planning questions there are the long-term issues that every teacher is aware of but which are so often pushed into the background because of the urgency of present problems. These are questions about the purpose of the work: What are we hoping to achieve? Might it be done more efficiently and effectively in other ways? At this level of questioning, other teachers become involved, especially the head of the school (who has his own immediate and longer-term questions). The issues now become: What is the purpose of our school? How effective is our work? What changes seem to be called for and how might they be implemented?

Questions such as these are perhaps best viewed by stepping back from the immediate school situation to obtain a vantage point from which they can be seen in a broader perspective. The taking of decisions about the 'whole' curriculum in the middle years of schooling implies providing answers to three separate yet closely interrelated groups of questions. The first group concerns the broad educational issues discussed in our first report. These are the issues which exist irrespective of the structure or design of schools and schooling. They are as much political as educational in that they span basic problems such as why we place children in schools at all and what education is for. Questions such as these raise problems which range from the extremely broad – the purposes of education, for example – through a series of more sharply defined issues which bring in judgements about content and method, to some very precise and specific questions, the answers to which provide the teacher with the objectives for particular sets of learning experiences. In the second group, questions are forced upon us by the operation of our particular educational system. Roughly these are of the following order: What should children do in their middle years *because* they emerge from one type of school (a first school or a primary school) and must later go on to another type of school (an upper school or a secondary school)? What, therefore, are the constraints on a middle-school curriculum because the children come from one or more first schools and must later go on to one or more alternative upper schools? These questions are created because of the system itself and they could be called 'system-bound' questions. In a third group are questions which could be categorized as 'school-bound' questions. These are about the constraints on a middle-years curriculum engendered by operating it in a particular type of school, for example, a primary school with a tradition of non-specialist class teaching, a secondary school with an affiliation to a curriculum which has been thought through in terms of so many discrete subject

9

fields, or a newly established middle school forced to reconcile the traditions of several primary and secondary schools. The answers to this third group of questions will depend to some extent upon the answers given to the other two groups of questions.

The line of argument proceeds thus: given these ideas about what the educational system as a whole is charged with achieving, given these particular local circumstances (and bearing in mind that these may provide opportunities as well as constraints), *this* is what these middle-years children should be enabled to learn in this school. Teachers have usually had very clear ideas about the last step in the argument and these have been articulated in the syllabuses and curricula to be found in our schools. They have recognized that these prescriptions make assumptions about the prior stages outlined above but they have been slow – perhaps because of the political implications of the value judgements implied by broad statements of purpose – to give to these prior stages the prominence they require. Indications of changing and perhaps conflicting views about these larger questions together with the curriculum development movement itself have caused teachers to become less reticent about the earlier stages in the argument. Indeed there is very little in education today which can be taken for granted.

These larger questions are discussed first before moving on to a chapter on planning the work, and a series of statements from the point of view of a particular subject or area of the curriculum. The fact that separate chapters have for convenience been devoted to particular subjects must not be taken to be a statement of advocacy for the separate treatment of subjects in the curriculum. Chapter XIV on integrated approaches is a sufficient reminder of the extent to which in the middle years of schooling the boundaries between the areas of knowledge have not always and with all age-groups been found helpful. The final chapter includes some speculations about future developments and seeks to return to that 'whole' view which is the concern of the first chapter.

For convenience teachers and headteachers have been referred to throughout this report as 'he', although there are more women than men teaching middle-years children and more male than female headteachers.

# I. The whole curriculum – aims and content

There are so many different things that *could* be done in school; there are so many different things that *are* done. How are we to decide what *should* be done? It is particularly important for British teachers to ask this question, for our system is noteworthy for its relative lack of central direction. In many countries the teacher is able to say: 'I teach this and I teach that because the official curriculum requires me to do so.' A British teacher (or perhaps more accurately a head) can say: 'I teach this and I teach that because in my professional judgement it is the right thing to do.' Our first report, *Education in the Middle Years*,[1] emphasized the fact that value judgements are constantly being made in deciding what shall and shall not be done with the children. The considerable freedom possessed by British teachers makes it all the more important to consider the criteria for choosing the elements which go to make up a whole curriculum. It is perhaps even more important for middle-years teachers to give careful thought to this. At the first-school stage, though methods may vary in detail, there is a wide measure of agreement about the main emphasis of the work. At the upper-secondary-school stage, external public examinations and the task of easing the school-leaver into the world of everyday work act as constraints. Teachers of middle-years children are more free from outside pressures, especially when transfer is achieved without an external assessment. Unlike the first-school and upper-secondary-school teacher, the middle-years teacher receives the child from a school and sends him out to a school. A greater measure of freedom brings with it greater responsibility for decisions about the curriculum.

There are many questions to be asked. Why do we do what we do and why do we not do the other things we could do? Is there an overall shape to the curriculum? Has it coherence? Cynics have suggested that the curriculum of many schools is the result of unexamined tradition warped by the excesses of enthusiasts. Teachers should respect tradition and should listen to the enthusiast, but the thinking teacher will seek criteria by which the various claims may be judged. The point of view taken in this chapter is firstly that any curriculum should be the result of conscious planning as well as intuition, and secondly that planning is of particular importance in middle-years education since these years are so important in the development of the child as a thinking person. This viewpoint may well be resisted by those teachers – perhaps primary-school teachers in particular – who regard planning as the enemy of freedom. The writers can vividly recall visiting a primary school in which each day ended with the only timetabled session of the day – a discussion of what to do tomorrow. There can be no doubt that it is possible for highly gifted teachers to develop, over a period of weeks and without formal planning, a programme of work which, though it seems to be derived solely from the children's declared interests, is, in an acceptable sense, balanced, rewarding and full of rich learning experiences. From time to time the children's interests may have to be nudged in the direction considered by the teacher to be desirable, but the whole programme could nevertheless be seen to flow entirely from what appeared to be the children's spontaneous interests. However, it would not be realistic to assume that all teachers could, or indeed should, be expected to organize their work in this way. There is also room for doubt about the extent to which short-term day-to-day planning, even in skilled hands, can be relied on to provide a properly articulated programme of work for older junior- and lower secondary-school children. Careful planning of the curriculum need not exclude the possibility of pursuing fruitful lines of inquiry further than originally intended or of encouraging those unusual turns of thought and action which often attract the term 'creativity'. Indeed all plans should encompass and even plan for unplanned developments. Much that is lasting and valuable in learning is the result of the happy accident, and good planning will always recognize this. Whether the curriculum is planned in detail or not there can be no doubt that the children themselves will leave their mark on it. The curriculum is nothing more than the back-cloth and the lighting for the action of children actively learning and there will be as many ad lib or forgotten lines as there will be scripted passages.

In this chapter we look at the curriculum as a whole. There is a sense in which the curriculum may be regarded as the sum of its parts, the parts being various activities, subjects or whatever sub-category the commentator prefers. There is also a sense in which it is more than the sum of those parts. A common reaction when asked to draw up a curriculum, whether it be for 8-year-olds or 13-year-olds, is to draw up a list of subjects and then to begin to give 'weightings' to these – two periods a week of this, an hour of that, and so forth. Even when the initial assumptions are not in 'subject' form the process is similar. The weightings given usually reflect the tradition for these activities and any specialist can mount convincing arguments for a significant part of the resources available to be given to his or her specialism. Indeed, those who try to look at the curriculum as a whole rapidly reach the conclusion that any one aspect of the curriculum can be shown to be capable of providing almost every conceivable learning outcome. It may be taken for granted that all subjects that are in the usual curriculum (and a good many more that are not) are essential to an understanding of the world and for future survival, provide unique opportunities for the development of cognitive, affective and psychomotor skills, are almost a full education in themselves, require specially trained teachers and specialist facilities, are undervalued in the schools and require more time on the timetable. It is easy to see how cynical the whole-curriculum thinker becomes after a series of such 'unanswerable' cases has been heard. Clearly the only solution is a forty-hour teaching week! With little more than half that number of teaching hours available, each subject (or activity) must justify itself in a highly competitive situation. The approach used here is to begin not with the list and all the assumptions already implicit in the acceptance of these sub-categories but with three major and interrelated dimensions of the problem. These are the aims of education in the middle years, the activities through which those aims might be achieved and the content of the activities. The three are interdependent and provide a model to help the thinking teacher in making decisions.

## Aims of education

*Education in the Middle Years* argued the case for giving attention to this first significant step in the task of reasoning a way through to a curriculum.[2] The aims which teachers have in their minds are an amalgam of ideas (articulate or not) about the individual and his development, with other ideas about society and its evolution. It is perhaps misleading to differentiate aims in this way, for the interdependence of the individual and the society he shapes, and which in turn shapes him, is so great as to defy complete separation. It should also be pointed out that the aims an individual teacher may have, even if described as 'purely educational', have political implications in the sense of making judgements about what kind of life, what kind of society is 'best', what kind of ideas are 'worth' passing on and which individual skills are 'desirable'. All the quoted words imply a scale of values against which the judgement is made and it is possible to argue that scales of value of this kind are as much political as educational.[3]

For present purposes attention is directed first at the aims which, in so far as they can be separated out, could be called societal. Schools seek to pass on to each new generation of children the knowledge, skills, ideas and feelings which are judged necessary to make it possible to live – and live well – in our society. This calls for an understanding of the process by which the norms of our society have been evolved and in this sense the school stands for tradition and for conformity. Societies change, however, and in modern times they change quickly. Indeed it is now a truism to say that the one permanent feature of our society is change. It follows then that the societal view will be forward as well as back and schools will seek to provide not only experiences which enable a child to

13

grasp the essentials of our world as it is but also experiences which will make him ready to fulfil himself in a world which will be very different from the world of today. In this sense the school stands not only for tradition and conformity but also for the future and a willingness to accept – even to provoke – change. It is here that the teacher realizes that political questions are not far away and the professional task of the teacher is to make the nice judgements called for while transmitting the culture as it is and at the same time developing in the young the capacity to adapt that culture to the changed world of tomorrow. Some schools catering for middle-years children have already decided that problems such as race relations, population policies and environmental pollution are significant enough to merit attention in the formative period of 8 to 13. But the future makes its impact on method as well as content and it can be argued that since we cannot know with certainty what knowledge will be most relevant to the needs of the year 2000 we should concentrate upon the development of attitudes needed to cope with a rapidly changing world. Attitudes which accept change, which tolerate the differences to be found in an increasingly pluralist society, and which arrive at a view after open discussion, are seen by some teachers as desirable and have their impact upon the ways of learning practised in the schools.

The problem may, however, be seen from the point of view of trying to provide the opportunities each child needs to develop and fulfil himself as a person; in fact to provide for that child the experiences which will enable him to become the best kind of person he is capable of becoming. Even if the value-laden word 'best' is allowed, it is clear that fulfilment of this kind is only possible in a social setting. The approach which takes the child's personal development as its starting point could also be regarded as the culmination of the approach which begins with a view of society. However strongly personal development and self-fulfilment is held as an aim, it cannot be followed through without reference to wider social aims. Those who take personal development and self-fulfilment to its extreme produce schools (sometimes called 'progressive') in which the pupils decide on their own curriculum. In many schools catering for middle-years children opportunities are created for children to choose particular activities which interest them but there can be few schools which can provide anything like the range of activities which could, quite reasonably, be asked for today. If a middle-years child can fulfil himself in the study of science, mathematics, or on the football field, he is more likely to find what he needs in school than the child whose development as a person would be enhanced with coaching in diving, instruction in a less usual musical instrument or by learning Greek. If the range of activities which can be provided is to be extended it will be necessary to think of extending the school day and of making all the educational

14

facilities of the area available to all the children. Clearly the means as well as the end must be willed, but if middle-years children are to be allowed to seek out and pursue their special interests it will be necessary to move away from the concept of the single school as the provider of all that is needed. It is important too to develop this idea not merely as the means of providing 'enrichment' for the gifted. If the point has validity at all it has validity for all children.

At this point a further extension of the argument is possible. It could be said that the personal development of the child cannot be planned or even provided for without involvement with many people and institutions which exist outside the educational system as narrowly defined. Schools are increasingly seeing themselves as part of the community they serve and it is therefore legitimate to think of the curriculum being as much community-based and involved as school-based. The strongest links with the community are the parents and their participation in the work of education is likely to increase.

The broad aim of providing opportunities for self-development and self-fulfilment is capable of taking the curriculum deviser a considerable way, possibly in directions away from those which are traditional. The middle-years teacher has a particular responsibility here because the years 8 to 13 are those in which children begin to decide how best they may develop and fulfil themselves. Ideas about what they would like to do and what they find rewarding emerge. If the educational system is to develop the potential of each child, it is important for middle-years teachers to keep the range of activities and experiences as broad as possible. Our system has long been successful at seeking out, reinforcing and developing potential for success when it is clothed in the academic form which teachers themselves display. Today we realize that talent may display itself in other ways and it is important for our curricula to reflect this realization.

## Activities

In this section we consider those activities through which aims of education in the middle years might be achieved. The term 'activities' is used not in the sense implied by the phrase 'activity methods' but in the broader sense of what the children are to be led to do or experience if the aims are to be achieved. For example, if it is decided that a suitable way of allowing some children to fulfil themselves would be to learn to play the recorder with sufficient competence to give pleasure to the average listener and to be able to accompany a hymn sung at assembly, the checklist of activities related to this would include such things as distinguishing pitch, breath control, control of fine finger movements, the ability to read a simple line of staff notation, perhaps also the ability to accomplish simple transpositions, and many other skills, all of which would have to be broken down into stages and graded. But playing the recorder involves something more than intellectual and physical skills; it involves, to use a common phrase, the heart as well as the head. Furthermore, it involves the co-ordination of all these activities. It has been found convenient to classify these activities partly as a way of judging to what extent particular curricular contents cover the spectrum of possible activities and partly as a way of analysing what has to be done if the total activity is to be accomplished. The checklists of Bloom[4] and Krathwohl[5] will be familiar to many. The three categories in this typology are: firstly, the cognitive (that is, activities of the intellect); secondly, the affective (that is, to do with the feelings, emotions and attitudes); and thirdly, the psychomotor (that is, those involving physical skills, but remembering that these have an intellectual element as well). Most school activities involve two or three of these categories simultaneously but for the purpose of analysing what we are about a rational separation is convenient.

Most schools give more weight to activities with a strong cognitive content; the affective and the psychomotor areas seem to come off worst. These weightings reflect the history and tradition of education in this country as much as any positive curricular decision. It is apparent that there cannot be a 'right' answer but there can be no doubt that in the middle years those schools thought to provide examples of practice worth imitating ensure that cognitive objectives are never achieved at the expense of unfavourable affective outcomes. To put the point more directly, good schools do not purchase rapid intellectual advance at the expense of long-term emotional attitudes.

Gagné[6] classifies the 'learning domains' in a somewhat similar way. He distinguishes five: motor skills, verbal information, intellectual skills, cognitive strategies, and attitudes. The first and last have parallels in the Bloom–Krathwohl list; the middle three are refinements of what Bloom and Krathwohl call the cognitive, and have particular significance for middle-years teachers. Verbal information refers to the facts, principles and generalizations out of which knowledge is constructed. Gagné describes intellectual skills as 'the discriminations, concepts and rules that constitute the basic skills of the elementary curriculum . . . and the elaborations of these that occur throughout more advanced subjects.'[7] Verbal information makes it possible for a child to know something; to be able to use and apply that knowledge demands what Gagné calls intellectual skills. This distinction is a valuable one for those seeking to determine the learning activities most likely to enhance the intellectual progress of the pupils. A further development is, however, possible. The cognitive strategies which Gagné distinguishes represent an advanced form of learning in which the skills have become 'internalized', that is, instead of being able merely to apply the intel-

16

lectual skills, the child has developed a new way of seeing problems and of obtaining solutions to them.

Whatever the analysis used, it is clear that the teacher of middle-years children in planning the children's learning activities has a range of types of learning to manipulate. Some, such as motor skills and cognitive strategies, improve with practice; some, such as verbal information, depend for meaning upon the context in which they occur; and some, such as attitudes, seem to follow no general rule. In thinking a curriculum through, the teacher should consider not only matching the type of learning to the content but also seeking within the content opportunities to extend the child's range of learning skills. The content is there to develop the learning as much as the learning to encompass the content.

## Content of the curriculum

It is difficult to discuss aims and to analyse activities without thinking about the content through which the aims are achieved and the activities pursued. Knowledge of what? Attitudes towards what? What kinds of skill? These are the questions which teachers quickly ask and the answers which first come to mind contain the traditional subject titles like mathematics, religious education, physical education, and so forth. The phrase 'so forth' is particularly apt here, for learning in the middle years can for many children be a voyage of discovery to many subject lands, some familiar and frequently visited and some less so. To list the many subjects that are or could be learned would not greatly assist the case even if one were to add to the list all the various forms of integration which may now be discovered. Clearly a selection has to be made and an attempt is made here to produce some guiding principles. The attempt stems from a somewhat arbitrary four-fold division of the field of knowledge and skills which has been arrived at after studying the writings of Hirst,[8] Phenix,[9] Whitfield,[10] Peterson[11] and others. The four content areas suggested are: basic learning skills, empirical studies, aesthetics, and morality. Like all categorizations, this simple division has its defects and it is obvious that a subject may be classified under more than one heading. English, for example, at one stage may be thought of as a basic skill, but at another as being in the aesthetics category. For present purposes subjects are allocated to the category where their strongest contribution appears to be made. For the curriculum deviser the problem is less one of placing subjects into categories and more one of examining the work of a school under each of the suggested content areas and asking whether or not the children have had sufficient opportunities of rewarding experiences in each.

17

The basic learning skills are a sine qua non of learning and may be classified as those to do with language (speaking, listening, reading, writing), with number (counting, calculating, measuring, estimating), and with physical control and movement. This category owes something to what Phenix calls 'symbolics', referring to the communication that takes place through symbols. There are, of course, other forms of symbolic communication (for example, art) but these are perhaps better listed in the category where they make their most powerful contribution. In the case of art this is clearly aesthetics.

One of Hirst's forms of knowledge – mathematics and logic – is parallel. It is recognized that many children 'pick up' these basic skills in the course of work primarily directed towards the achievement of other goals. The fact that they are listed separately above does not imply separate teaching but it does imply the desirability of specifying for different age levels, and perhaps for particular individuals, what behavioural objectives are appropriate. In reading, for example, the child's future educational progress is clearly related to his making appropriate advances in reading between 8 and 13. It should be noted that the behaviours mentioned in this first category are all skills and it may be pointed out that skills develop best under conditions of well-motivated, supervised, successful and enjoyable practice. However it is tackled, there can be no doubt that the middle years should provide a systematic programme for the development of the basic skills of oracy, literacy and numeracy, and for the social and motor skills without which development as a person is impeded. If a second language is to be included it should in the middle years be regarded principally as a communication skill. It follows that its objectives should be expressed in terms appropriate to this section of the curriculum.

For the middle years the importance of planning the development of the basic skills is so great that a further proposal is now made – that this first category should be subdivided into: **a** the basic skills themselves (facility according to age and ability), and **b** the developed form of their operation which renders them worthy of the Phenix term 'symbolics' or Hirst's 'mathematics and logic'.* Mathematics (which could be defined as the language of science) and language are clearly of paramount importance. It is assumed that provision will be made for children to acquire facility in the fundamentals of their use. The importance of these skills as a means whereby the individual develops understanding and control of his environment is such that they probably merit a separate subclassification of their own. Placing them here must not be taken to exclude

---

* The larger physical skills as developed in physical education may in their developed form fit more happily into the aesthetics category.

those aspects of their further development (for example, in aesthetics) more appropriately listed elsewhere. The importance of this group in the middle years cannot be over-emphasized and the fact that practice, not all of it intrinsically interesting, is required should not be baulked. Fortunately the success which comes with the mastery of these skills itself reinforces their acquisition, and once this is achieved so many further developments in learning are made possible. It is obvious too that the level of skill attained should advance with the years from 8 to 13.

EMPIRICAL STUDIES

The second category is one which appears in various novel forms – environmental studies, finding out, projects – as well as in a series of subject headings such as history, geography, nature study, social studies, science, and so on. The nearest category in the list by Phenix is 'empirics', implying by this the use of the empirical method to verify statements about the world about us and thus to arrive at concepts of importance in seeking to interpret everyday phenomena. Hirst, too, gives special place to the physical sciences. What is significant about this group is the mode of inquiry employed. Perhaps the most powerful of learning strategies is the empirical method; it is used in the infant school and in the university laboratory. The experimenter observes as accurately as he can, he measures if possible, he records his observation. He then refers to the literature or other authorities to place his observation in the context of related observed and recorded phenomena. He then draws what conclusions may reasonably be drawn from the recorded observation and he reports the findings. There can be no doubt that the intellectual component in this cycle is a powerful one and it has led some enthusiasts into claiming that the important thing is not *what* you do but *how* you do it. The 'what' is also important because it provides the child with a culture, an understanding of his world and a preparation for his future. It can also provide a means of self-development and self-fulfilment. But the 'what' can also be significant in terms of the subject fields from which it is drawn. In choosing material the teacher will be particularly attracted towards inquiries which centre round a point of significant knowledge – significant because it represents a key concept in developing understanding of a particular part of the map of knowledge.

The benefits derived from the study of a subject such as history are not, of course, all to be listed under the empirical heading. The development of the imagination belongs to another category, but a significant part of the case for history in the middle years turns on its contribution to developing an understanding of the methods by which an environment may be interpreted.

For 8-year-olds it is conceivable that the whole of this category could be

19

covered by some all-embracing title such as 'environmental studies', but by 12 or 13 the sciences will have been hived off, leaving the history–geography–sociology side. Even then emphases will vary according to the locality and the decisions of the teachers. Some of the different emphases possible may be demonstrated by reference to three Schools Council projects:

Environmental Studies[12]

Social Studies 8–13 (leading to the History, Geography and Social Science 8–13 Project)[13]

Project Environment.[14]

Though science may be used with 8-year-olds as part of a general exploration of the environment and as part of a programme designed to develop skills relevant to systematic inquiry, sooner or later it emerges as a separate sector. In the present climate of opinion (bearing in mind the probable future of our children) the trend is for it to emerge sooner rather than later. Some teachers attach such great significance to this aspect of the curriculum that they would prefer to regard it from the start as a distinct sector. For our purposes in this report, it is regarded as part of the general field of empirical studies. Those who favour developing home economics (in its extended form) as a field of study would see it as belonging to this category. There are many paths which could be followed; but not all can be followed at once, and it is important to see that a wider range of objectives than those strictly pertinent to the particular subject area chosen for exploitation are kept in mind. It might be suggested that the syllabus of what is to be attempted should include material of significance from other fields, deliberately incorporated because the field to which that material properly belongs is not included. Again there are projects with much to offer, notably the Schools Council Science 5–13 Project[15] and the Nuffield Combined Science Project.[16]

AESTHETICS

The third content area put forward for consideration is akin to what Phenix called 'aesthetics', and again has a parallel in Hirst's list. Into this category fall art, craft, music, drama, poetry, literature (including, perhaps at age 13, literature in a second language), movement, games and much of the work in physical education. This category is concerned with providing opportunities for children to gain the experiences needed to develop an understanding of this part of their culture, to develop the skills needed to practise these arts and above all to find within them means of self-expression. The importance the group is given depends on the judgements made by those who devise the curriculum. In this area the judgements made are more obviously judgements of value than any others made in curriculum construction. Some of those who give weight to deriving a curriculum from estimates of the kind of life the child is likely to have after school regard this sector as one which must be developed more than in the past because there is likely to be a very much shorter working week by the end of the century. A case can also be made out on the basis of arguments concerning the quality of life made possible by the environment we create, which reflects to some extent the aesthetic judgements we make.

## MORALITY

So far, the headings which have been found to be useful have had a rough parallel in the lists of Phenix and Hirst. These authors have three further categories which are here brought into one, and grouped together as 'morality'. The title chosen must not be misconstrued. The concern here is to enable children to discover more about themselves, physically and psychologically, to understand the regulation of relationships between individuals, groups and peoples, and to have some awareness of what have been called the ultimate questions. Of course, this has to be worked out in relation to the developing powers and experience of the child. The category covers work in physical education (including health education), moral education, religious education, parts of the history, literature and geography programme, some of the sociology now introduced into schools, integrated approaches such as those provided by a humanities programme and, above all, much of what is imparted by the hidden curriculum of the school. Casual remarks, formal talks, assemblies, punishments, traditional procedures and standard practices – all these speak to the child no less clearly than lessons. It must be recognized that the whole area of moral and religious education is one of great difficulty because of the legitimate differences of view held by substantial groups in society.

## SUMMARY

It should be pointed out that the four categories used above are not intended to be mutually exclusive and separately timetabled divisions; they represent nothing more than convenient headings under which can be listed most of the named school activities which could be regarded as fulfilling the general aims of middle-years schooling. Although a subject or area of study may be listed in one category this indicates merely the point of its most significant impact and does not imply that it has no relevance in other categories. The argument so far can be summarized as follows.

*Category I – Basic skills*
These are: linguistic; numerical; physical. Two levels are suggested: **i** basic computational, language and manipulative skills; **ii** more complex mathematical and linguistic skills involving a hierarchy of logical concepts. The development of these skills may more properly fall into Category III – Aesthetics. The general aims should include the ability to communicate in an appropriate form.

*Category II – Empirical studies*
These may be subdivided into two: **i** environmental (history, geography, sociology), and **ii** scientific (natural and physical science). The aims should include understanding of the world and the development of a disciplined method of inquiry. Home economics in its extended form would fit in here.

*Category III – Aesthetics*
These include art, craft, drama, movement, games, physical education, music and developed forms of mathematics and language. The aims should include opportunities for self-development and expression.

*Category IV – Morality*
This covers understanding of self, of relations with others, of the value systems required by a pluralistic society and an opportunity to develop a personal standard of values. The category covers work in physical, moral and religious education as well as literature, history, geography, sociology and the hidden curriculum of the school.

We discuss later the question of balance in the curriculum. It is convenient here to note that a curriculum for the middle years which does not provide for significant experience in each of the categories listed above cannot be said to be balanced. It is perhaps particularly appropriate for teachers in England and Wales to reflect on this question. The abandonment of the grouping system in favour of the single-subject examination at age 16 may be thought to have been an indication of a turning away from that 'all-round education' which was often praised. The same trend finds its expression in the later middle years in the abandonment of subjects and even whole categories of the above scheme. The plea made in our first report, *Education in the Middle Years*, for keeping the options open is directed at such curricular decisions.

## The whole curriculum

It is now possible to bring together the three major dimensions of the curriculum discussed so far. The analysis has been in terms of aims (what it is hoped to achieve), activities (by what means) and content (through what material).

Curricular models of this kind must be used with caution. The analysis may have identified a component within the activities area called cognitive strategies and an element in the content area called environmental studies. It would be foolish, then, to decide that at one date, time and place there would be a lesson aimed at developing cognitive strategies while exploring environmental studies. On the other hand, if the environmental studies programme as it developed from 8 to 13 *never* provided opportunities for developing and practising cognitive strategies then there would be cause for concern. Analytical models tend to categorize, but life as it is lived by children in schools is a synthesis and so too is a curriculum. Though it may be valuable to separate the strands of thought, the interweavings of content and the overlap of methods which can be observed in schools, it does not by any means follow that the day is to be divided into times when this aim (not that) is met, when this subject (not another) is being learned or when one method (and no other) is being pursued. Analysis is needed so that we can clear our minds about the task before us, but the plan as enacted is synthetic. To take an example from that part of the problem concerned with content, even if it were decided to treat English as a separate subject it would be impossible to provide learning experiences in that area which did not spread over a range of objectives and which did not overlap into other subject areas. Nevertheless, the act of having analysed what the English periods are intended to achieve will have been of value, not least, perhaps, in making it possible for those with conflicting viewpoints about the teaching of English to recognize the source of their differences. The teacher who gives cognitive outcomes greater emphasis than affective outcomes will produce a different scheme from someone who has the opposite order of priority; yet neither can keep the learning of what they regard as the lower-order priorities out of the curriculum, for the two cannot in practice be separated. The choice is between situations more likely to enhance one outcome without excluding the other, and the choice is ultimately one of professional judgement.

There is one other factor which curricular models must take for granted but which may well have as much significance as any of those already mentioned. It must always be assumed that, to develop properly, children should feel secure, healthy and loved. The atmosphere both at home and at school undoubtedly affects the capacity of the child to respond to what is offered to him. The child who lingers in a corridor for fear of being bullied in the playground, who malingers to avoid PE or other activities which involve uncovering a physique he has come to regard as defective, the child who does not feel wanted, is one for whom the curriculum is irrelevant to what for him are the major problems of life. There may not be a case for a full counselling service in the middle years but, given the importance of what might be called non-academic factors and given the need for the educative process in the middle years to include a diagnostic element, there can be little doubt that properly organized guidance and pastoral care are needed across these years. What we call the whole curriculum is only a part of that wider whole, best summed up as the total life experience of the child. In planning the curriculum we cannot ignore what happens in that wider whole.

## Additional factors

Curriculum models are often criticized for being mechanical and therefore ill-adapted to the special circumstances which distinguish a particular class or school from its neighbours. A model of the major parameters of choice must recognize that those who use it will refine, adjust and occasionally ignore it in the light of the many changing circumstances which shape the day-to-day and term-to-term curricular decisions taken by practising teachers. The following discussion of some of these curricular variables is prefaced by some comments on the growing trend towards more formal planning of curricula. The Revised Code of 1862 and the many school syllabuses which followed it represented a tradition in which a declaration of the content of the curriculum was considered a sufficient indication of the curriculum as a whole. The content assumed the agreed method; the objectives and methods of evaluation were similarly taken for granted. With the 'progressive' schools, assumptions of this kind could not be made; primacy of the children's interests, the insistence upon self-discovery, topicality and upon developing whatever situations occurred, all meant that it was difficult to declare a content and thus write down a syllabus of the traditional kind. There can be no doubt that the essential spontaneity of such teaching is an essential part of good practice in middle-years education. Increasingly, however, these practices are being accommodated within the framework of more positive planning. Such terms as 'structure' appear frequently in discussions, and the packaged materials produced by curriculum development projects often incorporate a precise plan of work.[17] There can be no doubt that the middle years provide an opportunity for incorporating the best of the progressive methods of learning into an approach structured in terms of enlarging the child's understanding, skills and personal qualities. It would be unreasonable to assume that such structuring will occur in the course of a series of spontaneously generated events. If the curriculum is to be thought of as a series of planned happenings, the case for reviewing systematically the criteria for curricular choice is a strong one. Some of the additional factors which require consideration when making such choices are: age, ability, the nature of the subject, and balance in the curriculum.

*Education in the Middle Years* described the changes which occur between the ninth and fourteenth year. From what developmentally is known as middle childhood the child moves into the changes associated with adolescence. For any one age the variations provided by a large sample of individuals may be as great as the changes occurring in a single individual between 8 and 13. It must also be remembered that the pattern of organization in schools may provide for the children of a single age group being taught together, or for two or more such groups. Clearly, therefore, the curriculum has to be thought through first for the whole group concerned (8 to 11, 11 to 13, 8 to 12, 9 to 13 or whatever the relevant group is) and then for particular segments within it. The decisions taken in relation to, say, the 11 to 13 group must make sense in themselves but should also make sense within the wider span, and those in turn should make sense within the whole pattern of education. The point of focus at 11 to 13 will naturally differ from that at 9 to 11, for example. Perhaps it would not be inappropriate at this point to challenge the assumption that a curriculum focused on the 9 to 11 age range (or for that matter the 8 to 12 school) requires less resources than that focused on the 11 to 13 range (or the 9 to 13 school). The curriculum planner must also think of the variations needed within a particular group because of individual differences within it. This problem is best considered under the heading 'ability'.

## ABILITY

The spread of ability, however it is defined or its effects measured, is greater than that of age. Unfortunately for the planner, ability in one sector of the curriculum does not necessarily imply ability elsewhere. This problem, and sometimes problems created by age differences within a group, can to some extent be solved when the content of the curriculum is carefully structured. The gradual building up of a conceptual structure provides opportunities for children working at different levels of sophistication and experience. There are considerable implications here for method and organization.

The two preceding sections may best be summarized by pointing out that an overall view of the 8 to 13 curriculum must inevitably be followed by a closer look at the stages within that span. Provision for development through the period itself automatically allows for changes of level but has implications of considerable import for teaching method especially in the unstreamed situations which are now so common.

## THE NATURE OF THE SUBJECT

A case can be made out for teaching any subject. Similarly there is no part of any subject which cannot be shown to be capable of offering something to any child. Problems of choice occur, therefore, within as well as between subjects. The teacher should give first consideration to what opportunities the subject provides for exploiting and developing the child's powers of learning.[18] This calls for an understanding of the nature of the subject or area of study concerned. There are first-order disciplines (such as mathematics) and second-order constructions (such as geography) created by drawing upon other subjects.[19] There are subjects which – in their structure if not in the way particular children may approach them – have an inherent logic, and others which normally are developed in the mind of a child as a result of a succession of seemingly casual experiences. It must not be assumed that the child will necessarily learn best if the subject is presented in the sequence found pleasing to the adult specialist whose insight may well come from possessing a range of cognitive strategies not open to the middle-years child. Indeed the art of the successful teacher includes the ability to identify the learning strategies which are most likely to be successful for particular children in particular settings and in relation to particular subject areas. Any artist must respect the materials being used and the task of the teacher as he surveys the content of the subjects at his disposal is to remember not to do violence to the child's nature or to that of the subject.

The criteria of choice within a subject area are two: significance and interest. Interest is, of course, all-important for without it learning cannot be effective. But interest for the sake of interest cannot be satisfactory. The interest should be there to enable the child to learn something worth learning. Hence the material should also be significant. The significance may not appear to the child – therein lies the art of the teacher and the deviser of teaching materials. It may be significant because it gives practice in a skill which in turn forms part of a process which is capable of leading a child from a proposition or a concept which he has already grasped to another which forms the next part of the structure being built by the teacher. The child who has been shown how to measure the length of time a weight fixed round an upstairs pulley takes to reach the ground will do the exercise and report. The objectives here have as much to do with scientific method as with understanding gravity. The idea of experimental error is important and the next step is to plot the results of several observations and then to take the mean. Notice that the process involved leads to a concept which can be readily generalized. There are, then, many things that could be done. The teacher selects those things which are significant (in terms of the learning outcomes) and interesting. If the item is not intrinsically interesting (but has an essential part in the structure) the teacher strives to make it interesting, but if it cannot be made so it is also part of the teacher's task to motivate children to tackle, practise and perfect learning which though apparently uninteresting is judged to be an important requirement for future progress. This is not drudgery for the sake of drudgery but application for the sake of achieving something worth achieving. Worth-while learning can be, but is not necessarily, fun. The structure being built up is a structure of coherent knowledge, a congerie of consistent attitudes, and a set of skills. It follows that a degree of planning is needed; a map has to be drawn, a strategy evolved and a sequence decided. The teacher, as he encourages the child to move from one stepping stone to the next, will remember that some children will find different and unexpected pathways towards the same end. This too is part of the plan – recognition of the probability that there will be unexpected as well as intended learning outcomes.

BALANCE

Many of education's clichés deal with the concept of balance in the curriculum. 'Mens sana in corpore sano' makes the point; so does 'a good all-round education' and such phrases as 'many-sided', and 'wider interests'. C. P. Snow's famous Rede Lecture[20] was a contribution to this theme and so was that remarkable passage in the Crowther Report which sought to rationalize and justify the English and Welsh (though not Scottish) devotion to subject specialization.[21] The trend of recent years has been in the opposite direction, however, and the first report from this project made a strong plea for keeping all the curricular options open until 13 at least;[22] in other words, to provide a balanced curriculum. The rest of this chapter is devoted to a consideration of the idea of balance in relation to the curriculum in the middle years. The request for 'options open until 13 at least' implies that there should be a balance between the different areas of knowledge that are explored, balance in terms of content. But balance is a concept of significance in other parts of the curricular model as well. For example, there is a case for ensuring a balance between the various broad aims of education and the objectives derived from them, and balance in the types of learning behaviour evoked in children, as well as balance in terms of content. Balance should not, however, be thought of in terms of equal quantities; the balance referred to here is a judicial balance rather than a mathematical one. Behind the judgement lie estimates of minimum requirements, legitimate weightings and special justifications – all, of course, varying according to the professional view taken in the light of the particular circumstances. Tradition pulls strongly, and there can be no doubt that many a hard-pressed teacher of religious education with a relatively small book allowance has wondered how different life would be were there some error and the allowance for English or mathematics was given to the religious studies department. As an exercise it would be an illuminating experience to begin with the assumption of parity of treatment in time, resources, and staff and then justify, step by step, the deviations from the initial position made necessary by the practicalities of decision-taking. In facing these difficult

27

decisions many teachers recall the familiar distinction between must, should and could. There are things which *must* be done – the minimum requirement; there are others which *should* be done, but are less vital; and beyond that again is the area of *could*, and the choices made here give a school, year group or class its distinctive ethos.

*Balance between aims*
Balance should be considered first in relation to the aims. In the case of the broad aims outlined in this chapter the questions to be asked are as follows. Are there sufficient opportunities for the children to get a grasp of the culture they are inheriting? Are they being given an inkling of the kind of world they and their generation will control? Are there sufficient opportunities for the children to pursue their particular bent? It is obvious that these aims are not discretely achieved; just as a particular subject content may be highly relevant to more than one aim so may the pursuit of one aim (say personal fulfilment) simultaneously achieve another. Overlapping of this kind makes any attempt at achieving a mathematical balance illusory, but the question must still be asked if only to help teachers face the implications of their judgements.

*Balance between types of learning activity*
Balance should also be considered in relation to types of learning activity even though there is here just as much overlap as in the other dimensions. There are different kinds of learning behaviour and the concept of balance clearly implies giving the child appropriate experience of the different kinds of learning, keeping in mind a range of types of learning as well as a hierarchy of increasing complexity within each.[23] Children have ways of behaving – some would prefer to call them ways of learning – which change, develop and become more powerful as a result of making a way through networks of ideas, feelings and activities of increasing complexity and interrelatedness. The art of the educator lies chiefly in contriving a sequence of meaningful experiences which help the child to understand one part of the network and then to use this as a base for exploring adjacent and probably more complex parts of the structure. While it is true that this learning cannot be done in isolation – *something* must be learned – and these processes cannot therefore be divorced from the content, the pathways through the learning maze are important enough for some curriculum devisers to focus on them and to call for a balance between the different types of learning behaviour. The current stress on behaviourally expressed objectives is in part a result of the determination of psychologically-oriented curriculum developers to express in precise terms the sequence of behaviours which amount to the ability to 'know', 'feel', or 'do'. These objectives are expressed in a hierarchy of com-
28

plexity which is the modern equivalent of the old-fashioned rule of thumb: 'from the known to the unknown'. The traditional school textbook presents the subject in terms of an analysis of the subject as a subject. The psychologist would prefer to think of the problem in terms of analysing the children's ways of learning. What the curriculum developer needs, however, is not the analysis of the subject nor of the child but of the child learning the subject, and this may be something distinct from the other two. It will also be important to keep in mind those exceptional, so-called 'creative' children who prefer to take unusual paths through the maze.

The activities in schools catering for middle-years children cannot be neatly classified into psychologists' categories. Dance is strongly affective as well as physical and parts of mathematics may for some be as much affective as cognitive. But if a rough assessment were made it would be seen that the cognitive domain receives most attention, the affective is the next most significant and the psycho-motor receives least notice. As children go through the years from 8 to 13 this statement becomes more rather than less true. The balance in a music school is clearly different from that in a traditional preparatory school. The balance in the middle school that was formerly a secondary school often seems to the observer to be different from that in the middle school that was once a primary school. Again it has to be emphasized that there is no right answer and the variations that exist are a demonstration of the freedom, and responsibility, of the teaching profession.

The balance usually struck in favour of activities with a strong cognitive content is justifiable. The middle years are years in which important changes take place in the child's ways of learning. The child changes gear, as it were, and can henceforth proceed at a better pace. There can be no doubt that, as long as the child is not being over-pressured, the earlier he achieves succeeding conceptual levels the better. Just as the child who effortlessly grows into reading at an early stage has had opened to him a range of non-direct experience closed to his non-reading contemporaries, so does the child who without undue difficulty acquires new levels of understanding at the earliest possible moment become the possessor of powerful learning tools without which his education, in the full sense, cannot proceed. Hunt[24] goes so far as to suggest that the environment should be matched to the child's conceptual level. In the British situation (increasingly unstreamed) this is done in a group rather than a class situation and is achieved by ordering and arranging the material. Teachers who focus on the learning processes will order and arrange (or 'structure') the material in such a way as to bring the child to the realization of a new concept at the earliest convenient time. The cycle of facts–concepts–generalizations runs strongly through such teaching. The lower the conceptual level of the pupils, the greater is the

29

need for structural materials. The converse is also true. Students who have mastered the concepts involved in an assignment may be left to seek their own autonomous (and perhaps creative) ways. The teacher's day-to-day task is to achieve the right balance between free exploration and directed experience in order to achieve the maximum intellectual growth. Hunt suggests further that what is involved here is something more than the mere modification of existing behaviour.[25] If the child is to establish the new conceptual levels he needs to develop himself further as a learner, there has to be a structural reorganization (within the affective and possibly psychomotor domains as well as the cognitive) which has in total the effect of enabling the child to become a different type of learner. It may therefore be a question not merely of changing gear but of acquiring an entirely new and more powerful model. These are the significant changes in learning which the curriculum of the middle years must seek to foster. They are changes which are lasting, transferable, fundamentally different from what went before, and they are achieved not without difficulty. The greater the difficulty likely to be experienced, the greater the need for structure in the presentation. From the traditional primary school comes an important warning that structure without prior relevant experience does not readily produce established concepts. The term 'structure' implies the putting together of items specially selected because of their significance. In a sense the teacher, on behalf of the child, does what the intelligent learner does – discards the redundant and focuses upon the significant. The emphasis is on the stage-by-stage building up of the total structure or, in other words, on the process rather than the content. In this sense it could be suggested that the content is there to enable the process to be experienced and not the process to enable the content to be acquired. This excursion into the significance of the cognitive aspects of learning in the curriculum of the middle years, though part of a discussion of the need to retain an overall balance between different types of learning activity, has perhaps concentrated overmuch on the cognitive. A programme of work that restricted itself to cognitive goals would certainly not be a wholesome one. The case for activities which give pre-eminence to affective outlets and to the development of psychomotor skills cannot be denied. The task of the teacher and especially the head-teacher is to strike the balance between the claims.

*Balance in content*
The aspect of balance most readily discussed is that of balance in allocation of resources – most notably time - between subjects. It is here that warring lobbyists are at their most strident. Teachers do not need to have this quart-into-a-pint-pot problem spelled out to them. No matter how stringently the specialists differentiate 'must' from 'should', and that in turn from 'could',

30

the minimum requirements for all the subjects that could be taught in the middle years exceed the time available. The problem is eased if the number of claimants is reduced and integration is one way of achieving this. This involves abandoning, to some extent, the discipline-centred approach typical of upper-secondary education though now becoming less common in the middle years. The disciplines are valuable in that they cover significant parts of the world of knowledge, ideas and skills in a well-worked-out and carefully-structured 'package'. It is becoming increasingly apparent, however, that not all that teachers wish to do – especially in the middle years – can be embraced by the traditional disciplines, even when children have reached the stage when the boundaries between the disciplines can be seen by the pupils to be meaningful. The first stage of removal from the discipline-centred curriculum is to a multi-discipline approach, and this leads to an integrated and possibly to a problem-centred curriculum. The teacher's choice between a disciplinary and a non-disciplinary approach will reflect his assessment of how best to achieve curricular aims. His concern with the problem of pollution (given high priority because of its significance in the world of tomorrow) may, for example, lead him to prefer mounting a project directly on this theme, involving studies in the natural and physical sciences, geography, sociology and aesthetics, rather than to twist an existing science syllabus in the preferred direction. A series of such studies would sample a large number of disciplines without ever giving systematic training in any one of them. Clearly much will depend on the sample drawn and the extent to which the projects involve the use of structured knowledge of the kind most familiar to subject specialists. The project which runs across several disciplines leans heavily for justification on relevance or interest. It must be recalled, however, that if the subject is to be justified in terms of what it can do for the child's learning powers the same criterion should be applied to multi-disciplinary approaches. It might then be suggested that relevance or interest is not a significant criterion. It must also be asked how far the work covered has provided opportunities for developing the child's learning powers and for mastering the essentials needed for discipline-centred post-13 courses. To put the point directly: the head of physics in a secondary school has traditionally organized a coherent series of learning experiences in physics covering the years 11 to 16. The proposition now being put is that he should restrict himself to the three years 13 to 16. The question facing the middle-years teacher is what experiences will replace the former diet of two years of elementary physics. A full commentary on this problem must refer to the aims of the total educational system. Just as the shift from tripartite to comprehensive secondary education should be preceded by clear statements that aims are now different and are not to be evaluated by the old standards, so here it should be plainly recognized that the school is engaged in a different task. As in so many cases, a compromise is needed and this compromise must be arrived at after answering several questions. Is it proposed that all the children will be educated in the 11 to 13 stage as if they were all destined to become professional physicists? A case can be made out for providing highly specialist (and therefore unbalanced?) education for a small percentage of highly gifted children, but this is not the proposition being discussed here. Is it proposed that the courses in science should recognize that children will use it for many purposes including, for some, that of becoming a professional physicist? What are the essential elements of physics which must be grasped by the age of 13 if the future physicist is not to be stunted in his development? Can these elements be incorporated in studies of wider interest with perhaps additional work provided for the more gifted and for the less gifted? What contribution can these elements make to the achievement of general educational aims? The point of this catechism is to suggest that in the middle years all subjects shall be seen as vehicles for the general development of all children as well as for the specialist development of some. With these questions answered the physicist might be in a position to ask for certain key concepts to be established by 13 and these would then become nodal points in a network of centres of interest around which structured materials could be used to develop learning pathways. The record card passed on to the secondary school would list not so much the topics covered but more the concepts of significance that had been grasped. The need for structured-learning materials is particularly important in integrated problem-centred curricula where there is perhaps a slightly greater risk of not ensuring the progressive development of learning skills needed in the creation of a conceptual map. Those who plan curricula will look with particular interest at specifications from different subject areas which are related to each other. Such coincidences can lead to carefully worked out integrated projects offering the double benefits of saving space on the timetable and of providing simultaneously the basis for the future development of several subjects.

Problems associated with the integration of subjects will be considered further in Chapter XIV. The preceding paragraphs seek to demonstrate how elbow-room can be obtained by integrating subjects which abut one on the other. Though this helps, it cannot solve the problem of overall balance between the various kinds of content. The move back from subjects to integrated subjects gives a broader view but a further step back is needed before the teacher is in a position to make the overall judgement which the concept of balance requires. In the scheme suggested earlier, content was divided into four areas: basic skills; empirical studies; aesthetics; morality. The claims of an individual subject may be considered in terms of how well that subject is capable of contributing to the achievement of the overall aims of that part of the curriculum. What is it we hope to achieve in the empirical area? Can this be done best through separate subjects? Through integrated subjects? By a combination of both? Is the answer for children at 8 different from that at age 13? Clearly there are different answers for different people and different places. In one school rural studies may well be the principal means of achieving aims in the empirical category while in another school there may be no environmental studies but a highly-developed home economics course.

For present purposes it is important to stress the idea of balance between the four areas suggested above. The basic learning skills must be grasped and developed between 8 and 13. There should be sufficient experience of finding out in the environmental or the scientific side; there should be experience of a wide range of artistic media, and a measure of skill achieved in at least one of them. Finally, there should be an awareness of the existence of moral problems and signs of the emergence of a personal moral code. The 13-year-old would thus have had many avenues opened to him. The question of balance in the content of the middle-school curriculum is therefore less one of arbitrating between conflicting subject claims and more one of ensuring that there is adequate experience in all the main types of learning, in developing knowledge, feeling and skill.

*The overall balance*
The idea of balance has been discussed to illuminate the problem of judgement which faces every curriculum deviser. Holding the balance between the aims of education as applied to the middle years of schooling will ensure that children have a grasp of the culture they inherit as well as an understanding of the changes being wrought around them and a vision of the future to which the changes of today are merely the prologue. In terms of the learning outcomes, the idea of balance implies adequate experience according to the abilities of the child in the whole range from the psychomotor skills through the varying types of cognitive behaviour to those activities which are so significant in establishing the child's capacity to be educated. In content, as we have just seen, there is a sampling across the main areas to make sure the curricular options remain open. The plea is therefore for a broad general education, a whole curriculum for the whole child, as a preparation for what is to come, whether that is to be specialized or not. The balance being sought is one that takes into account the dynamic of the child's own development; the balance at 8 (with greater emphasis on the basic learning skills) will be different from that to be held at 13 (when there may well be stronger emphasis on the empirical studies and correspondingly less, for most children, on the development of the basic learning skills). The subjects used to achieve the aims within particular areas may vary from one age

33

level to another. Nor is the significance of any one area and its impact on the children to be quantified in terms of timetabled hours. (For example, it is not suggested that there should be a timetabled moral education period.) The learning outcomes being balanced are the result of the impact made by the school as a whole and it is obvious that the labels on a timetable are not precise indications of the learning that takes place.

Finally there is that finely adjusted balance which is contrived for particular children and particular groups. The curriculum for the slow learner must clearly be different from that of the highly gifted though in both cases the requirement of balance remains. There is therefore no such thing as *the* curriculum for the middle years but *a* curriculum (one of many possible) for a particular middle-years school and within that school there is, ideally, a curriculum for each child. Yet, whatever the variations, each curriculum should, like a work of art, be well contrived in the sense of having distinctiveness, design, shape, coherence and balance.

## References and notes

1. Schools Council Working Paper 42, *Education in the Middle Years* by E. H. BADCOCK, P. B. DANIELS, J. ISLIP, A. G. RAZZELL and A. M. ROSS (Evans/Methuen Educational, 1972).
2. Ibid., pp. 11–24.
3. For a development of this point see M. D. F. YOUNG, 'On the politics of educational knowledge', *Economy and Society*, **1** (May 1972), 194–215.
4. B. S. BLOOM, ed., *Taxonomy of Educational Objectives: the Classification of Educational Goals*, Handbook I: Cognitive Domain (Longmans Green, 1956).
5. D. R. KRATHWOHL, B. S. BLOOM and B. B. MASIA, *Taxonomy of Educational Objectives: the Classification of Educational Goals*, Handbook II: Affective Domain (Longmans Green, 1964).
6. R. M. GAGNÉ, 'Domains of learning', *Interchange*, **3** (1972), 1–8. (Ontario Institute for Studies in Education.)
7. Ibid., p. 3.
8. P. H. HIRST in R. D. ARCHAMBAULT, ed., *Philosophical Analysis and Education* (Routledge & Kegan Paul, 1965).
9. P. H. PHENIX, *Realms of Meaning* (McGraw-Hill, 1971).
10. R. C. WHITFIELD, ed., *Disciplines of the Curriculum* (McGraw-Hill, 1971).
11. A. D. C. PETERSON, ed., *Arts and Science in the Sixth Form* (Oxford University Press, 1960).

12. Environmental Studies 5–13 Project (1967–71), based at Cartrefle College of Education, Wrexham, Denbighshire, directed by Melville Harris. Publisher: Rupert Hart-Davis Educational.
13. Social Studies 8–13 Project (1968–70), based at the Institute of Education, University of London, directed by Dr Denis Lawton. For the report from this project, see Schools Council Working Paper 39, *Social Studies 8–13* by DENIS LAWTON, JAMES CAMPBELL and VALERIE BURKITT (Evans/Methuen Educational, 1971). The continuation project, History, Geography and Social Science 8–13 (1971–75), is based at Liverpool University and directed by Professor W. A. L. Blyth and R. Derricott (publishers: Collins Educational and E.S.L.).
14. Project Environment 8–18 (1970–73), based at the Department of Education, Newcastle University, directed by R. W. Colton. Publisher: Longman.
15. Science 5–13 Project (1967–74), directed by L. F. Ennever and based at the School of Education, University of Bristol. Publisher: Macdonald Educational.
16. Nuffield Combined Science 11–13 Project (1965–69), directed by J. Elwell, and based at the City of Birmingham College of Education. Publisher: Longman.
17. For an interesting comment on this theme by a practising primary-school teacher, see C. M. RICHARDS, 'Trends in the curriculum of the primary school', *Journal of Curriculum Studies*, **4** (May 1972), 3–10. The reader may also wish to refer to pp. 33–6 of Schools Council Working Paper 42, *Education in the Middle Years* (Evans/Methuen Educational, 1972).
18. See *Education in the Middle Years*, p. 20.
19. For this distinction see P. HIRST, 'The logic of the curriculum', *Journal of Curriculum Studies*, **1** (May 1969), 151.
20. C. P. SNOW, *The Two Cultures and the Scientific Revolution* (Cambridge University Press, 1959).
21. Central Advisory Council for Education (England), *15 to 18* (HMSO, 1959), Volume I, Chapter 25.
22. Schools Council Working Paper 42, *Education in the Middle Years* (Evans/Methuen Educational, 1972), pp. 22–3.
23. See above, pages 16–17, for the typologies of Bloom and his collaborators, and of Gagné.
24. D. E. HUNT, *Matching Models in Education*, Monograph series No. 10 (Ontario Institute for Studies in Education, Toronto, 1971).
25. Ibid. Hunt contrasts the so-called phenotypic changes with genotypic changes.

35

# II. Planning the curriculum

This chapter looks at some of the practical aspects of curriculum planning and seeks to identify some of the factors which influence teachers in planning a middle-years curriculum. It also offers some suggestions for their consideration – and the project team recognizes it is not alone in doing this. Indeed we may envisage the teacher as being at the centre of a network of communicators all of whom wish to inform, advise or persuade him over matters concerning his role. This network may be conceived as being in two separate but integrated parts, the first part being the communications network established within the school, and the second the network established by the system of which the school is a part. The communicators in this second network include the local education authority, the Department of Education and Science, the Schools Council and its field and curriculum officers, colleges, universities, and, in recent years, the teachers' centres, bodies such as the National Foundation for Educational Research in England and Wales, subject associations such as the Historical Association, the Geographical Association, the Association of Teachers of Mathematics, the National Association for the Teaching of English, the Association for Science Education, the Association for Teaching Social Studies, the professional associations and many other organizations. Radio and television are used as media for dissemination, as well as being originators of communications in their own right. There is also a large number of individual authors and their publishers.

The resources made available to teachers through this network may be grouped as those offering professional information and those supplying teaching resources. The first group would include material dealing with philosophy, psychology, sociology, curriculum theory, curriculum practice, developments in the various subject areas, research findings, and so on. The second category includes those materials designed for the teacher to use directly with the pupils – textbooks, visual aids, radio and television programmes for schools and some of the educational apparatus and equipment.

When we look in particular at the communications directed towards teachers working in the middle years of schooling there is at present a further important way of observing the available curriculum information. This is to consider whether it is designed for teachers working in secondary, middle or primary schools, or whether it is intended to encompass the whole middle-years age-range irrespective of any institutional framework. For example, some of the

36

recent curriculum development projects seem to be producing materials which have been conditioned to some extent by the type of institution in which the project envisages middle-years children to be. Projects which are concerned with providing resources at the secondary-school level frequently offer textbook courses designed to be used directly by children, in addition to any other support books for the teacher. By contrast, projects which are designed for junior schools or for the whole middle-years age-range tend to produce materials for the teacher, either in the form of information books, guides, or units of work, or other source material for the teacher to study, adapt and develop for use in his work with children. These primary or middle-years projects seem much less likely to produce a course in the traditional sense. Recent examples of these two approaches can be seen by contrasting the materials originating from the Oxford Junior Science Project, the Nuffield Junior Science Project, and the Science 5–13 Project, with the materials produced by 'secondary' projects, such as the Nuffield Physics, Chemistry, and Biology texts and the Combined Science texts.[1] Again, the teachers' guides produced by the Nuffield Mathematics Project (5–13)[2] are different in kind from the textbook resources produced by the various secondary mathematics projects. If we extend the range of examples to look at middle-years curriculum projects such as those dealing with English, art and craft, environmental studies, history, geography, social studies and science, all appear to be following the pattern of providing materials for the teacher. They suggest approaches and ideas, and frequently provide selected examples of possible content, but the essential common element is in the provision of teacher material. After studying this material the teacher has the task of devising his own ways of developing the work with the children in his care. Nuffield Primary French[3] seems to be the one exception at present.

An outside observer without previous knowledge of our educational system might be excused for wondering why such marked differences have developed between school institutions classified as 'primary' and those classified as 'secondary'. After all, he would observe that the first year of secondary education is virtually an overlap with the final year of primary education, as far as age is concerned. Some juniors are 11 years 11 months old at the time of transfer; other children of identical age will be completing their first year of secondary-school work. There is, of course, a much greater overlap if levels of intelligence, attainment, maturity and other factors affecting learning are given consideration. This is not in any way to suggest that the system of transfer is wrong, but simply to question the educational reasons for the common lack of continuity between primary and secondary education. How many junior children actually complete their course in, say, primary mathematics just at the time of transfer? Are some of the more able, older juniors ready for a secondary course to begin before the

September date of transfer? Are the materials currently being produced by curriculum projects covering the middle years of schooling more likely to appeal to teachers working in primary, middle or secondary schools?

The influence of institutional bias either in favour of the secondary school or in favour of the primary school, as far as the provision of information and resources for the teacher are concerned, throws into relief a number of curriculum questions which are of concern to all who teach in the middle years. The teacher's access to information and his choice of resources are vital factors influencing the implementation of the curriculum. A school which purchases some hundreds of copies of a given textbook series is likely to provide a course of study significantly different from that provided in a school which has a number of guidebooks for teachers and a range of source books or reference books for children. An examination of the curriculum for the middle years is likely to raise issues about how the curriculum ought to be planned. The provision of resources which have been designed for a 'primary approach' or for a 'secondary approach' are of considerable significance when assessment is made of how the curriculum is actually planned. One of the major questions which emerge after a detailed examination of the types of communication addressed to primary teachers and those addressed to secondary teachers is the extent to which these approaches have an historical rather than a currently valid educational basis.

To some extent, the school curriculum of the past was planned with a fairly 'closed' content in mind. The kind of learning which was felt to be relevant in English, arithmetic, history, geography, nature study and religious knowledge was capable of being conveniently produced in the form of elementary texts designed for children to follow. Domestic science, art, crafts, physical education and music fell outside this category, but they could be adapted to fit into the kind of learning environment dominated by the requirements of the more academic subjects. In more recent years the new secondary schools and junior schools have developed different identities, the former building on the academic tradition of the past and devising new forms of external examinations open to a wider range of pupils, the latter coming under the influence of the infant-school tradition and the 'liberal' educators of the past. More recently still, the advent of middle schools and the growth of interest in the concept of a middle-years phase have focused attention on how primary and secondary schools plan their curricula. Since an 11-year-old may now be at the top of a junior school, the bottom of a secondary school or midway through a middle-school course, it seems reasonable to predict the eventual emergence of some common approaches to curriculum planning irrespective of the type of school institution.

This relatively new interest in the middle years with its transitional emphasis has made us more conscious of two extra-institutional factors, both of which are

38

likely to influence the planning of the curriculum. The first is the so-called 'knowledge explosion' which has opened up a much wider range of possible content in all subject areas. Material at one time regarded as outside the scope of young children's learning has taken on a new significance; some of the old knowledge is now outdated, or its significance has declined in the light of new discoveries. The second factor is that which questions the wisdom of providing a curriculum that leans too heavily on the learning of facts and skills, and suggests the need for a wider range of objectives in children's learning. It is obvious that much of the new factual material is still capable of being produced as a set course in textbook form. History books, for example, are now likely to make some mention of the Second World War and give correspondingly less attention to some of the wars in the distant past. Elementary texts in geography are less likely to take the form of 'little peeps at other lands'. Mathematics texts are likely to contain fewer practice examples in arithmetic and to offer instead elementary work in symmetry, statistics, probability, topology, and so on. However, some of the new kinds of *learning* designed to meet the wider objectives in the middle years are less easy to document in this way. Aspects of history, geography, social studies, environmental studies and science will almost certainly call for time to be given for direct observation, experiment, the collection of evidence, the production of reports, and so on. The nature of the exercises undertaken will at times be influenced by the particular locality of the school – whether, for example, it is urban or rural. Even in the unlikely event of two schools adopting identical objectives and following similar methods to achieve those objectives, what is observed, discussed, collected and recorded may be quite different, for the available resources in the two environments are not likely to be identical. To offer a practical example, the project team observed children in one urban school investigating the survival of plant life in town streets – the gutters, pavements and verges were just three of the areas investigated and they provided a surprising range of examples. By contrast, a rural school had pupils investigating the survival of plant life on the sea-shore and contrasting this with the survival of plant life in the hedgerows surrounding the playing field. As a side-issue, it was interesting to note that while the rural school was able to make use of a good many information books dealing with plants of the sea-shore and hedgerow plants, the urban school was somewhat deprived of relevant printed material designed for this age-range of children. It is this enormous range of valid possible content that makes it increasingly difficult to produce a national textbook offering a complete course of the type which had such an appeal in the past when the emphasis was more on providing an acceptable but limited content to all readers (the traditional chapters in the nature text dealing with the oak, horse-chestnut, daisy and dandelion, the hibernating hedgehog and the fieldmouse).

Irrespective of their relative institutional flavour, the materials which have been produced by projects and by many individual authors do tend to emphasize one concurrent necessity. This is that there should be as much flexibility as possible in middle-years timetabling arrangements if children are to be offered experience in a wide range of learning activities. It may not always be convenient to fit the work which is planned into a programme consisting entirely of lessons of a fixed duration; furthermore it may be difficult for some of the work undertaken to be given a precise subject classification. In the example of the two schools quoted above some of the children were spending as much time on what might be classified as 'practical mathematics' as they were on 'botany'. For others, the work had major elements of art and English. This is far from suggesting that the only reasonable alternative is a completely unstructured curriculum set in an integrated day.

There are five statements which can be made at this stage about the practical aspects of planning a middle-years curriculum:

1    Teachers are at the hub of a complex web of communications designed to inform and influence them.
2    There is a considerable increase in possible content for the curriculum and the selection of what is regarded as of prime importance calls for wise decision-making.
3    Many teachers now accept a fairly broad range of objectives as being desirable in the middle years, and this may call for a variety of different kinds of learning activities.
4    Some important activities do not fit precisely into the traditional list of subject headings while other activities do.
5    While the formal pattern of a timetable divided into 40-minute periods or double periods is a useful structure for some learning activities, it is not always the best structure for all activities.

Planning the middle-years curriculum in the light of what has been said about the nature of information and resources, the teacher and the communications network, and the major transitional questions involving middle-years children, suggests an undertaking which makes more sophisticated demands of the teacher than curriculum planning did in the past. Without being critical, it would seem that a reappraisal of curriculum planning in many schools is called for. From visits to observe the work in the lower forms of secondary schools the project team found that it is not uncommon for the timetable to be revised at least once a year. At this time there is a review of the various subjects taught and each is likely to be allocated a number of periods depending on the weighting thought to be desirable for that particular study. When this has been agreed, a senior member of staff has the complex task of devising a new timetable, allocating rooms, forms and teachers to their weekly programme (although the programme may be based on a unit longer than the five-day routine). What seems important to stress is that at this stage in planning vital decisions have already been made which may radically affect the content and implementation of the whole curriculum even though the curriculum itself may not have been discussed, except in terms of subject weightings. Specifically, this can result in an historian being in the position of planning one aspect of the curriculum within the pre-determined framework of two 40-minute periods each week with a range of different forms which will meet with him in certain specified form-rooms. While there is obviously much about history that can be, and is, learnt in such situations, there are historians (and of course others) who have become frustrated by the difficulties encountered when trying to vary the fixed routine in order to provide experiences for their pupils which do not fit the organization. When the bulk of the curriculum is conceived within such a framework, and perhaps *all* the learning in some subjects, it may well be that teachers are likely to develop a more restricted view of the scope of their subject in the middle years than is desirable.

It was mentioned in the project's first report, *Education in the Middle Years*,[4] that the project team found that many primary-school heads were frequently concerned with the organization and teaching methods followed in their schools. But while they were prepared to discuss at length their reasons for adopting vertical grouping, the integrated day and the ways in which they had planned for group activities to be undertaken, it was much rarer for them to speak with equal assurance about the actual content of the curriculum. Having established the kind of framework within which teachers and pupils were to work, it was not uncommon to find that responsibility for what the children were encouraged to learn was delegated to the staff who often planned their work individually. In some schools it would not be an unfair comment to claim that there was little co-operation between classes or co-ordination of the work throughout the school, so much so that in some cases each class seemed to be operating virtually as a miniature one-year school. The modern mathematics which flourished in one third-year class might or might not be developed in the fourth year. Crafts which were introduced in the first year might or might not be developed in succeeding years. Much, perhaps overmuch, is left to wise decisions being made informally and on an ad hoc basis when teachers meet in the staff-room or elsewhere. From this a common factor emerges, that of the somewhat isolated or fragmented planning of the whole curriculum, frequently within the class structure at the primary level and within the subject structure at the secondary level. In drawing attention to this, there is an implicit assumption that there is a need for a new conception of priorities in planning a middle-years curriculum, and

41

an urgent need for teachers to have more time in which to carry out this work.

One of the most important observations we have been able to make is that almost universally teachers do not have time to plan the whole curriculum of the school. It seemed that in lively schools with energetic staff and a great range of extra-mural activities there was the least time for planning. There can be no doubt that the work of the teacher has become more complex and demanding than in the past, and that curricular options have increased enormously, yet schools seem to have been able to provide no more time for planning the curriculum than they did when little more was required than a simple syllabus, probably based on a given text, for each of the main subject areas. It is rare to find a school able to devote as much as one week in the year, without other distractions, to evaluating the work already undertaken in the school, to examining alternatives, to considering what innovations seem to be called for and how they might be arranged, and to deciding the relationship between new elements and the curriculum as a whole. While the provision of a planning week each educational year would not, in itself, guarantee the creation of a better curriculum, there is evidence to suggest that the present lack of time prevents adequate consideration being given to the whole curriculum offered to many children in the middle years.

What are the positive suggestions that can be offered regarding the planning of the curriculum? The theoretical aspects have been considered in Chapter I, and what follows are more practical, organizational considerations; means to an end in that they seem likely to facilitate the planning of the curriculum in a manner that is neither pre-conditioned by an inflexible organization, nor relying too much on individual choice and planning which may lead to a fragmented curriculum. Firstly, in schools with a reasonably stable teaching staff, the case for the enterprise being tackled by the team of teachers who will be involved in implementing the curriculum seems extremely strong:

1    We have probably already passed the stage where the headmaster can study all curriculum options in sufficient depth to assess effectively their relevance and degree of importance to the work of the school, and to construct in the light of his own knowledge the curriculum he wishes his staff to implement. To suggest a team approach does not undermine the responsible position of the head any more than the ultimate responsibility of the chief education officer for the work of the schools is weakened by delegating responsibility to the heads of the schools in his authority.

2    If there is to be a whole curriculum for the school, planned and constructed to achieve the school's objectives, it nevertheless has to be implemented by individuals who are responsible for only a *part*. It seems reasonable to

42

assume that individuals can deal with their part of the curriculum more effectively if they have previously been involved in planning the pattern of the whole.

3 Most curriculum innovations have to be based initially on informed opinion, and consensus of informed opinion is likely to result in sound, balanced decisions being made. Furthermore, such changes are more likely to be well implemented if they are the result of a team agreement rather than a unilateral decision.

4 Team planning allows for patterns of learning which cut across established subject boundaries to be given serious consideration.

A practical example may serve to illustrate the value of some form of team planning. Social studies is not at present a component of all middle-years curricula, but Schools Council Working Paper 39, *Social Studies 8–13* (the report of the Social Studies 8–13 Project)[5] argues a case for its inclusion. The claim is made that such studies are distinct from history, geography and the physical and biological sciences, and an outline scheme of work is proposed, based on an allocation of some 20 per cent of the school timetable. It seems unlikely that many schools are immediately in the position of finding what amounts to a full day each week readily available to devote to such work, but serious consideration should be given to the basis of the social studies claim. A school is still free to reject the claims that have been made, but it seems reasonable to say that the decision should be arrived at after considering the evidence. Furthermore, it ought not to be considered in isolation, but needs examination by the teaching team in the light of the whole curriculum being offered in the school.

Secondly, a decision to adopt a team planning approach to the design of the school curriculum raises two practical issues: **a** what is a desirable size for such a team; and **b** how best might the team operate? To the first of these questions there is obviously no precise answer for much will depend on the size of the school. However, it suggests an important supplementary question which has a bearing on the matter and that is concerned with the degree to which specialist teaching is desirable in the middle years. Although there are now many exceptions, the general practice is still for children at some point between the ages of 11 and 12 years old to move from a school where they are taught by one teacher to a school where they are taught by a number of teachers (nine seems about the average). Administratively this is a convenient procedure, fitting in well with the organization of most primary and secondary schools, but for a variety of reasons changes are now taking place. There are primary and middle schools organized on a team-teaching or year-group basis, thus *increasing* the number of teachers normally involved with a group of children, and there are also secondary schools

43

where the number of teachers working with the first- and second-year forms has been considerably *reduced*. Although it is too early to know whether these changes represent the start of a general trend, if it should become fairly general practice then one of the major organizational differences between the two institutions would cease to exist at the middle-years level, and a more gradual transition would replace the present abrupt change.

The second question – how best might the team operate? – raises the issue of planning priorities. *Education in the Middle Years* stressed the value of a school establishing aims, and Chapter I of this report has already considered how a curriculum might be developed in order to achieve these aims. At the initial planning stage it seems important that all teachers concerned with implementing the curriculum should be involved, for there are certain basic questions about which decisions ought not to be made in isolation. These would include:

1    How best can the objectives of the school be met through activities which belong specifically to the subject areas and may be best dealt with through a subject approach?
2    What kinds of learning experiences are there which cannot be so easily categorized?
3    Are there aspects of the curriculum which might benefit from having either a co-operative or an integrated approach?
4    With the available resources and the available amount of time, what is the best programme which can be devised to implement the curriculum?
5    In the light of these decisions, how can the school best be organized to facilitate the work of the teaching staff?

Of course this is an over-simplification of the task, and the five broad issues cover a range of other important decisions that have to be made. Question 4, for example, will involve the difficult matter of sorting out priorities in the light of the available time, money, space, teaching staff, and so on. These are likely to be the questions which dominate the thinking of the practical curriculum planners and frequently involve side issues of tantalizing complexity. Nevertheless, the approach suggested here does leave questions about the school organization to be answered after more important decisions have been made. A school exists as an institution devoted to learning and teaching, and the way in which it is organized must be planned to facilitate the purposes for which it has been created. No school organization should be regarded as a major conditioning factor when starting to plan the curriculum. Timetabling, the use of rooms and other details must flow from prior and more fundamental decisions about the purpose and content of schooling in the middle years, and must not pre-empt such basic decisions.

The chapters which follow deal with some of the subjects of the curriculum and it is necessary to make some preliminary points about what many regard as a major problem in writing about the curriculum in primary and middle years. Chapters about recognized subjects may be taken as implying that separate teaching of these subjects as subjects is justified and even commended. Yet the same authors may already have made the point that subject boundaries are, in some cases, of little validity. The Department of Education and Science pamphlet, *Towards the Middle School*,[6] does not, in fact, provide any 'subject' chapters at all; the Plowden Report, *Children and their Primary Schools*,[7] made the case for integration in chapter 16 but in the following chapter considered various aspects of the curriculum under a series of subject headings. This is not, as some writers have implied, a contradiction, for the chapters are complementary to each other. The fact that one school follows a curriculum implemented under a number of separate subject headings, while another school follows a largely integrated curriculum does not imply that the content of the curricula of the two schools is completely different. Children in both schools are likely to make music, to follow a physical education programme, to paint, model, develop concepts in mathematics, learn to read and write, to be involved with aspects of history, geography, science, religion, and so on. The main difference is likely to be in the methods adopted to implement the curriculum rather than in the actual content. In this report subject chapters have been written since this is a convenient way of looking at parts of the curriculum. Separate subject treatment is not thereby implied, nor for that matter is integration.

Whatever the mode of curricular organization adopted, it is important for a school to keep under review a 'profit and loss' account of their activities which asks not only, 'What have we gained through this form of organization?' but also 'What have we been unable to achieve because we are organized in this manner?'

Another major point must now be made. In writing these subject chapters the project staff had the considerable literature available in some of the subject areas, papers written by sub-committees of the Schools Council's subject committees, the publications and materials produced by the various curriculum development projects, the opinions expressed by the many hundreds of teachers in the project's discussion groups, and many other sources of advice. However, the chapters have not been written by subject specialists offering advice on the teaching of their subject in the middle years. In this regard, the members of the project team do not claim to be 'jacks', much less 'masters', of all trades. However, they feel they are in some way close to the position of heads of schools, who do to some extent have to arbitrate between rival claimants for resources. While the specialist expert has much to give, and curriculum development could not proceed without this help, the curriculum in this undertaking is the whole

45

curriculum, and the problem lies in finding a framework which will accommodate all the separate (some would say 'subject') parts. The project team has often been impressed by the outstanding work which some schools produce in some subject areas but has, from time to time, been tempted to consider how far the excellence of subject $x$ in one school is achieved at the expense of subject $y$. Certainly the authors of a report such as this cannot but 'live dangerously' in the sense that they are compelled to comment upon the claims made by specialists! It has to be stressed, therefore, that the chapters which follow are to be regarded as a statement of the views of the project team, arrived at after considering the evidence presented to them and bearing in mind the need to relate the claims of one area of the curriculum to those of the others. The judgements on particular subjects made by experts in those subjects will no doubt differ from those made by a group which is attempting to consider all subjects. The judgements that matter are not, however, those made by subject specialists, by pressure groups, by project teams, or indeed by inspectors and officials; the judgements that matter are those made by teachers, and the intention in these chapters is to offer for their consideration a view by non-specialists of the claims of specialists.

## References and notes

1. The Oxford Junior Science 5–13 Project (1964–67) on the formation of scientific concepts in children was based at the Oxford Institute of Education. The Science 5–13 Project (1967–74), established to consolidate and extend the work initiated by the Nuffield Junior Science Project, was based at the School of Education, University of Bristol, and directed by L. F. Ennever (publisher: Macdonald Educational). The Nuffield O-level Biology, Chemistry and Physics texts were published by Longman/Penguin Books in 1966–68. Nuffield Combined Science 11–13 Project (1965–69) was based at City of Birmingham College of Education and directed by M. J. Elwell (publisher: Longman).
2. Nuffield Mathematics Project 5–13 (1964–71), organizer Professor G. Matthews (publishers: W. & R. Chambers and John Murray).
3. The Nuffield Foreign Languages Teaching Materials Project (1963–67) began by producing French teaching materials for the age range 8–13. After two years the scope of the project was extended to include materials in Spanish, Russian and German for the age range 11–13. In 1967 the Schools Council began sponsoring the production of continuation materials for the age range 13–16. The continuation project, Modern Languages Project (1967–75), is based at the Language Teaching Centre, University of York, director (from January 1973) D. Rix. Publisher: E. J. Arnold.

4. Schools Council Working Paper 42, *Education in the Middle Years* by E. H. BADCOCK, D. B. DANIELS, J. ISLIP, A. G. RAZZELL and A. M. ROSS (Evans/Methuen Educational, 1972).
5. Schools Council Working Paper 39, *Social Studies 8–13* by DENIS LAWTON, JAMES CAMPBELL and VALERIE BURKITT (Evans/Methuen Educational, 1971), report of the Social Studies 8–13 Project (1968–70), based at the Institute of Education, University of London, directed by Dr Lawton.
6. Department of Education and Science, *Towards the Middle School*, Education Pamphlet No. 57 (HMSO, 1970).
7. Central Advisory Council for Education (England), *Children and their Primary Schools* (HMSO, 1967), Vol. I.

# III. Art

There are four questions which must concern every teacher of art working with children in the middle years of schooling. Firstly, why should such a subject be taught? Secondly, what sort of content seems desirable? Thirdly, in what ways might it be taught? Fourthly, what is the relationship between art and craft and the rest of the curriculum?

Art and craft formed part of the curriculum in every school visited by the project team, and despite considerable inquiries, we were unable to find a school catering for middle-years children where art and craft did not form a part of the curriculum. Since it appears to have obtained general acceptance as a desirable study, and it would be generally agreed that expediency and tradition are not in themselves sufficient justification for its inclusion, there should be reasons which indicate the desirability of continuing with work in art and craft as part of the middle-years curriculum. Why is art to be preferred to more science, mathematics, French or history, or to some other at present unrepresented experience – say, conservation or survival studies? The justification either for what it should be, or why it should be there at all, is not always explicit, yet the issue is an important one, for in order to assess the value of a course it is essential to know why it is being done and what it is intended to achieve. Unless the rationale and the objectives of the course are relatively clear there is no reasonable way of judging now or in the future whether or not it has succeeded or failed. This is an important signpost in rational curriculum planning. Undoubtedly, many able art teachers have established a rationale and a set of objectives for the art work in their highly successful schools. However, it is less easy to express this in a generalized statement about the aims and objectives of art teaching throughout the middle years, and even more difficult to make such a statement in a manner which is likely to be widely acceptable.

The Department of Education and Science publication, *Art in Schools*, considers the attempt made by Sir Herbert Read, after a lifetime of concern for art education, to define its aims:

> His knowledge of, and sympathy with, contemporary art was unrivalled yet his suggestion was a simple one: the aim of art teaching in schools should be to discover how forms arise in nature and then use that knowledge to construct forms that are equally vital or organic. Many art teachers would find this an important (if limited) aim, but it provides a starting point.[1]

48

There can be no doubt that at the present time it would be highly optimistic to expect more from any discussion of art in the middle years than a development of starting points.

Like other aspects of the middle-years curriculum, art is affected by differences in schools, their organization, curriculum structure, timetabling, environment, facilities and material resources; and by differences in teachers, their aptitudes, interests and abilities, type and degree of training, energy, enthusiasm and the freedom or constraints within which they operate. There are considerable differences in the children they teach in age and in aptitude. At the prescriptive level account has to be taken of the ideology of primary-, middle- and secondary-school teachers and their guiding conceptions of good and bad middle-years art education. The reasons why teachers hold such ideologies are subtle and vary from teacher to teacher. General philosophical and aesthetic beliefs about art education may be held with different degrees of conviction by individual teachers, expressed with different degrees of articulation and put into practice with different degrees of rigour and effectiveness.

There is an additional hazard in considering art, for despite a number of broad areas of agreement the subject remains, in the words of Dick Field,[2] 'a very personal discipline'. He sees the artist operating 'not with previously fixed and agreed symbols or signs, since these would be inadequate to explore the highly personal experiences with which he is concerned, but with original images, which he invents as he proceeds.' Furthermore, 'while he is working, the artist must develop and sustain a highly individual scale of values, peculiar to the particular work upon which he is engaged. We must not underestimate the sensitivity and discrimination required; and we have to admit that we do not really understand the process by which decisions are made evaluating the complex relationships of art forms.' Art has certain common terms such as colour, space, form, texture and design, but it is doubtful whether artists would accept a set of general rules governing their use. To quote Field again: 'At certain times, rules have been formulated for composition, ideal proportions have been proposed, colour has been regulated, in the interest of the organization of the work of art as itself. Today's artist rejects such external controls.'

In seeking to establish certain general aims for art education, therefore, there is little hope that the final result will be received with universal acceptance. However, the exercise might be considered worth while if it does no more than clear the ground for more productive thinking by others – 'No, not that . . . rather this!' The procedure adopted has been to select common elements from a number of sources and make some attempt to group these together.

The Newsom Report, *Half Our Future*, suggested that 'to make people more observant of the world about them, more responsive and more discriminating, is

49

potentially to enrich their personal lives a great deal'.[3] The Plowden Report, *Children and their Primary Schools*, after praising the efforts made by schools, expressed concern at the state of the environment: 'Much of the rest of the environment, rural as well as urban . . . is all too evidently the product of a crude indifference to aesthetic values, and of an insensitiveness to many of the deepest human needs.'[4] It was obviously felt that good art teaching might help counteract this crude indifference, and the idea has had many supporters from William Morris to Sir Herbert Read.

The idea of making people 'more responsive and more discriminating' indicates that certain changes in behaviour might be anticipated as a result of art teaching, but these are non-subject-specific objectives and can be grouped with others which fall into a similar category. One secondary-school art department, for example, has included such objectives as the development of sensitivity, the development of an awareness of the needs and the individuality of others, the capacity for reasoned controversy and the capacity for accurate communication. In a school where fairly rigid subject boundaries are established, objectives such as these might well appear in other aspects of the curriculum – for example, religious and moral education, English, and environmental studies. They are certainly evident in the Science 5–13 Project publication, *With Objectives in Mind*.[5] It would seem that the Plowden Committee had some of these broad objectives in mind when they suggested that art was not so much a subject, more a way of life:

> Art is both a form of communication and a means of expression of feelings which ought to permeate the whole curriculum and the whole life of the school. A society which neglects or despises it is dangerously sick. It affects, or should affect, all aspects of our life from the design of the commonplace articles of everyday life to the highest forms of individual expression.[6]

There would seem to be a wide measure of agreement that one group of objectives in middle-years art should be concerned with exposing a child to experiences which will change him for the better as a person. These may be expressed in a variety of ways such as: fostering taste and discrimination; providing an insight into the meaning of the phrase, 'a quality of life'. As a result the child will become more sensitive to the beauty and ugliness in his surroundings. He will learn sensuous enjoyment through the use of artistic media; he will learn to respond with pleasure to objects of beauty. In fact, through exposure to a broad range of artistic activities, in which he is encouraged to explore and develop skills and interests, he will gradually undergo a cluster of desirable changes in his personality.

50

Another major group of objectives is that concerned with heightening children's observation, developing powers of discrimination, encouraging the growth of perception – visual, spatial and tactile. *Art in Schools* has a whole chapter devoted to the development of visual discrimination, and other writers have referred to the prevalence of 'visual illiteracy' and the need to help children 'learn to see'. Since other aspects of the curriculum can be shown to have objectives concerned with observation, it is necessary to establish the particular contribution of art to this process. Obviously children can see in the physical sense without the need for a study of art, or any other aspect of the curriculum for that matter, but this is plainly not what is meant here. The implication is that there are different ways of seeing, and that successful art teaching can make a unique contribution to visual education. At one level there is guidance in seeing more accurately what is before our eyes – the physical environment; but at a deeper level there is the *response* of the trained artist to what is seen – its fitness, its significance, its crudity or its beauty. Value judgements are involved, and with good training these judgements are more likely to be sound ones.

A third group of objectives is completely subject-specific. Art in the middle years provides the opportunity for children to operate as artists, and through this activity to come to an appreciation of materials and an understanding of criteria akin to those of artists themselves. Through this process children are also enabled to realize and formalize their experiences. 'The part of the curriculum which we identify as art concerns itself to a marked degree', say the authors of *Art in Schools*, 'with the development of the faculties of seeing, touching and responding, as well as with thinking, reasoning and remembering.'[7] Through the process of working as an artist there is practice in the development of desirable skills, a growth of knowledge about materials and techniques and, with experienced teaching, the development and appreciation of good standards. Others have listed objectives which are related to a knowledge of art as a factor in human behaviour – 'to see art in its historic and social contexts'; 'to understand art as an element in the growth of human beings'; 'to provide sufficient worthwhile experiences to enable children to judge in what ways art might continue to be meaningful to themselves.'

Keith Gentle, reporting on the work of the Schools Council Art and Craft Education 8–13 Project,[8] observes:

From our observation, two forms of art and craft seem to emerge: one which observes the child's experiences and develops from this the values implicit for a visual, tactile and spatial education; the other one observes what is provided for him in the form of learning structures, based on things we feel he should know and be able to do, and assesses how he works within them.[9]

51

Gentle would appear to be making a cautious distinction between art education which has its focus on the child as a developing individual, and art education which is concerned with art as a discipline into which a child should be initiated. Undoubtedly some schools exist where such polarities of thinking can be observed, but in reality few teachers are likely to have a completely 'child-centred' or 'discipline-centred' approach. Many, perhaps most, would probably claim allegiance to both positions, only differing in their relative emphasis or stress on one or the other. But the two positions do suggest different objectives worthy of consideration and may therefore call, if not for a different allocation of the teacher's time and physical resources, then for a difference of approach and methodology. Such differences seem to crystallize a crucial problem – namely, how do we identify and ensure progress in art in the middle years of schooling? As in other aspects of the curriculum, this is a more sophisticated process today than it was in the past. At one time attainment and progress, say, in arithmetic, could be assessed by observing the complexity of the sums attempted and marking them either right or wrong. Drawing was frequently assessed by an equally simple judgement based on the degree of accuracy in the reproduction made of the orange, the teacher's handbag or another given object. This was a fairly rudimentary assessment, based almost entirely on the end products. Today we still have end products, and while few teachers would now regard them as ends in themselves, few would go so far as to claim that since 'the process is all' the end product can be ignored. It has been said of Cézanne that at times he would abandon a completed painting in the hedge, and there are probably few children who have not been equally glad to abandon a piece of their work in the classroom equivalent of a hedge – this may or may not be a measure of their degree of involvement in the process of creation, but the skilled teacher's assessment of the degree of involvement is certainly one of the criteria by which the success or failure of the art work can be judged.

As children progress through the middle years and have experience in handling the tools and media of the artist, as they are involved in the talk that surrounds the subject and the attitudes and values of their teachers, there is every reason to expect that such influences and practices should give rise to greater skills, greater insights and greater sensitivity. This is no longer the simple measure of the skill in isolation, but the skill advancing hand-in-hand with the sharper awareness and the deeper insight. It is here that there needs to be a synthesis of child-centredness and knowledge of the subject, for if the two are out of harmony there is a danger of failure in the teaching. The wise teacher is aware that whatever heightened sensitivities may be developed in the children, they are frustrated if they cannot find a satisfying outlet because of lack of knowledge about materials and techniques and an absence of standards of workmanship.

Alternatively an over-emphasis on the skills and techniques can result in some-what sterile attitudes and a lack of creativity. The assessment of successful teaching now involves much more than the marking of a series of end products, but nevertheless those end products will reveal a great deal about the richness or barrenness of the teaching.

In answer to the question 'Why should art and craft be taught in the middle years?' a number of reasons can be put forward and well defended.

1   There are the long-term reasons, frequently containing utilitarian under-tones, which characterize so much of William Morris' writing and which have echoes in both the Newsom and Plowden reports. They suggest that as a result of good art teaching, children will become more sensitive to the environment, will display more care and concern, and human living will in consequence be enriched. 'It also has a significance for our standards of living and the quality of our industrial products' (Newsom).[10] 'Education may therefore be defined as the cultivation of modes of expression – it is teaching children and adults how to make sounds, images, movements, tools and utensils' (Herbert Read).[11]

2   There are reasons concerned with developing powers of discrimination, heightened awareness, the growth of perception – visual, spatial, and tactile.

3   There are reasons concerned with art as an effective means of communica-tion and expression. 'An essential means of communication and a useful tool for a wide range of studies' (*Art in Schools*).[12] 'But art is not only a matter of the emotions, and for many boys and girls it can offer a rewarding discipline of hand and eye and intellect. Here is a training in perception and selection, a way of looking and a means of communication' (Newsom).[13] 'Art is both a form of communication and a means of expression of feelings which ought to permeate the whole curriculum and the whole life of the school' (Plowden).[14]

4   There are the reasons which emphasize the value of art as a study in its own right; children should have a chance to work as artists because it is a good and satisfying thing to do for its own sake. Under this heading might also be included ideas already mentioned, such as: the importance of seeing art in its historical and social contexts; to understand art as an element in the growth of humanity; to provide sufficient worth-while experiences to enable children to judge in what ways art might continue to be meaningful to themselves.

The views expressed so far are not likely to be completely acceptable to all artists or to all those teaching art in the middle years, but they represent some

53

of the views held by some teachers and artists at the present period. As such they may have value if only in helping us to arrive at clearer and more precise statements. While most, if not all, schools have found a place for art and craft in the middle-years curriculum there are considerable differences to be found in the content of the courses provided. There are compelling arguments in favour of diversity in this area of the curriculum, for selection can be made from a large number of possible options – although this must not be taken to imply that virtually anything is suitable for inclusion in the middle-years curriculum. A brief description of some of the approaches which the project observed in schools may serve both to illustrate some of the different ways in which the subject is being covered and to enable some comments to be made about them in the light of the preceding discussion. The brief and at times over-simplified descriptions which follow do not give a complete picture of the approaches which can be currently observed in schools, and they are not intended to represent such a survey. Rather it is hoped they may serve as models from which an answer can be developed to the second question this chapter investigates – 'What sort of content seems desirable in the middle years?' Each of the six descriptions which follow is based on a cluster of schools which were following a similar, if not identical, approach and in no case should they be taken as representing a single identifiable school. Nevertheless, all mention of specific lessons or examples of art work quoted are of those actually taking place in schools visited.

## I. Primary models

*Primary school A*
Here each teacher provided a regular series of twice-weekly lessons, one of which dealt with art and the other with craft. The lessons were generally of a little more than one hour's duration, and most of them dealt with a self-contained unit of work. Occasionally a topic might be introduced which took two or even three weeks to complete. In most cases the teacher prepared beforehand the requisite materials, enlisting the help of the class if something special was required (for example, a supply of empty containers, or a potato for making a potato-print). Most lessons began with the teacher describing or demonstrating what the children were to do and the class was then set to work to undertake the exercise. The art work was predominantly painting with tempera colours but occasionally wax crayons or charcoal might be substituted. The title of a picture or the description of some pattern work was given by the teacher at the start of the lesson. Sometimes a small group of children was selected to paint a 'mural' on sheets of sugar or craft paper which were stuck together to form a long panel. Large paintings like this were most often associated with some topic being

54

studied in, for example, history or religious education. The rest of the class might contribute cut-out paintings of houses, people, animals, etc., which were later stuck on to a large sheet. A typical classroom might display on the walls three or four of these large paintings depicting such subjects as Tudor London, Jesus feeding the five thousand, an underwater scene, firework night, and so on. There might also be a display of recent paintings done by individual children. A sequence of craft lessons might cover such exercises as:

the making of a model house in thin cardboard which was then painted and decorated;

making a potato-print;

making papier mâché to apply to the outside of jam jars which were then covered with pasted paper and painted to form a type of decorated vase;

making a model lighthouse or windmill from an empty washing-up liquid container;

making a small model ship or aeroplane from balsa-wood;

making model animals in clay and painting them with tempera colour when dry;

making a picture frame from strips of thin cardboard bound with strands of different coloured raffia.

About 10 per cent of the working week was allocated to work in art and craft, and most often the head had decided for one reason or another that it would not be an advantage to provide teachers with a syllabus or scheme of work which gave some indication of the content of the course. The weekly lessons were isolated, almost random, experiences having little or no discernible link with each other, nor did they form part of an overall plan for the development of any specified skills or desired attitudes towards aesthetic values. There is no doubt that at times the teachers might be somewhat at a loss to know what to provide for the next lesson, and the ideas and suggestions which appear in some of the popular educational journals were regarded as extremely valuable. The fact that outline lessons appear with such regularity in these publications seems to indicate that there is a demand for guidance at this level on a fairly wide scale. By the end of the school course it was not anticipated that the children would have progressed through any specified stages of development in the use of any medium, nor was there any deliberate attempt to foster observation, growth in discernment, appreciation or skills in the use of colour, texture, shape and pattern in the making of pictures. Certainly there might be some development in the children's ability to handle some basic tools such as scissors and brushes, but there was frequently a general lack of understanding on the part of both pupils and teachers of how much more there might be to both art and craft than

55

was offered in the school. The stream of end products made by the children during the craft lessons might frequently be lacking in real merit, no matter how well the exercise might have been carried out. Some of the major criticisms of such courses seem to be:

1    They offer content which is unlikely to result in children developing the skills, abilities and attitudes which might be expected in artists and craftsmen, for the work they are doing is not, in the main, the kind of work undertaken by artists and craftsmen.

2    Although these lessons were regarded as being – and often were – extremely popular with the children, and were frequently claimed to have value in this respect, this defence ignores the fact that there are other and possibly more worthy experiences which could be offered and which could at the very least be equally appealing.

3    There was no marked progression in the work being undertaken. The clay work and print making, for example, showed very little development at the 11-year-old level when compared with that undertaken by 8-year-olds.

4    The fact that the content frequently lacked intrinsic merit made it unlikely that one of the outcomes would be a heightened sensitivity towards, and greater awareness of, those values and attitudes which seem to be desirable for the personality of middle-years children.

*Primary school B*

Although the school had no written syllabus or scheme of work, the head had provided some detailed notes for guidance which covered his ideas on education and the approach he expected his teachers to follow. Art and craft were allocated no set periods during the week but were available as two of a number of options which could be chosen at different times of the day. The emphasis was on providing as wide a range of resources as possible. These included different kinds of paints, brushes, dyes, inks, pens, crayons, markers and pencils; variety also characterized the supply of papers and cards. Each room was provided with a clay bin, a carpenter's bench and a supply of basic tools. Shelves contained a collection of craftsmen's materials in the form of string, cords, cotton, pins, clips, wires, plaster, glues, pastes, etc. There was a large fabric box, a box of timber off-cuts, and several containers of 'junk' materials. The timetable was unstructured and it was not easy to ascertain how much time the children spent on art and craft activities, although the teachers kept a watchful eye on individual choices to ensure that the working week had some balance. Although it was unlikely that there would ever be more than six children working in the art and craft area at any one time, many more children might be engaged on these activities in the room or elsewhere in the school. There is little doubt that considerably more than 10 per cent of the time was spent on this aspect of the curriculum.

In contrast to the free choice which characterized much of the creative work, the italic hand was specifically taught and carefully practised in the early middle years. The older children spent some time in carefully producing 'best copies' of pieces of their written work and they were taught to pay considerable attention to the layout and design of the page, with encouragement to incorporate sketches, colours and patterns as an integral part of the work. The attention given to these aspects in this part of their work clearly marked it out as belonging to the art and craft section of the curriculum rather than, say, to English. There was incidental direct instruction as, for example, when a teacher pointed out to an 8-year-old that a polystyrene tile was not likely to stick well to a corn-flake packet if the child used powder paste, and added that there are different glues and pastes for different materials and situations and that it was good practice to sort out the best for the job in hand.

Progress in painting was achieved partly by individual, group, or even class discussions on finished work, the teacher going to some trouble to encourage a child to be explicit in describing how he achieved certain desired effects, etc., and partly by offering stimulation and encouragement so that children were able to maintain their interest and absorption in a painting for a longer span of time than that of the traditional period or lesson.

Such a school might be considered as having several characteristics which together form a complete course in primary art and craft:

1    The provision of a wide range of materials in the use of which children were given considerable freedom to experiment.
2    In the field of handwriting and display, the powerful influence of the teachers was most apparent. Not only were these skills taught but there was a clearly observable progression in the development of skills, and older children were capable of producing highly sophisticated and aesthetically pleasing work.
3    The teachers had high standards of writing, lettering and display.
4    Teachers arranged displays of children's work, work by adults, and materials from which artists and craftsmen have derived inspiration – rocks, fossils, growing plants, grasses, etc. These were not regarded as simply enhancing the appearance of the school ('We are not a mini-Habitat!'), but as source material for close observation of pattern, shape, texture and form.

**5**  Children's paintings, drawings, sketches and models were treated with respect by the staff and discussed in detail with the children. Such creations were regarded as an important part of the school's work and children were made aware of the significance of what they had achieved, how it had been achieved and of the strengths and weaknesses of what they had created.

A course such as this would seem to make provision for the development of skills, to a minor extent through craft activities but principally through the direct teaching of handwriting and display and through discussing with the children their creative work. A wide range of materials and freedom in their use seems likely to go a long way towards providing the children with pleasurable and satisfying pursuits. Finally, the high standards set by the teachers themselves, the variety of displays throughout the school and the quality of the artefacts and natural objects seen in the school are the cause of much unconscious but no less effective learning.

*Primary school C*
Some of the features common to the second model were also observed here, but in craft there was a deliberate policy of developing progression in the use of clay and in print-making. The craft of the potter and the print-maker were considered highly suitable for middle-years children. Other resources, similar to those of the second model, were also available and used in much the same manner. On entry to the middle years at the age of 8, the children had already experienced a year of virtually free play with clay and using fingers, hands and a variety of objects in simple print-making. During the following three years of the junior course they were given a fairly structured course leading from the making of thumb pots and coil pots to the use of the wheel in pot-making. They were also given help in making clay models and the use of moulds. All the children were expected to be familiar with the process of preparing clay for use – drying, crushing, soaking, draining, wedging, etc., and they produced models and pots for firing in both home-made kilns and in the school's electric kiln. While the range of craftsmanship developed by children at the top of the school varied, some showed considerable technical skill, creative ability and a sophisticated approach to the medium. There was a deliberate attempt to foster the study of two specific crafts in some depth, and a ready acceptance by the staff that this policy inevitably limited the range of other art and craft experiences which could be offered. To what extent this might be regarded as a weakness is a matter of opinion. What cannot be overlooked is the obvious enjoyment, involvement, and unmistakable pride shown by the children in work resulting from a relatively high level of technical skill.

58

## II. Secondary models

*Secondary school A*

The school we describe for this model had a spacious, purpose-built design centre separated from the main school building, in which art, metalwork, woodwork, domestic science and other crafts were taught. For four days the pupils were in the main building following a fully structured timetable, but for one complete day each week they worked in the design centre. All the work here was under the direction of the head of department who, together with the staff in charge of each section, had planned an integrated course of studies which stressed both the development of technical skills and aesthetic appreciation. Not only were there carefully arranged displays of pictures and artefacts, but middle-years children worked alongside sixth-formers who were engaged in advanced-level studies, and thus they had the opportunity of observing older and more skilled craftsmen at work.

The content of the course was based on a group of major themes which were investigated by the children through a range of media. There was no division of the sexes, and within the framework of a common theme children undertook a variety of different studies, using the available resources of each section of the design centre. The course was structured so that while each child spent half a term on one particular section, the exact nature of the work undertaken was not predetermined. Although this meant that groups of children had undertaken studies in different aspects of art, craft and domestic science, they had all been exposed to the possibilities and limitations of several media which they had used to develop their interpretations of the topic studied. The centre was fortunate in having a team of specialist craftsmen and an extremely wide range of technical resources. At times the teachers gave clear and specific instructions, which were obviously essential when machinery for heavy crafts was in use, but for most of the working day advice, help and guidance were offered only when necessary. There was no problem over girls using, say, metal and enamels to create costume jewellery any more than there were problems over boys undertaking cooking and other work in the domestic science area. The teaching staff allowed the children to use the various machines under supervision and took every possible precaution to ensure the pupils' safety.

The quality of the work displayed in the design centre and the wealth of resources did not appear to spread into the rest of the school and there was evidence of a division between developments in the centre and the remainder of the middle-years curriculum. It was not simply a contrast between the white-coated overalls of the design team and the black gowns of the rest of the teaching staff. The creation of the centre had permitted the staff working there to evolve

59

a different working pattern and with it a different approach to learning from that followed in the main school building.

This school could quite clearly claim considerable success in providing a meaningful course for their middle-years children and this was evident from the number who chose to continue their studies to an advanced level and eventually left the school to take up a career in which they could put their abilities in art, craft and design to good use.

*Secondary school B*
Again we describe one school though features are drawn from several typical of this model.

Here specialist teachers were responsible for courses in art, woodwork, and metalwork. The teachers concerned had planned their schemes of work independently of each other and worked in different parts of the building. In woodwork during the first term certain basic skills were taught with emphasis on the proper handling and correct use of tools. In the second and third terms some simple items were made – a toy, a small wooden steamer, a pencil box and finally a small hanging bookshelf. In the second year slightly more complex models were made, culminating in the construction of a folding stool and a carved fish on a wooden stand. Metalwork followed a similar progression from elementary skills in handling tools to making such items as a coat-hanger, a latch for a gate, a small decorated dish or ash-tray, a poker and a pair of book-ends. The art work included different forms of picture making, and instruction in a range of techniques such as stencil-making, lettering, lino-cutting, and print-making. Middle-years children had a double period of art each week and a double period of craft, with groups in classes alternating between woodwork and metalwork. There was no attempt to integrate the work in art and craft with any other aspect of the curriculum, nor was there any indication of aesthetic influence spreading from the centres where subjects were taught into any other part of the school building, either in the form of displays of pictures and artefacts, or in less specific ways.

This was an extremely traditional and elementary course, followed without deviation by all the pupils, the emphasis being on developing skills in the handling of tools. In woodwork and metalwork the skills were put to use in reproducing a copy of the teacher's model through following a number of carefully directed steps. It was not until the children had progressed beyond the middle years that they were allowed to exercise some choice or show any creativity. There seems little doubt that the course in art and craft formed a popular part of this school's curriculum but it is equally clear that there was little concern shown over providing experiences which might have a value in develop-

60

ing desirable aspects of personality, apart from possibly carefulness in conserving materials, a concern for good order and accuracy in measurement.

## A middle school catering for children aged 9 to 13

The school was new and had had little time to develop its own character and methods of working. Physical provision included resource areas for art, woodwork and metalwork but at the outset it was anticipated that work in art and craft would not be completely isolated in these special areas of the school. The teachers agreed that consideration should be given to displays 'tastefully colourful, regularly changed and neatly and tidily arranged', and that there should be a deliberate policy of fostering high standards: 'Our great objective must be to see that children become awakened to their environment, attracted by texture, colour, patterns, shapes; to help their eyes to see, their minds to be active, their senses to be re-active, and the opportunities given to be creative through any of the media of the curriculum . . . By the time they leave the school, pupils should be able to pass critical opinions about many themes, to question, to comment on beauty, ugliness, atmosphere, to be repelled or attracted by their environment.'

While specialist teachers were responsible for heavy crafts, domestic science and art, their work was not exclusive to these areas, and conversely, every teacher was regarded as a teacher of art and craft. In the first few terms of the school's existence there was good evidence to be seen of the efforts made in setting high standards of display. Considerable progress had been made in following the policy of integrating art and craft with the projects, topics or themes followed by different year groups, and sometimes work was developed independently of other aspects of the curriculum. It is too early yet to discern any permanent pattern, relationship or balance between studies in which art and craft are central (undertaken for their own value), or peripheral (forming part of a project or topic followed by a year group). The staff recognized the value of having both aspects in the curriculum, just as they recognized the value of including some teaching of skills and techniques and some opportunity for 'discovery' or 'free exploration' in a medium. It may be some time before there is general agreement that the best balance has been effected between these sometimes conflicting values and it may be, in view of the other important curriculum priorities in the school, that this is not really a vital matter.

In view of the great variety evident in the above typical approaches, what can be said about the content of an art and craft course in the middle years? Firstly, there appears to be little use in producing a catalogue which attempts to list suitable content. If such a list seeks to be definitive it becomes too long; if it is

61

selective there are almost insoluble problems of criteria. While certain studies might be regarded as having some general claim for inclusion, others which are no less valuable appear to be virtually unique to the school or the environment where they are practised. This is certainly true of the excellent work being undertaken in a small number of village schools where a new generation of children is being taught some of the rural crafts which were on the verge of extinction – crafts which have ceased to be generally followed as a trade since they are no longer an economic proposition, but which are now recognized as having a new value at the artistic, aesthetic level.

However, while it might not be possible to produce a list of suitable content, there are certain criteria which can be applied to any programme of art and craft in the middle years. In setting up these criteria the project team has been greatly helped by informed comment from specialist teachers of art and craft in secondary and middle schools, from teachers working with children in the primary schools, inspectors and advisers working with local authorities, HM Inspectorate, lecturers in art and craft working in colleges of education and from the directors and members of the Schools Council Art and Craft Education 8–13 Project. While the project team acknowledge the value of these contributions, in fairness to all it should be pointed out that the following criteria do not necessarily represent the views from any one of these sources.

1   The course must contain variety. Middle-years children are too young to have had the opportunity of finding out very much about the range of materials and resources used by artists and craftsmen. To offer them a highly specialized training in one craft or one aspect of art would both limit their creative experiences and prejudice their chances of making a choice from a known selection of options at a later stage of their education. This criterion received general approval, one group of informants going so far as to state that the course should include 'the broadest possible experiences of every conceivable material and tool within the scope of the child. An infinite variety of source material both physical, abstract and imaginary, everything that is within the range of the child, but always attempting to extend that range.' However, most of our informants suggested that caution was needed and pointed out the danger in unlimited variety, in children flitting from one experience to another. The advantages were those that appeared to have been gained by the children described in the third type of school mentioned, where teachers used their own expert knowledge in some particular aspects of art to extend the abilities and understanding of the children. Perhaps the most important suggestion was that of the importance of providing variety between classes of activity – two-dimensional and three-dimensional, controlled and free, using tractable and intractable materials.

**2**  While there is need for variety, there seems also a need to provide some deeper study of a craft or crafts. 'Thou O God dost sell to us every good gift, but only after very great labour', wrote Leonardo da Vinci. Every craft disciplines its practitioners and it would be unfortunate if older middle-years children were not given the opportunity not only of knowing what those disciplines are, but also of experiencing a little of the freedom which craftsmen have once they have mastered their discipline.

**3**  In addition to material resources, children need to have the opportunity of seeing the results of good craftsmanship and of handling things which have been well made. This means that the school should provide good displays. There should also be a plentiful supply of natural objects from which artists and craftsmen have derived their inspiration. These displays should form a part of the art and craft course; they should be discussed, their significance made manifest, and close observation of them encouraged.

**4**  There appear to be four stages of development which need to be recognized when children handle new materials and resources throughout the middle years. Although they are categorized into four separate items it should be made clear that they do not form a simple time sequence, beginning with the 8-year-old and culminating with the 13-year-old; it is more of a spiral progression which needs to be followed through with varying degrees of emphasis at each stage, whenever new materials are introduced at any period throughout the middle years.

**a**  Opportunity to play, experiment and to discover what can be done or made with the materials. Some of our informants criticized the use of the word 'play' as being too frivolous in this context, but it seems quite appropriate to describe the early experiences of getting used to and handling the materials in a reasonably free and unstructured situation. Junior teachers will doubtless be aware of a similar stage of development necessary when introducing children to any form of structured apparatus in mathematics: children are encouraged to play with the apparatus for some time before they come to terms with it and can make full use of it as mathematicians.

**b**  During this period some incidental teaching will be needed for a variety of reasons, including safety, to enhance the value of the experimental period to the child, to prevent undue wastage of time and materials in limited supply, and so on.

**c**  As children come to terms with the materials, there comes a time when, to quote from one of our informants, 'the urge to fashion the materials by dint of some creative imperative leads to the need for skills which have to be learnt – and taught.' These then become essential for any progress or

63

development to be made in handling the materials. There are two serious dangers here. One is that in allowing children too much freedom teachers may fail to offer positive help and the poor results which follow are no longer satisfying to the child and lead to frustration and loss of interest. The other danger is to overburden the child with rules before he has had enough opportunity to handle materials and experiment on his own. Sometimes this is done to the extent of teaching conventions as rules and this in turn can lead to the death of creativity and an equal loss of interest.

d  Freedom to explore the medium creatively once the basic principles, limitations, and possibilities have been experienced. Here the children begin to work as artists and craftsmen.

The third stage gave rise to more critical comment than any other when this chapter was read in its original draft by our informants. Stages **a, b** and **d** were generally accepted and agreed. The nub of the issue was clearly over stage **c**, and this part has been rewritten in the light of the comments made. Even now, in its revised form, it is doubtful whether it offers any full explanation of the subtle ways in which some of the skills of the good teacher become the skills of the pupils. The consensus of opinion suggests that although it is legitimate to categorize section **c** in the manner shown, in reality the process is one which takes place with varying degrees of significance all the time children are handling the materials. There is an intangible 'right teaching moment', recognized by the skilled teacher who is working with children in a particular situation.

5  Although not all those who teach art and craft to middle-years children are likely to have specialist training, it seems essential that all teachers should have some knowledge of what they teach. We should be appalled at the idea of illiterate teachers teaching reading but there are grounds for thinking that we still tolerate visually illiterate teachers teaching art. If one of the desired outcomes of a course in middle-years art is a heightened sensitivity and an awareness of beauty, then these qualities should be apparent in the teaching staff of the school. At the start of the chapter we quoted the Newsom Report on one of the expected outcomes from teaching art: 'to make people more observant of the world about them, more responsive and more discriminating.' It would seem that to achieve this aim there is a need for art to be taught by teachers who are more observant of the world about them, more responsive and more discriminating. The Plowden Report spoke of 'a crude indifference to aesthetic values and an insensitiveness to many of the deepest human needs.' To counteract this, there would appear to be a need for teachers who are not indifferent to aesthetic values, and who are sensitive. This is not to suggest that middle-years art should be taught only by specialist trained teachers but simply to emphasize

that there are many ways in which teachers can improve both their skill and understanding of what they undertake to teach.

6 Art and craft should contain a verbal element – art and craft is something that is talked about and thoroughly discussed as well as being something that is done. This has already been hinted at in 3 above, but from the evidence available it would appear to be a neglected element in some schools. Not only is it suggested that children's painting and models should be discussed and children encouraged to take a critical attitude towards their own work, but this discussion should be extended to the work of other artists and craftsmen. We are claiming for art and craft in the middle years what has already been established in music and literature. Children should not only be exposed to good music, poetry and prose but, equally important, efforts should be made to allow children to see work produced by skilled artists and craftsmen. They should also be helped to observe closely their own environment, and to consider both its beauty and its ugliness. 'To discover unseen things beneath the obscurity of natural objects', as one medieval painter expressed it.

While there is a fairly general acceptance of the view that art in the middle years should show considerable diversity in its content, there is also some feeling that an outline of suitable content should be specified. Even if this is not taken to mean the spelling out of a list of desirable practical activities, the task is still a major undertaking. The second and third chapters of *Art in Schools* indicate a little of the diversity of practices to be found in the 8 to 13 age range at the present time, and will provide a starting point. It might be useful here to question the traditional subject title of 'art and craft'. Whatever value there may have been at one time in linking art and craft together, is it still of use today? Might it not be a positive hindrance to clear thinking about a whole curriculum to spend time considering art, woodwork, metalwork, needlecraft and perhaps pottery but ignoring, say, music? This would be a powerful argument if the alternatives were mutually exclusive, but this is by no means so. Having considered at some length one aspect of the middle-years curriculum we are now able to review other aspects of the curriculum which have elements in common and possibly similar, or even identical, objectives. At a later stage we can go on to consider the relationship between such studies and the whole curriculum.

So far as art is concerned, one of the cluster of objectives put forward as an argument for including it in the curriculum is that such study is a means of achieving desirable developments in personality – sensitizing children, making them aware of beauty, encouraging them to explore their own imagination, to be creative, etc. Objectives such as these seem also applicable to other aspects of the curriculum – drama, music, literature, for example – and there are also links with physical and religious education. An overview of all that schools intend to offer in these aspects of the curriculum will help to ensure a balance between these objectives and the others which the school considers desirable, and also that the experiences themselves make up a harmonious whole.

Whatever approach to teaching art a school may adopt, there is little doubt that an occasional review of what is actually happening may reveal the need for some changes or modifications in procedure. What was once accepted as having a high value may, almost imperceptibly, have slowly degenerated to a routine chore. At the primary level where project work has had an extended history and is now fairly widespread in practice, it can happen that some studies which have important values in their own right – and art is one of these – are in danger of being either stifled or distorted. Art may become little more than a means of providing painting or other illustrative work for a succession of projects. By contrast it would seem that many secondary schools have not yet established a system for inter-specialist liaison for the middle years, and frequently art and the various aspects of craft are divorced from each other and from the rest of the curriculum. Where this is the case, a review seems to be called for, if only to ascertain that middle-years children are being offered the best course of studies that can be arranged.

## References and notes

1. Department of Education and Science, *Art in Schools*, Education Survey No. 11 (HMSO, 1971), p. 65.
2. R. FIELD, in R. C. WHITFIELD, ed., *Disciplines of the Curriculum* (McGraw-Hill, 1971), pp. 162–74.
3. Central Advisory Council for Education (England), *Half Our Future* (HMSO, 1963), para. 378.
4. Central Advisory Council for Education (England), *Children and their Primary Schools* (HMSO, 1967), Vol. I para. 685.
5. Science 5–13, *With Objectives in Mind* (Macdonald Educational, 1972).
6. *Children and their Primary Schools*, Vol. I para. 676.
7. Department of Education and Science, *Art in Schools*, Education Survey No. 11 (HMSO, 1971), p. 2.
8. The Schools Council Art and Craft Education 8–13 Project (1969–72), based at Goldsmiths' College, University of London, and directed by Audrey Martin, Dr Renée Marcousé and Michael Laxton. Publishers: Van Nostrand Reinhold.

9. KEITH GENTLE, 'From random experience towards positive directions', *Ideas*, Nos 16 & 17 (January 1971), 11–15 (Journal of the Curriculum Laboratory, University of London Goldsmiths' College).

10. Central Advisory Council for Education (England), *Half Our Future* (HMSO, 1963), para. 378.

11. HERBERT READ, *Education through Art* (Faber, 1943), p. 11.

12. Department of Education and Science, *Art in Schools*, Education Survey No. 11 (HMSO, 1971), p. 94.

13. *Half Our Future*, para. 378.

14. *Children and their Primary Schools*, Vol. I, para. 676.

# IV. English

In writing this chapter the project has drawn extensively on an unpublished paper, 'English in the middle years of schooling,' produced by a sub-committee of the Schools Council English Committee. In acknowledging this, we are in no way implying that the Committee is necessarily in agreement with all this chapter contains.

Douglas Barnes has described the position of English as follows: 'The mother tongue has a unique status in the curriculum, because English at once indicates a subject area and a medium of learning and teaching.'[1] English in the middle years has therefore two closely related elements. One is mainly utilitarian and is concerned with the development of the four communication skills: listening, speaking, reading and writing. The other, which has an aesthetic bias, uses these skills and includes the use of poetry, prose and drama. Precise statements about the balance between these two aspects are not possible, for in striking a balance, even a theoretical balance, it is necessary to try to polarize the two elements on either side of a fulcrum. Not only is it extremely difficult to separate the two parts, but the position of the fulcrum itself is an important variable. In practice, balance is conditioned by the particular teaching situations which face individual teachers. For example, a child may be unable to function well in history or geography because of a lack of skill in reading and writing. Sympathetic help in the basic skills of communication may well enable him to reach his potential across the range of curriculum studies. At another level, a child who has these skills may be unable to respond adequately to the set of poems the class is reading. He is also disabled, although the reasons for the disability are different.

Throughout the whole of the middle years there are some children who cannot read, who cannot write and some who may appear orally inadequate. Obviously there are more of these children at the 8-year-old level than at 13, but the older children who lack these communication skills are likely to present a greater problem to the teaching staff, for such slow learners will often have behind them some years of school failure. At the other extreme, there are children who enter the middle years with good reading ability and some skill in spoken and written language and who, by the age of 13, frequently show considerable maturity. For most children, however, the middle years represent the period of schooling when considerable development in language skills takes place. Development is uneven, and teachers may be faced with any one of a number of different situations,

68

or indeed a mixture of situations. Probably the three most common are as follows:

1   The primary teacher who is responsible for all or most of the curriculum for a class of children. These children may have developed good language skills, they may have made little progress or, more likely, they may represent a range of ability levels.

2   The English specialist who is responsible for teaching a single subject to a large number of children throughout the secondary school. In some selective secondary schools all the children may have developed good language skills, while other schools are likely to have children covering a wide ability range, or there may be a preponderance of slower learners.

3   The specialist teacher responsible for teaching a subject other than English. This role will almost certainly involve some participation in language development. In extreme cases teachers may be faced with a major problem in helping youngsters with poor language skills to undertake satisfactory learning in other aspects of the curriculum.

Clearly English requires the co-operation of the whole staff in reaching agreement on objectives and procedures, at least with regard to language skills. It is obvious that the greater the ability shown by the children in such skills, the greater the chance of their being able to tackle other aspects of their work without facing the handicap of blocked channels of communication. It is also clear that since teachers work in a variety of different teaching situations their opinions on, and attitudes to, the teaching of English are likely to vary. There are also differences to be found in the relative importance which they attach to different aspects of teaching English.

In speech and the written word, children have access to two *means* of communication; however, in language they also have access, as the Barnes quotation implies, to a *medium* of communication – the medium in which learning and teaching are carried out. Children use language to communicate with others; they also think in language and respond through language to a very considerable extent. Their relative skills or disabilities in the use of language affect both intellectual and emotional development. What they become as people, how they relate to other people, and the ways in which they perceive the world, are closely bound up with their access to, and prowess in, language.

A framework of language functions would therefore be a very useful aid to teachers. The Schools Council English in the Middle Years of Schooling Project (1970–72)[2] developed and put forward one theory for such a framework. It is a sophisticated formulation which throws light upon the problem of language as a medium of communication. In this theory, a person is conceived of as being, at any one time, in one or two operational modes or stances, in relation to experience, knowledge and behaviour. The stance of a child may therefore be either the 'role of spectator' or it may be the 'role of participant'. The distinction between these two roles is basic to an understanding of the theory: the differences between them may be hinted at by asking the reader to consider the difference between *reflecting* on events, a spectator role, and *behaving* in them, a participant role. Expanding the distinction further, the spectator role involves going over what has already happened, rehearsing what might happen, and contemplating the behaviour of others, whether imagined or real, in order to relive, recreate, evaluate and savour the experience; the participant role involves *using* what one already knows, or finding out what one needs to know, in order to behave appropriately in the present circumstances. In the words of the English Committee's sub-committee, to be in the role of spectator is to be 'concerned with events not now taking place (i.e. past events or imagined events) and to be concerned with them *per se* (as an interruption to, or holiday from, the march of actual events) and not as some ongoing transaction with the actual.' To be in the role of participant is to be engaged in the world's work, to be behaving as buyer or seller, instructor or learner, confronter or appeaser, etc., when one is primarily concerned with 'getting things done'.

Within these two roles three functions of language may be plotted on a continuum:

Transactional ———————— Expressive ———————— Poetic
(participant role)                                                                (spectator role)

The English sub-committee in their paper on English in the middle years of schooling described the three functions as follows:

*Transactional language* is language adapted to the manifold purposes of getting things done in the world. Adaptation to different kinds of task (or transaction) sets up formal differences as striking, for example, as those between a running commentary on a race and an electioneering address, or a recipe and a psychiatric case-study. In general, its form is such as to articulate at any point with the practical, professional or intellectual concerns of those it is addressed to.

*Poetic language* is the medium of an art: it is language adapted to constructive, artistic purposes, to the production of objects of contemplation. Thus, its form is such as to *resist* piecemeal articulation with the practical, professional, intellectual concerns of a reader (or listener) and strive for

70

internal relations that give it a unified structure and make it a unique object.

*Expressive language* is language close to the speaker (or writer). It verbalizes his current preoccupations, displays his mood of the moment. Centrally (i.e. in its purest form for, as we noted, the line on the diagram represents a continuum), it is utterance at its most relaxed, utterance as free as possible from outside demands, those of a task or of an audience. It is informal, intimate language, and the person addressed (if there is one) is regarded as an intimate. What is said is likely to reveal more about the speaker's opinions and feelings about the world than it reveals about the world itself. Much of what is said would be ambiguous or meaningless to a listener who did not know the speaker, his general circumstances, and the circumstances of the utterance.

The theory is designed to allow the teacher to have a clear perspective of the comprehensiveness of a child's language experience, irrespective of subject divisions in the curriculum and, in a broader context, irrespective of whether the child's experience is located in the school or in the world outside the school. It underlines the significance of language as a medium and in doing so provides insights for the broader issues of English in the middle years. Similarly it offers some clues about the opportunities provided in the classroom. Thus a child who is deprived of the opportunity to write, read and listen to stories and poems is not only kept from experiencing language with a poetic function, with all that that might bring, but is also rendered less of a person. If we could obliterate the effects on a man of all the occasions when he was 'merely a spectator', it would profoundly alter his character and outlook. On the other hand, the pupil who does not have the opportunity to explore and use at his own level transactional language of an increasingly complex and diversified kind will be at a great disadvantage in making headway at the upper end of the secondary-school curriculum. Expressive language in general, and expressive speech in particular, is regarded as a developmental priority, for it is in speech above all that a person makes his first steps in sorting out and framing his hypotheses. To put it more bluntly, speech is the single most important language skill related to new learning.

The failure to demand active involvement of the pupils has gone hand in hand with a failure to demand that they verbalise their learning, that is, that they use language as an active instrument for reorganising their perceptions. It is not that there is too much language, but that it is not fulfilling its function as an instrument of learning. Rather, language is seen as an instrument of *teaching*.[3]

Skill in the English language is one of the most obvious goals of the schools, the level of achievement in this directly affecting the chances of success in all other cognitive attainments[4] and selection for particular educational opportunities. The 11-plus and other similar streaming devices depend heavily upon measurements of attainment in language skills, most often in written form. But however these skills may be taught, under whatever subject labels and sub-divisions English may be learned, it is clear that priority must be given to the development of speech.

> Not only does speech come before writing in all human experience, it comes before it in importance, because it bulks so much larger in the lives of ordinary folks and is so much bigger a factor in what we might call their social adequacy.[5]

'Reading is not our first problem in the curriculum', said the headmistress of an urban primary school. 'Speaking is. Many of the children are not just inarticulate but are incomprehensible outside the home environment.' The situation is not unique to urban areas for a similar statement was made by the head of a small rural school with an enrolment of children from isolated hill farms. Giving children many opportunities for developing and improving their skill in talking is clearly an important priority. Teachers will also be concerned in widening the range of subjects for discussion and the contexts in which talk takes place. Children in the middle years of schooling have many vicarious experiences from the mass media of television, radio, cinema and comics, but there is no dialogue with these particular audio-visual stimuli. They warrant allocation of school time for investigation; discussion with others may enable the children to learn modes of critical appreciation. Further experiences, more direct and with personal involvement, are desirable, and when teachers plan these they often have not only linguistic objectives in mind but also goals related to other social and cognitive attainments.

Teachers take pupils to the theatre, to dance festivals, to museums and fire-stations, to the local park and to the sea-shore. Here there are not only shared experiences which generate the need for spoken language, but also sources of new knowledge and enriched vocabulary. Going outside the walls of the school, costly though it may be in time, may well result in higher achievements within the school. The science department of one secondary school devoted an afternoon each week to local projects undertaken by first-year pupils. Most of the work was practical and initially the children were not expected to undertake written work; the emphasis to start with was on encouraging the practice of accurate and concise oral reporting. The two chief objectives were the successful handling of scientific equipment and precision in the verbal reports of their

72

inquiries and discoveries. High achievement in these skills would, the teachers believed, aid pupils in the more formally organized science programme in later classes where the balance would shift from verbal reporting to written reporting. The teachers recognized that the development of the appropriate spoken language was in itself a major undertaking.

James Britton has claimed that the development of the appropriate spoken language is in itself a sufficiently exacting task, demanding a more precise form of linguistic construction than the usual expressive modes of daily converse. He recorded the talk of a group of first-year secondary pupils. Afterwards he observed:

> I believe that the movement in words from what might *describe* a particular event to a generalisation that might *explain* that event, is a journey that each [pupil] must be capable of taking for himself – *and that it is by means of taking it in speech that we learn to take it in thought* . . . The spare look this language has may mislead us into thinking that it can easily be learnt. But the task is not that of learning a language; rather it is that of acquiring *by the agency of the language* the ability to perform these mental operations . . . *a child's language is the means.*[6]

From a primary school the headmaster and staff took the fourth-year pupils to a good hotel on the south coast to provide experiences which were almost completely outside the lives of council estate children. Simply learning how to order a meal in such a setting was, he thought, a desirable accomplishment. The journey provided a number of new situations which offered scope for language development as well as growth in other directions.

> If language is a behavioural response then it can only take place meaningfully where there is something to which the pupil can respond. The nature and quality of the context also become important. The teacher must first ensure that the contexts he uses will throw up ideas and concepts which will stimulate his pupils and give scope for behavioural response in language . . . Necessity is the mother of learning in acquiring language skills, and it is the job of the teacher to devise contexts which are likely to throw up such points of necessity.[7]

It is not only in such extra-mural contexts, of course, that language stimulus may be found, but also by providing appropriate experiences within the classroom where, after all, most schooling takes place. (The outside can also be brought inside.) As Douglas Barnes says:

73

The uses to which language is put by the pupils in any lesson depend not merely on language tasks explicitly required by the teacher, but on each pupil's perception of the whole situation which provides a context for language use . . . there is reason to believe that children differ from one another in the extent to which their performance is determined by context.[8]

There is a need, therefore, to provide different contexts in order to help all pupils, not merely by the interest aroused for something new but by the challenge and opportunities for language development which are entailed. Which kinds of activities will be of most worth can only be decided by close and careful study of the pupils, their attainments, environment and probable interests. Although the aim must include maximum pupil involvement, it will almost certainly be desirable to plan for small groups with minority tastes. Anyway, some children respond better in a smaller group than the class. Within such groups opportunities may be provided for testing and expanding ideas aroused in earlier experiences. The teacher will be testing the success or otherwise of the programme and procedures, the children trying out new phrases and new knowledge.

The teacher may not be the encouraging leader or participant he thinks he is. His questions may not sound to children as encouraging as they were meant to be.[9] So many questions directed at the class are intended to elicit a specific response desired by the teacher. The child knows that the questioner has the answer and that speculation or even sensible guesswork will be unacceptable. It may be of some assistance in the learning process for a teacher to analyse the kinds of questions he uses and how different kinds may be related to different objectives. While every effort may be made to encourage verbal participation by all pupils, even in the most successful groups there will be some who contribute less frequently than the others and all pupils will be silent sometimes. Yet even the silent ones may be taking part. In an unpublished paper from the Schools Council English in the Middle Years of Schooling Project, B. Newsome writes: 'One cannot very well discuss talk without referring to what the silent members of the group are doing. Talk, after all, is social interaction.' The success of the social interaction will depend to some extent on the degree of individual successes among the members. Whatever the curricular subject may be, each child has a need for recognition of his contribution and an expectation of success, at least sometimes. This success will be closely associated with his general language ability which can be fostered by every teacher in the school.

So far this chapter has placed considerable emphasis on the importance of speech. Next to it in importance is reading. Much has been written about the various methods, approaches and schemes for teaching reading and it would be

74

quite impossible to give even a summary here of the main arguments contained in the literature. However, there are three questions which seem worthy of being mentioned. The first is concerned with the extent of the relationship that exists between reading and writing. To what extent can encoding the written language be linked with decoding the printed word, and ought the two processes to develop hand in hand? This question is examined by David Mackay and Brian Thompson in *The Initial Teaching of Reading and Writing: Some Notes toward a Theory of Literacy*.[10]

Ronald Morris discusses the second question in his article, 'What children learn in learning to read':[11]

> Basically the argument is that psychologically speaking it is difficult to learn anything neat. We cannot set out to teach a child the skills of reading and succeed in doing just that. The invitation to learning that we offer a child brings many guests, some unwanted, to the party.

He stresses the importance of the teacher ensuring that learning to read takes place in a situation that is relevant to the child, that it is not an activity like solving a crossword puzzle but is associated with a purpose – *what it is* that the child wants to read, write or understand. Morris further suggests that the development of other channels of communication have made some changes in the reasons why a child needs to be able to read.

> Reading is not quite what it was, or what it was thought to be, thirty or forty years ago when most of the dominant techniques in use today were developed. In particular, while reading is still thought of in many quarters as the only or most effective way of extending vocabulary and acquiring vicarious experience, both these claims are questionable in contemporary society blessed as it is with an abundance of communication through non-literary channels. It can therefore be argued that it may be better to think of reading today and in the immediate future as taking its main significance from the contribution that it can make in helping the individual to reflect upon, organise and understand at a deeper level some of the ideas and information that reach him first through other channels. The view that it is only, or mainly, through book learning that we can enlarge our command of language and knowledge of the world has had its day and should cease to be.

The third question is concerned with the relationship which exists between the experience of the reader and the content of what is read – what is behind the phrase 'to read with understanding'. Very little is yet known about this, and it

75

is doubtful if it is possible, in the present stage of knowledge, to make first generalizations about all children. Certainly not all arrive at the level of understanding described by Lord David Cecil:

> To train our taste is to increase our capacity for pleasure: for it enables us to enter into such a variety of experience. This is indeed the special, precious power of literature. In actual life our experience is inevitably restricted both by the limitations imposed by our circumstances and by our own character. No one person can ever know in practice what it is to be both a man and a woman, a mystic and a materialistic, a criminal and a pillar of society, an ancient Roman and a modern Russian. But books can teach us to be all these things in imagination.[12]

Three other aspects of reading in the middle years must be briefly mentioned. Firstly, there is the importance of the teacher's sharing prose and poetry with the children. The good story well read is vital at the early stages and its value has by no means vanished at the older age-level. Secondly, there is a need for the provision of an adequate supply of books to be readily and freely available to children throughout the middle years. In some of the larger secondary schools where first- and second-year pupils are not permitted access to the main library or where its use is, for them, restricted to one period each week to permit the changing of a story book, then it seems essential to establish a separate reference library for the lower school. The pattern of having books readily available in infant, junior, middle, upper-secondary schools and in universities ought not to be suspended during the first years in secondary education. Thirdly, this chapter is being written at a time when considerable interest has been aroused over the question of standards of reading ability in schoolchildren. The Plowden Report, *Children and their Primary Schools*,[13] indicated the considerable proportion of homes where books were either non-existent or held in low esteem. Although standards in reading ability are a matter of concern, the actual skill of reading is only one aspect of the whole problem. The task of the teacher in the middle years is the wider one of developing and cultivating in children a taste for books of all kinds, and there is a danger that an over-emphasis on the need to increase reading skills may distract some teachers from the wider and more fundamental objectives of literacy. Some of the schools which the team visited have adopted schemes which help children to become not only book readers but also book owners and an increasing number of teachers are offering middle-years children help and guidance in beginning their own home library. The skill of reading is not something to be considered in isolation, for in practice it is closely linked with all the books used by children in school and with the study of literature itself. Perhaps one of the greatest strengths of the primary-school organization is that it facilitates the task of the teacher in arranging for the natural integration of literature with other aspects of the curriculum. Because he is aware of the 'whole', the experienced primary teacher is able to see that appropriate literary experiences are used to enhance the teaching of other aspects of the curriculum. He can draw from the range of historical novels, from stories of exploration and discovery, from natural history tales and from the store of poetry, those books and extracts which will contribute to the children's learning. This practice is followed to an increasing extent at secondary level, but at present there are still many schools where even a basic element of co-operation across the curriculum is lacking.

One of the most interesting examples of co-operative planning that the project team was able to observe was in a secondary school where the role of the specialist teacher was held in high esteem but where it was recognized that it was difficult to provide a sufficiently wide range of learning experiences within the confines of a rigid, subject-based timetable. For short periods during the term the timetable for first-year pupils was suspended while staff and pupils undertook a full-time investigation of some aspect of the local environment. At the time of the team's visit the children were studying the cause and effect of the east coast floods which had inundated part of their town some years earlier. The English specialists had a key role and they undertook the organization of the children's interviews with police, fire-brigade, other social and welfare officials, with people whose homes had been flooded, and with officials in the municipal offices. The English team was also responsible for co-ordinating the bulk of the written work, the editing of tapes and the selection of appropriate poetry and prose dealing with man's recurring battle with the elements. They also supervised the flow of creative writing generated by the investigation. This, by itself, might be considered a valuable experience for the children although it would have been extremely difficult to organize within the confines of the normal timetable. However, the whole study was enhanced by the work of other specialists. The scientists and geographers considered with the pupils the how and why of the flood's occurrence. The history specialists offered the children their expertise in showing how an historian sets about investigating an historical happening, where records might be found and evidence collected. The art and craft team undertook responsibility for mounting an exhibition of paintings, drawings, photographs, written reports, maps, diagrams and models. They also undertook the supervision of the making of books and folders to contain a more permanent record of the investigation.

While there was complete agreement over the value of the exercise and it was recognized that the pupils were highly motivated and produced much work of an excellent standard, there was some disagreement over whether such an

77

approach to learning could be allowed to make greater inroads into the normal timetable. The majority of teachers felt that they would be unable to sustain either their own or the pupils' energy for a much longer period and that the law of diminishing returns might begin to operate. They felt that the exercise, carried out occasionally, gave relevance to all that the school was doing and served as both a 'harvest-time' for much that had gone before and a point of reference for work to follow. The work of this school has been reported in some detail because it offers a useful description of one way in which the pattern of learning, common to many children attending primary or middle schools, can be adapted and extended with considerable profit at the secondary level, and where full use was made of the enhanced resources and specialist expertise in such schools.

One of the problems in considering English as part of the middle-years curriculum is to deal adequately with its various aspects. The terminology in common use is frequently ill-defined, and is also capable of arousing strong feelings because of the various schools of thought with which certain terms have become associated. The project team looked at twenty schools in one local education authority and found that English was included either in the timetable or in an outline curriculum under some forty different headings. Obviously many of these naming words are synonyms but even when these have been clustered together, it is still apparent that the groupings reflect some of the different emphases which schools have in the teaching of English. Some schools chose to adopt broad headings such as English, humanities, aesthetics, integrated studies, projects, or assignments. Others subsumed the bulk of their work under headings such as basic skills, optional work, creative activities, topics, group and individual work, television and radio. Others adopted a more specific or fragmented approach: speech, drama, handwriting, writing practice, mechanical English, spelling, dictation, comprehension, grammar, compositions, essays, diaries, poetry, literature, library, stories, oral discussions, reading, and so on. Other headings were: English talks, language, language skills, language development, group and remedial reading, reading laboratory, literary experiences, written language, written expression, creative English, creative writing, free writing. While such a list of headings gives only an imprecise indication either of what the head of the school intends should happen, or of what individual teachers are actually doing, nevertheless it might be felt that such a list gives some indication of the approaches to English to be found in just a small sample of schools in one locality.

Between the ages of 8 and 13 most children will be developing the ability to write with a reasonable degree of fluency and, one would hope, with a fair hand and with increasing accuracy in spelling and sentence construction. In our visits

78

to schools we met a great variety of opinions about approaches, procedures and priorities as far as the teaching of written English is concerned. At one extreme are those who see the chief priority being the maintenance of the freedom of the child to 'express himself through his writing'. At the other extreme are those who believe it important to offer a structured programme involving spelling, dictation, handwriting, essays and the teaching of various aspects of grammar. While only a minority of teachers seem to have opinions that are quite so strongly polarized as this, most appear to be clear about their priorities. These tend to be strongly held and are most often expressed in language that is either 'left or right of centre' – that is, they place greater emphasis on the fact that writing skills grow and develop from the actual practice of writing, or they claim that it is important to spend time specifically teaching spelling, sentence construction, grammar and so on as a means of achieving 'satisfactory standards' in their children's writing. Both approaches can be seen to work well when adopted by skilled and efficient teachers with a sensitive approach to children's learning, but unfortunately it seems equally true to say that neither approach guarantees success. From visits to many schools recommended as outstanding for their work in the teaching of English, certain common characteristics seemed to emerge. Without presenting these in any order of priority they are:

1   A plentiful supply of good fiction and reference books available for children to use and an interest and concern shown by the teachers in what the children read.
2   Good prose and poetry read by the teacher to the children. Much conversation with the children, as distinct from talking to them.
3   A deliberate attempt to ensure that written work has a relevance that is apparent to children. Hence a frequent linking of English with other aspects of the curriculum, and written work based on children's direct experiences.
4   Children's written work carefully considered to enable wise judgements to be made about the degree and kind of help it would seem best to offer them.
5   Following from 4, the exploitation of teaching situations that arise from discussions of the children's own written work, frequently at an individual level, but also considerable group teaching to deal with common factors.
6   No adoption of 'class standards' of good work, but a recognition that children will be working at a variety of levels depending on their ability and level of attainment. (Perhaps a belief in the truth of Adler's dictum, 'If you can't praise a page, praise a line; if you can't praise a line praise a word; if you can't praise a word praise the way a letter has been formed. The point of success is the point of growth'.)

**7**    An awareness that different types of writing call for different skills and the adoption of a long-term policy to extend and develop those skills. This is far from needing a detailed syllabus setting out any given progression but it is equally far from a random, haphazard approach to the development of children's written work.

**8**    High standards adopted by the teachers and forming part of the ethos of the school. Thus neatness and tidiness are not made a fetish but are seen to make sense in a crowded school community. Frequently handwriting will be taught as an art form and stressed when written work is to be displayed or preserved.

In the paper on English in the middle years of schooling (unpublished) from a sub-committee of the Schools Council English Committee, the following comments were made on expressive language:

We believe that in favourable circumstances a great deal of speaking and writing by children of 8 to 13 will lie within the band we have labelled 'expressive', for these reasons:

**1**    Much of the talk that goes on in families is expressive, so that such talk presents an influential model from the start.

**2**    Children have to learn to take into account the needs and point of view of a listener, i.e. their early attempts at putting their ideas into words are highly egocentric. Those who know them best learn to interpret their meaning where a stranger cannot. This egocentricism reinforces the tendency to use expressive language in the middle years.

**3**    Closely allied to this, but a more powerful reason, is the fact . . . that a new idea will tend to find its first formulation in words that meet *our own* requirements but are not subjected to any further demands from elsewhere. For this reason we may nourish an idea by talking about it with a close friend who shares our interest – that is to say by discussing it in expressive language: and only then go on to the formulation intended for the target audience – a formulation either in transactional or poetic language as the case may be.

Thus in so far as schools set out to foster the use of language at the children's own initiative (the use of language to serve the user's own purposes), they are likely to meet utterances at various stages along the continuum from the expressive outwards in both directions. And the ability to move outwards will be an indication of growth in linguistic competence.

The same Schools Council paper included some useful notes on writing and reading and these seem to offer an appropriate summary to what has been written here:

Observation of school writings over a wide range would suggest the following hypotheses:

1 The main stream of activity in writing in the middle years will lie within the expressive category, and the principal form of development will be increasing differentiation in the directions of both the transactional and the poetic.

2 Expressive writing is the form most directly channelled to the resources of a child's own speech: it is the form that presents the fewest obstacles to writing-for-one's-own-purposes.

3 Major influences in the process of moving towards transactional and poetic writing will, however, be familiarity with written models.

4 Deliberate imitation of written models is much less likely to blend with the speech-activated flow of expressive language than are the internalized after-effects of reading for its own sake. Deliberate teaching of a written style is likely to be ineffectual for a similar reason.

That such teaching may miscarry is suggested, we believe, by the following from a ten-year-old girl:

'Our new house was very conspicuous from the narrow lane and even though the place was very old we were very pleased with the garden, which was quite large and very untidy.

'Daddy and my big tall brother were in the dirty shed, cleaning out the rubbish and making room for the well used car of ours. I joined them and gave them each a cup of strong coffee, which they received with gratitude.

'In the kitchen, Mummy was sorting the furniture, wearing her pretty overall to protect her from the thick dust. "Come on Sally," she called, "your coffee is gradually getting cold." "Coming," I yelled back loudly . . .'

The next writer, also ten, seems, in a quite average way, to be in the process of *learning* to write, and shows promise for the future:

'Gloomy house: there is nothing nice about it. It has no colour in it. It is all a dirty grey misty colour, all the paint is scratched. Then when the sun comes out it is gay, the whole house lights up with a lovely bright pink and so does my old dull face with a pink too.

'The flowers on the window ledge open out with happiness in them. The grass turns green with delight . . .'

**5**    Learning to write cannot be separated from learning to read: in both processes we improvise actively upon our own representations, our stored experiences. In writing, the selecting and ordering of the material is our own task; in reading, our task is to order the elements in accordance with the structure given by the writer. Moreover, our ability to 'remake' in this way the experiences of others will depend upon the degree to which language has for us its roots in first-hand experience. Since these roots are grown above all in speech, and particularly in early speech, the reading ability of the 13-year-old will probably depend a good deal upon the talking experiences of the 8-year-old.

**6**    If expressive writing forms the main stream of activity in writing throughout the middle years, the main stream of expressive writing is likely to be 'autobiographical'. Hovering between the participant and spectator roles, such writing is capable of development towards the transactional (as in the first piece below), and towards the poetic – the fictional story or the poem, as in the remaining pieces:

'On Sunday I made some coal gas. I got a large peanut tin and punched a hole in the top. I filled it one third full with small bits of coal. Nothing happened when I first put it on the fire but after a while brown stuff came out. It was gas. I immediately tried to light it but it did not light. I tried to light it every five minutes. After fifteen minutes it lit. It lasted for eight minutes. My second try lasted for one hour three minutes. Each time it did not turn to coke. The back of the tin was red hot.' (Boy, aged 10)

'I awake, it's still early, I can hear my husband downstairs getting ready for work. A number of thoughts flood into my head. I remember it's Monday, I'm taking Form Three. 7.30, time to get up. I arrive in school two minutes late. I open the door and go in, nobody stands up, place my books on the wooden table and sit down. I speak. "Has anybody thought about the story I told you?" Hope answers, "please Mam but my mum said you shouldn't talk about books like that, she said it's . . ." "Okay", I say, "now who knows the author of Oliver?" Hope replies, "Er, Charles Dickens, wasn't it Mam?" "Yes," I smile, "now Paul did you know that," I say. He doesn't ask me why I said it as usual. He just looks out of the window. I shout, "Paul answer me" but he doesn't. To him I don't exist. I wonder if I do exist in their eyes or am I just a piece of furniture that speaks and isn't heard. Why don't they listen to me, is it because I'm dark. "What's wrong with me" I scream. They laugh and walk out – it's the end of the lesson. Paul shouts back, "Go where you're wanted." ' (Girl, aged 12)

'A Catherine wheel spins round
Seeming to say something you can't quite catch.
Swish – a golden rocket cuts through the air
And explodes where the stars seek refuge.' (Girl, aged 12)

This chapter has looked briefly at the uses to which language is put and at the varieties of speech and writing associated with those uses. In the primary school these varieties will be related in a multiplicity of ways in accordance with the activities the teacher makes available and with the interests of individual children. But where a subject curriculum is provided (and it is in the middle years of schooling that the shift to a subject-based curriculum takes place) how is the particular responsibility of the English specialist to be defined?

Curiosity in young children has few bounds for they are ready to be interested at some point in all that surrounds them. In the course of their schooling, their common curiosity has to be channelled into subjects that our educational system has marked out as areas where ideas of a particular variety can be conveniently handled. Their common curiosity about the natural and social environment is satisfied in part through geography, in part through science, in part through history, or maybe through environmental and social studies. But what English does is to focus upon a child's private, personal, individual experiences, all those areas of concern in which he is likely to be different from other children. It is no accident, then, that literature (in its traditional sense) is an important part of the responsibilities of an English teacher, since the concern of poets, novelists and playwrights is also, in essence, a man's unique and individual response to his experiences.

It is at this personal level that a child's experiences must be progressively drawn together to construct a relatively coherent, individual 'representation' or view of our common world as he progressively comes to understand it. And remembering that feeling and appraising as well as thinking are important elements of that representation, the major undertaking of English teaching is predominantly an activity in the spectator role, and not the participant. That is to say it is concerned not with knowledge and theory, but with assimilative or integrative processes. It indicates a concern for the unity and harmony of a child's total representation of experience. Thus talking and writing in the spectator role mark one aspect of the activity and a response to literature the other. There is a joint focus on literature (other men's representations of life in the role of spectators) and on children's opportunities, through talk and writing, of representing their own experiences in the role of spectator.

An English teacher also has a duty to perform with respect to a child's linguistic development in general, to his use of language as an agent in learning.

He needs to be able to communicate effectively and meaningfully and with ease in speech as in writing. This duty, it is suggested, has to be discharged in two ways. First, wherever paying attention to language as such, or learning things *about* language, proves to be a direct or indirect aid to using it (and this is a matter upon which we have to be pragmatic since evidence is scant and confusing) these approaches will be his responsibility. The second way is an indirect one. As a specialist he will need to help his colleagues to appreciate the important role that language plays in learning in all subjects, and convince them of the necessity of evolving a common attitude and coherent policy for language across all subjects in the curriculum of the school. In a middle school it may well be that the English specialist's direct and indirect responsibilities are closely interrelated. His own teaching, for a start, will provide him with some experiences of language activities across the spectrum. It is hardly desirable, and in any case hardly practicable, in a middle school for any teacher to confine his work to a single subject. Anyone who is acting as a 'consultant' specialist, rather than a 'practitioner' specialist, will be teaching more than one subject – or if the curriculum is defined in different terms, will be concerned with more than English alone. Thus, as a subject-based curriculum emerges, all who subscribe to the total language policy may have had some practical experience of its operation over a wide range, and hence have gained a clear idea of the other specialist needs with which, at the appropriate stage, their own must connect.

The secondary school presents a much sharper problem and one which, by all the evidence, has hardly been tackled. Traditional specialist teaching is often based upon practices of learning that take little account of the role of language. Not all teachers recognize the value to a learner of his own linguistic formulations. Writing, for instance, is for many teachers no more than a testing device, a means of retrieving information previously taught. Again, the efforts of many teachers to generate discussion may result in sessions which remain dominated by the teacher and his language. The possibility of moving from an initial tentative formulation in talk to a more reflective formulation in writing is still often unrecognized or ignored.

These are problems which can only be solved co-operatively by all the staff of a school. An English teacher has an opportunity of a particular kind, for it is in language activities in the spectator role that continuity from primary to secondary stages is likely to be least disrupted. A glance at one of the many collections of children's writing compiled in recent years may demonstrate some thread of development across the age-range in the personal writing, and stories and poems that children produce.

Development in participant role language is more difficult. It seems that writing of the kind quoted in the first example (the 10-year-old describing the

84

experience of moving into a new house) is rarely given the opportunity and encouragement to develop by gradual evolution into scientific reporting. Instead adult models are often prematurely insisted upon, and often enough these models are themselves second-rate writing. Again, when teachers of history or geography or other subjects invite children to take up the role of spectator – with participant activity eventually in view – whether in dramatic improvisation or in story-writing, there seems to be no consensus of understanding as to what is expected or on how the product is to be judged, or about what is to be gained from the undertaking. There exists, as we have suggested, a general air of uncertainty among teachers of all subjects as to what is the role of discussion – or the value of expressive talk – in teaching and learning; and as to how much talk from the teacher is profitable – of what kinds, at what stages and in what circumstances. These are not, of course, errors of perversity, but they arise from a general unconcern with language as a factor to be reckoned with in learning. Indeed some experimental thinking and teaching on the part of a few gifted specialist teachers highlights a matter of fundamental importance. A full consideration of the processes by which, in the middle years, transactional language begins to evolve from the expressive, seen in relation to the formation of the concepts proper to a specialist study, might well revolutionize the teaching of many subjects in the secondary curriculum. Perhaps the outstanding problem for the English teacher in the area of his main concern is that of ensuring progress in personal writing. We have suggested that there is continuity here from the primary to the secondary stage, but does that not sometimes appear as mere continuation without progress – a marking-time but no march? How in fact should progress be recognized? The earlier theoretical outline has suggested partial answers; a full answer in practical terms must await further analysis and further experiment. Meanwhile we shall content ourselves with suggesting two general and comprehensive roles for the English teacher.

1    The teacher as provider of material and experience. Once it has been understood that the reading of fiction, biography, etc., finds its value as a source of secondary experience, there can be no reason to exclude from the English teacher's concern such media as drama, film, radio and television, and by the same token not to take into the programme direct first-hand experiences as material for the children's own original presentations. Although a child comes to the class-room brimful of his own experiences (which, with the teacher's help, he will handle in language), the teacher will want to provide particular first-hand experiences both to the group as a whole and to individuals within it.

2    The teacher as stimulator, audience, confidant, critic, guide, instructor, chairman – and these are only some of the changing roles he bears vis-à-vis

children as language users. Many varieties of language usage have to be considered in planning any programme of activities. There is the kind of talk that accompanies and facilitates joint activity; the kind that maintains relationships between individuals in a group; the kind that seeks a solution or a consensus; the kind that supports individual reflection or interpretation; the kind that 'realizes' a text (or other form of presentation); the kind that leads to conceptualization and the kind that sanctions and modifies feelings and attitudes; dramatic talk; talk to inform or persuade. There is also writing of many kinds: factual, explanatory, informative, persuasive; personal, expressive; narrative, poetic, dramatic. We need to discover a great deal more, both by theoretical study and by the recording and interpretation of practical experiences, about how these forms relate to each other, and by what routes individual children arrive at a degree of mastery of some or all of them. This will involve, as we have suggested already, a consideration of a child's total educational experience and the way his work in English articulates with this total.

## References and notes

1. DOUGLAS BARNES, 'Language and learning in the classroom', *Journal of Curriculum Studies*, **3** (May 1971), 30.
2. Schools Council English in the Middle Years of Schooling Project (1970–72) was based at Goldsmiths' College, University of London, and directed by B. Newsome. Final report of project in preparation.
3. DOUGLAS BARNES, JAMES BRITTON and HAROLD ROSEN, *Language, the Learner and the School* (Penguin Books, 1969), p. 66.
4. See M. M. LEWIS, 'Language and mental development' in E. A. LUNZER and J. F. MORRIS, eds, *Development in Learning*, Vol. II: *Development in Human Learning* (Staples Press, 1968), pp. 144 et seq.
5. Report of the Advisory Council on Secondary Education in Scotland (HMSO, 1947), p. 63.
6. JAMES BRITTON, 'Talking to learn' in DOUGLAS BARNES, JAMES BRITTON and HAROLD ROSEN, *Language, the Learner and the School* (Penguin Books, 1969), pp. 114–15.
7. A. H. B. DAVIDSON, 'Rigour and concept in the project method', *Teaching English*, **4** (October 1970).
8. DOUGLAS BARNES, 'Language and learning in the classroom', *Journal of Curriculum Studies*, **3** (May 1971), 34.
9. For further discussion on this see DOUGLAS BARNES, ibid., and PAUL WILLIAMS, 'Talk and discussion', *English in Education*, **5** (Summer 1971), 18–30.

10. DAVID MACKAY and BRIAN THOMPSON, *The Initial Teaching of Reading and Writing: Some Notes toward a Theory of Literacy*, Programme in Linguistics and English Teaching, Paper 3 (Longman, 1968).
11. RONALD MORRIS, 'What children learn in learning to read', *English in Education*, **5** (Winter 1971), 8–19.
12. LORD DAVID CECIL, *Reading as One of the Fine Arts*, an inaugural lecture (Clarendon Press, 1949).
13. Central Advisory Council for Education (England), *Children and their Primary Schools* (HMSO, 1967), Vol. I.

# V. Geography

This chapter is derived from a paper prepared for the project by the Geography Committee of the Schools Council. Modifications have been made to avoid repetition of points made elsewhere and to eliminate differences in terminology. Additional illustrative material has been introduced at the request of teachers who read the paper when it was circulated for comment to teachers' centres throughout the country. Many schools will also be familiar with the materials from the Schools Council Project, History, Geography and Social Science 8–13 (1971–75), based at the University of Liverpool School of Education, and directed by Professor W. A. L. Blyth and R. Derricott. (These materials are published by Collins and E.S.L.)

## Geography and children in the middle years of schooling

Most children will, for most of their middle years, be in Piaget's stage of concrete operations.[1] Accepting, however, that the middle years of schooling include a changeover from the stage of concrete operations to that of formal operations, what do these terms mean in the practical learning situation, particularly with reference to the teaching of geography?

The stage of concrete operations is divided by Piaget into three sub-stages. The first is the period 2 to $4\frac{1}{2}$ years, when children are beginning to use language but lack clearly defined concepts to use with their language. Consequently their reasoning is not well structured. The second is the intuitive sub-stage, $4\frac{1}{2}$ to 7 years, when children begin to give reasons for their beliefs and actions and acquire a number of concepts. But their thinking may still be logically inconsistent. The third sub-stage is that of concrete operations proper, when physical actions or procedures may be internalized (i.e. carried out mentally). Thus children in this stage are able to arrange concepts into a hierarchy of classes, to arrange things, numbers, areas, etc., in order of magnitude, to understand that a group may be sub-divided into alternative classes (for example, the British Isles into Great Britain and Ireland or the UK and Eire). These children are also conscious that certain relations are symmetrical, that is, they are similar no matter from what point of view they are looked at – for example, measuring the distance from London to Birmingham is the same as measuring it from Birmingham to London. Similarly, they are able to handle 'multiplicative operations', that is, operations which demand the handling of two or more

88

quantities or qualities – for example, locating places on a map by use of grid references is such an operation.

Piaget, with special reference to spatial concepts, found that by the end of the final sub-stage of concrete operations, children could understand topological concepts, projective concepts (for example, perspective and cross-sections), and apply intelligently ideas concerning lengths, areas, angles and certain elementary properties of plan geometry. On the other hand, difficulties arose in the reproduction of three-dimensional models in two-dimensional space since these involved the use of two different systems of reference (horizontal and vertical) and two different scale systems. Further, the idea that the relationship between the various elements of a model remained constant, no matter from what point of view the model was seen, was also absent at that stage. Thus accurate map drawing is still a difficult art for most children in the concrete operations period. In general, children in this stage are still unable to make valid generalizations beyond what is to them concrete, finite, and visible.

The stage of formal operations is the stage when adolescent thinking is transformed into adult thinking. When complete, this transformation enables the adolescent not only to think logically, but to postulate hypotheses and to test them against experience. The pupil who has reached this stage is able to think both inductively and deductively and to understand the meaning and uses of generalizations and laws. Thus such a pupil may be able to infer inductively from statistics of rainfall and of height above sea level that there is a general relationship between rainfall and relief. He may then use his knowledge of the properties of air and the concept of relative humidity to postulate deductively a mechanism which would link causally air temperature and the amount of water vapour in the atmosphere, variations in air temperature with changes in relief, and variations in precipitation spatially with movement of air from areas of high relief. He knows that to check whether this generalization is valid he will have to measure the relative humidity of the air at various heights above sea level. In other words, the pupil who has reached this stage of mental development not only thinks in this manner, but is conscious that he does and knows the limitations and possibilities of these formal operations. He understands that if his premises are false, then his conclusion is false and he must start again.

Further concept development proceeds throughout intellectual development in the light of the individual's experiences of reality and his mental structuring of that reality. Consequently his mode of thinking will be helped or hindered by the mental concepts he has acquired at any stage either within or outside the school. However, we know that children, even within the UK, grow up in vastly different physical and social environments, that according to the experiences they have they will or will not develop certain concepts and even certain types of

89

language to express their ideas. The concept represented by the word 'moorland' may mean much more to the pupil living in Lancashire or Yorkshire than to the pupil living in Surrey or Kent. Similarly, children in contact at home with facilities for finding things out, or at school with stimulating teaching, may well develop their thinking much more rapidly than children whose homes and school are educationally unenterprising.

It may also be argued that as mental maturity develops, so will the need to structure learning along more formal lines. In geography this means that whereas in the early years children's investigations of their environment proceed without any consciousness of what particular discipline is being used, in later years they will become conscious of the body of concepts, rules and procedures belonging to a subject, and they will begin to appreciate whether a problem needs to be tackled by using the ideas and techniques of, for example, mathematics, geography or physics. But the advantage of the Piagetian model of intellectual development is that it is independent of whether teaching proceeds along subject or non-subject lines. It tells us that, in the middle years of schooling, there will be little point in teaching subject matter along formal propositional lines, except perhaps for a minority of pupils. Nothing in this model of mental development suggests that the content of geography is in any way unsuitable for this age-range. In fact our knowledge of children's curiosity suggests that they may be highly motivated towards the many aspects of geography.

## Objectives for geography teaching in the middle years

In order to arrive at a clear discussion of objectives it is necessary to make a distinction between two conceptions of aims, both of which are relevant to the teaching of geography. Firstly, we may conceive of broad educational aims. These may be achieved through the teaching of geography or through the teaching of other curriculum subjects, though in the practical school situation it is difficult to ascertain whether or to what extent this is so. In their breadth of conception these aims transcend subject boundaries: they are realistic in so far as they define the long-term education of a person. Secondly, there are aims which are specific or unique to the teaching of geography. These aims are more easily realizable in geographical attitudes, skills and concepts. They are easier to state as objectives. A useful way of emphasizing the distinction, in the words of N. J. Graves, is that 'we must realize that there is a difference between what we would like geography to achieve and what it in fact achieves.'[2]

EDUCATIONAL AIMS OF GEOGRAPHY

1    To encourage clear thinking, the acquisition of knowledge and the art of utilizing knowledge, which in itself can be interesting and culturally valuable.

2    To promote the development of intellectual skills, such as the ability **a** to perceive, select and record accurately, whether in the field, from books, pictures or other visual and audio aids; **b** to classify phenomena; **c** to analyse, synthesize, correlate and evaluate information; and **d** to generalize.

3    To heighten the appreciation of the link between individual phenomena and the whole of which they are part, providing abundant evidence of the interrelationships of subjects.

4    To help in the formation of favourable attitudes concerning social responsibility, tolerance and initiative, and international understanding (for example, to stimulate interest in local, national and world affairs and the growth of accurate, realistic ideas concerning other people).

5    To offer opportunities for aesthetic experiences.


AIMS SPECIFIC TO GEOGRAPHY

*Attitudes*

1    An awareness of the peculiar, dynamic relationship which exists between man and the total environment in every area studied, that is, an essentially human, ecological view. No other subject attempts to elucidate this relationship in such breadth. Geography involves some understanding of the many facets of man, revealed in anthropology, archaeology, history, economics and sociology, and of the equally broad spectrum of the physical world treated by the physical sciences and mathematics.

2    An appreciation of the elements of landscapes (including urban and rural), their evolution and integration to form coherent wholes, both physical and social.

3    An interest in inquiring into the nature and location of peoples and places.


*Skills and concepts*

Perhaps the easiest way to arrive at these aims is to attempt to state what the terminal objectives might be. By terminal objectives are meant the knowledge and abilities that many children should possess by the time they reach the end of the age-range under review. Such a statement of objectives must be guided by the past experience of teachers and by the experimental evidence given by Piaget and other psychologists as to what children are able to comprehend and do by the time they reach the age of 13. Since there is logically no end to the possible factual content of geography, it is necessary to delimit these terminal objectives by stating the skills and concepts which might be known. These could be derived from a series of experiences arranged by the teacher from fieldwork, studies of the UK and of other parts of the world, factual material from other subject areas being drawn upon as required.

The skills which might be acquired are:

1    The ability to use an atlas with a view to:
locating places with and without longitude and latitude grid;
describing elementary facts about relief, drainage, vegetation, population distribution and other simple distributions contained in an atlas;
measuring distances.

2    The ability to read large-scale maps (1:2 500 to 1:10 560) with a view to:
locating urban features (buildings, roads);
following a route;
plotting simple information (e.g. house type) on the plans.

3    The ability to read medium-scale maps (1:25 000 to 1:100 000) with a view to pupils being able to:
locate themselves in a well-marked position (e.g. a cross-road, top of a hill);
follow a simple road route;
abstract information such as that represented by the larger conventional signs (e.g. urban areas, woodland, water surfaces, A and B roads);
recognize the contour patterns representing valleys, spurs, plateaux and ridges;
state elementary relationships between physical features and communications where these exist;
draw elementary cross-sections based on contour lines.

4    The ability to carry out such field observations as:
the identification of simple relief features such as valleys, spurs, plateaux, scarps and ridges;
the identification of clay, sand, sandstone, and limestone;
the identification of soil by tactile tests – clayey, sandy, silty soils;
the identification of such vegetation groups as heathland and/or moorland, crop-land, and grassland;
the recognition of simple urban classifications, e.g. house type, industrial building, commercial buildings.

5    The ability to carry out observations of weather to include:
recognition of wind direction;
identification of cloud types (stratus, cumulus, nimbus);
the reading of maximum and minimum thermometers;
the reading of rain gauges.

**6** The ability to:
plot and read temperatures and rainfall on graphs;
draw simple histograms;
draw simple sketch maps.
**7** The ability to extract simple descriptive information from photographs of rural and urban landscapes including oblique aerial photographs.

Concepts might include, for example, an understanding of the following:

**1** That land may be worn away by: weathering in situ; erosion due to water and wind action.
**2** That deposition of sediments takes place by water and by air.
**3** That soils are made up of weathered rock and biological elements.
**4** That weather is due in part to the different characters of the air masses which pass over any given area.
**5** That agricultural land use is partly a function of soils and weather, and of other factors such as the prices of agricultural commodities.
**6** That urban areas may be divided into commercial zones, industrial zones and residential zones.
**7** That urban centres tend to be 'central places' serving the surrounding areas and are nodes of communications.
**8** That roads and railways between two urban areas tend to follow areas of least physical difficulty.
**9** That population density is often related to the availability of natural resources (water, minerals, heat, soils).
**10** That population migrations often occur from areas of low incomes to areas of higher incomes.
**11** That the world contains a variety of environments and that human response to similar physical environments is not necessarily uniform.

The next step in the argument is to decide whether such terminal objectives are or are not in harmony with the model of intellectual development proposed in the first part of this chapter. In other words, how far are the skills and concepts which it is proposed pupils should master by the age of 13 examples of 'operations' which could be performed by the majority of children who will be in the Piagetian stage of concrete operations. Experience and the work of various researchers on the map-reading and map-making abilities of pupils in this age range seem to suggest that the various skill objectives proposed are achievable, though inevitably there is likely to be a normal distribution of performance in any test given to check on these skill attainments. With respect to the concepts or 'understanding', it is much more difficult to be positive that these are in

93

harmony with the intellectual development of 13-year-old children, because how far these concepts will be meaningful will depend to some extent on the depth at which they are taught and on the methods used to teach them, as well as the vocabulary employed. For example, understanding the idea that an urban centre 'services' the surrounding area may be easily comprehensible in terms of shopping visits made by people in villages to the local market town, and this may be taught by reference to a survey of the shopping habits of certain families in the villages concerned. It may be much more difficult if the concept of a central place is formalized in terms of the functions of a town defined technically by various stringent criteria, or if an attempt is made to delimit the sphere of influence of a town by reference to a theoretical model using regular hexagons, and extending the argument to consider hierarchies of central places. However, the language used in the statements referring to the concepts which might be taught tends to indicate the level at which they should be treated. The implication is that at least at the end of the middle years of schooling some of the simple generalizations made would be meaningful to the children concerned. But as we have seen, it is still uncertain what proportion of 13-year-olds can make generalizations from available evidence.

## Teaching the subject matter

Identifying the terminal objectives does not, however, yield any information as to what procedures are to be used to reach them. It is therefore necessary to look into the ways in which teaching schemes might be organized so that, during the five years of the middle years of schooling, pupils might be led to a progressive mastery of the skills suggested. It is assumed that, though the skills and concepts were isolated for purposes of analysis, the teaching will not be structured so as to separate the teaching of skills from concepts. The two are complementary: some concepts are needed in the learning of certain skills (for example, the concept of scale for the measurement of distance on a map), and some skills are needed for the understanding of certain concepts (for example, the development of concepts about types of slopes depends on the ability to measure the gradient of such slopes either in the field or on a map). Thus the order in which the objectives have been stated in no way implies an order in the teaching schemes adopted.

How then may the teaching be organized? In setting forth certain views on this the following assumptions are made:

1    Much of the geography to be learnt will be learnt in the process of exploring the local environment both directly and vicariously.

94

2    Some attempt will be made to compare the local with more distant and different environments.

3    Growth in understanding will be achieved not by teaching certain skills and concepts at particular periods of time and then passing on to other things, but by revisiting these skills and concepts frequently, deepening their meaning for the pupils through their application in novel and increasingly more complex situations.

4    For part of the time, the pupils will be encouraged to discover certain principles or ideas for themselves, the teacher having to some extent structured the situation to enable this process of discovery to take place.

One possible way of dealing with the problem of structuring the learning process in this field is to suggest in broad terms the sort of activities for each year which might help the child progressively to acquire the skills and concepts identified as being desirable terminal objectives. For example, 5 in the list of concepts states: 'That agricultural land use is partly a function of soils and weather, and of other factors such as the prices of agricultural commodities.' What does this involve? Understanding such a proposition (not necessarily in the language used here) implies: some knowledge of the meaning of land use, and understanding that types of soils affect the yield of crops; that soil affects yields differentially as between crops; that rainfall, rainfall regime, temperature, and sunshine amounts affect the growing season and the rate of growth of crops; that a farmer in deciding what to plant or not to plant is influenced by the price he is likely to get for his crop.

It would seem that a beginning may be made by exploring the rural environment so that 8- to 9-year-olds become conscious of the nature of the rural landscape in terms of its fields, its farmhouse buildings, its roads and lanes. Possibly this is best done in high summer so that crops are clearly visible as well as animals. Vocabulary may be learnt in relation to such concrete things as farmyards, haystacks, potato-clamp, cereal crop, root crop, stony soil, damp pasture or whatever else happens to be relevant to the particular exploration. Back at school, suitable writing, number work or practical activity (drawing, modelling) may take place to reinforce and develop certain of the ideas gleaned during the field-work. There might also have been observation of the weather and a record made of whether it was fine, wet or showery. In the following year the 9- to 10-year-olds might well examine samples of soil taken from the school grounds, describe its texture and compare it with a contrasting sample brought in by the teacher. The children can be helped to develop the idea that soils differ in feel and may be described by such words as coarse, sticky, sandy with pebbles, and so on. The work on weather may be further developed by attempt-

95

ing to record over a short period of time the 'feel' of the air temperature, the nature of the cloud cover, the nature of rain when it fell, the existence of frost or any unusual phenomena such as hail or thunder. It may be possible also to examine pictures of certain crops at close quarters and label these so that consolidation of knowledge about farming develops. This might occur in connexion with a reading assignment. The 10- to 11-year-olds might, during the course of a farm visit (following a route map on the way), use a large-scale plan to locate the various fields of a farm, and map the crops (including grass) growing in them. Samples of the soil in each field might be taken back to school for subsequent description in terms of texture. Note might be taken of whether the soils appeared dry, moist or saturated with moisture, and such observations correlated with recent weather and the texture of the soil. An attempt might be made to see whether there was any connexion between the soils and the crops grown (there may be none). Map-reading skills would incidentally have been involved. In the following year (11 to 12) a month-by-month account of the activities on the same or another farm might be correlated with changes in the weather. By this year recording temperatures in degrees Celsius and rainfall in millimetres may be undertaken and graphs of temperature variations drawn. This might occur in a 'mathematical activity', but from this the rhythmical change in weather from season to season and its effect on crop growth can be noted. It may be possible to obtain figures of crop yields per acre (or hectare) over a number of years to see whether these change in response to changing weather conditions or not. The idea should develop that crops are affected not only by seasonal changes in weather but by differences in amounts of rainfall, sunshine or levels of temperature from year to year. In the year ending middle schooling, an exercise in English which included a discussion of incomes and prices might lead to a consideration of the nature of a farmer's income and how crop prices affect it. The reaction of a farmer to changes in crop prices might be gauged fairly easily by noting changes in cropping on a given farm over a number of years in response to changes in the guaranteed price for certain agricultural commodities. It would be noted, however, that not all farmers grew the high-priced crop and that even those who did grow it did not grow it to the exclusion of everything else. An awareness may therefore develop that land use is a function of several factors. At this stage it may be appropriate to show, by means of a simple game, that chance also plays a part in determining the cropping pattern on a farm, since the optimum crop combination may depend on the weather and the farmer may take a decision on a crop combination which is based on weather expectations which may or may not be fulfilled.

The pattern elaborated above is, of course, not the only pattern possible, neither has it any claim to be the best. In order to fit the geography ideally into

96

the rest of the curriculum nothing short of the total picture would be required. Further, in the classroom situation, patterns of teaching seldom follow exactly predetermined lines. Flexibility of approach, and fluidity in content is necessary. It may well be that for certain pupils what is really important is not the main concept the teacher was attempting to get them to learn, but a subsidiary or ancillary one which they have enjoyed developing. In terms of the example, some pupils may become far more interested in meteorology than in the factors affecting agricultural land use. Nevertheless, this does not absolve the teacher from clarifying his objectives, for only in the knowledge of these can he act rationally in guiding the learning of the pupils.

Such a vertical scheme running through the five years of middle schooling could be matched with a horizontal scheme in which for any one year topics dealt with would be integrated or linked. This would be particularly true of the earlier years when teaching would probably not be on subject lines. Thus if our topic of agricultural land use were used, then the mathematics, English, art, history, etc., which might be extracted from it, would have to be structured into an integrated whole.

For additional information on first-hand materials, secondary sources, and relevant techniques for using them, the reader is referred to the excellent resource books of the Geographical Association. *Geography in Primary Schools*[3] contains descriptions of rural and urban field-work carried out with primary-school children from infants to top juniors, together with details of techniques suitable for use by specialist or non-specialist teachers in the field or the class-room. *Geography in Secondary Education*[4] covers the age-range 11 to 18, with most emphasis on the age-group 11 to 16. The author, N. J. Graves, suggests that teachers in middle schools use this booklet in conjunction with *Geography in Primary Schools*. Both booklets have been written in the light of relevant research on child development and geography, and contain extensive references to audio-visual and written resources.

Here are two practical examples taken from *Geography in Primary Schools*.

The first describes an exercise in urban field-work, important in that most middle-years children attend urban rather than rural schools. In comparison with the rural example given above – designed to show how a relatively complex terminal objective might be pursued – this illustrates how comparatively simple short-term objectives might be realized. While the example was not originally conceived within the suggested framework of skills and concepts outlined earlier it might well be taken as falling under concept 7, an understanding 'that urban centres tend to be "central places" serving the surrounding areas and are nodes of communications.'

97

*A market survey*

The survey took place on a Saturday morning between 9.00 and 10.00 a.m., and this was why it was felt best for a group of six volunteers to undertake the project. Their age was 10+, and their I.Q. range was from 109 to 96. The children worked in two groups and were given a map of half the market each. The map had previously been checked and brought up to date. Each group had several copies of a questionnaire which they filled in for each stall.

*Questionnaire*
1. Stall number (from map)
2. What does the stall sell?
3. Where do the goods come from?
4. Where does the stall-holder live?
5. Does he come on both Tuesday and Saturday?
6. Does he go to any other market?
7. If so, where?

There were obviously some problems: some of the stall-holders objected to the questions, particularly No. 3, on personal grounds. Some stall-holders were too busy to answer questions, particularly towards the end of the survey. Problems like this will only ever be partially overcome. A previous visit by the teacher could verify which stall-holders would be willing to answer questions, and a sample of each type of stall obtained in this way. Inquiries at Hereford Butter Market showed that this would have been possible there.

After the discussion, the group decided upon the following presentation:
1. Map of stalls, shaded with colour key to show type.
2. Column graph, number of stalls of each type.
3. Map of Lancashire showing where stall-holders live.
4. Scale diagram showing other markets visited, then distance and direction from Kirby.
5. Pie-chart: stall-holders who go to other markets.
6. Writing: how the survey was done.
7. Writing: conclusions.

The teacher who conducted this survey comments: 'It is difficult to ascertain how much the children gained in knowledge, but they gained immensely in confidence of manner and also in the techniques of field-work and presentation. Therefore, from this point of view the survey was worth while.' He adds, too, that twelve children would have been a more satisfactory number; that it might have been profitable to repeat the inquiry on three successive market days; that results need to be compiled immediately to retain interest and that more attention could have been paid to conclusions.[5]

(For teachers concerned with difficulties over geographical techniques, and in this context with mapping techniques, see chapter III of *Geography in Primary Schools*.)

Much school geography is of necessity undertaken in the school or classroom, and the second example concerns secondary resources and techniques for using them. From among various possibilities it has been necessary to select one which typifies recent developments in geography teaching. While some teachers might question whether it is typical, one development which has certainly excited a good deal of interest and attention is that exemplified in the so-called 'role playing' or 'operational' games.[6] These games represent a serious attempt to make use in the school situation of quantitative analysis techniques developed in recent years by academic geographers. In the games, children simulate real-life situations – for example, planning factories or shopping areas, or discussing the implications of a new highways scheme. They are required to make decisions on the basis of available data, coping in the process with the element of random chance, and with a multiplicity of choices. The games are designed to cater for children of differing abilities, and in this respect may vary in simplicity or sophistication.

*A route-planning game*
This is an exercise in route planning rather than a game, and comes from Book I of *New Ways in Geography*. It could be easily adapted to the children's own area, and any urban school could devise its own version. Whereas a field-sketch type of picture and a related map are given in the book, an airphoto and a portion of the 25-inch O.S. map could be used to devise a local example. The object of the game is to plan specific journeys for a group of eight or so people or vehicles, which must be the quickest routes between the points named as their places of departure and arrival. All the journeys entail crossing the river which runs through the centre of the town by means of one of three bridges. The object of this particular exercise is to find out which people use one specific bridge. This is obviously a problem which town planners deal with daily, and variations on the theme will spring to mind: for instance, the river may not exist in a local example, but road works may present the same problem.

A further development of the game is the building up of a table on which the children are invited to fill in, between sets of co-ordinates, a 1 or a 0 to signify whether any journey crosses the river or not. The table lists people and destinations in the same order horizontally and vertically (like the distances-between-towns table at the back of an AA book). The table enables the plotting of every pair of journeys which can be made on the map, and can be filled in by the children individually, thus testing their skill in map reading and at the same time giving them a list of results from which further work might be done if the local area is being used for the game.[7]

It is increasingly unlikely that geography will appear as a separate subject in the curriculum of younger pupils; and many schools would pursue its aims through environmental studies, social studies, projects, and even literature. It is equally probable that older boys and girls pursuing a project would find themselves thinking along channels in which the cohesion of their thought would produce recognizable subject studies. While this might be going on with some pupils, others would undoubtedly still remain at the stage where subject disciplines as such would be inappropriate. Whatever form of organization is adopted the teacher would do well to examine the work from time to time to ensure that the skills and objectives of geography find an adequate place in the programme and are not neglected.

Finally, this chapter has been exposed to the often cogent and constructive criticism of teachers throughout the country. It might be salutary, and serve as a form of recapitulation, therefore, to conclude with one stringent extract from these comments. From one teachers' centre came the following views:

The group felt this was far too idealistic. Is it possible to have such complex structuring and still retain a flexible approach, fluidity of content, and opportunities for children to work at their own level and to follow their own particular interests? Does such structuring take account of the personality and individual strengths of the teacher? The paper does not indicate whether a continuation of the present primary-school situation of a class teacher is envisaged, or the use of a specialist in a class teaching situation, or team teaching. We felt that many of the concepts suggested in the paper would require specialist geography teachers. The demands on a class teacher would be too great if he were expected to teach all subjects as thoroughly as the paper suggests geography should be taught. Few general class teachers would be able to satisfy the higher IQs at 13 years in all subjects. We felt that the aims as set out in the paper could be achieved in a class teaching situation with a geography specialist! But what of the other subjects? It is doubtless possible to achieve these terminal objectives, given favourable conditions – *but at what cost?*

The reader may judge for himself the relevance and validity of these comments. However, it could well be argued that while they indicate very real teaching problems, they miss one important point, and this relates to the chapter's purpose. As stated earlier, 'The pattern elaborated above is, of course, not the only pattern possible, neither has it any claim to be the best. In order to fit the geography ideally into the rest of the curriculum nothing short of the total picture would be required.' What the chapter suggests is an approach to geography which may be utilized by primary, middle, or secondary teachers in the practical context of different middle-years institutions. It does not set out to be, and in the nature of the problem could never presume to be, a formula for the teaching of geography in the middle years.

In this chapter an attempt has been made to state the kind of skills and concepts that children in the middle years of schooling might learn specifically through geography or through a geographical approach as part of an integrated curriculum. These skills and concepts have been stated as terminal objectives that might be reached at the end of the period under consideration. Using the Piagetian model of intellectual development it has been assumed that much of the teaching would avoid the formal hypothetico-deductive approach, but would concentrate on concrete evidence to develop those concepts and skills which children could use in concrete situations, though it is expected that towards the end of the middle years of schooling some children would be able to develop abstract generalizations which would have meaning for them. The facts to be used in teaching have not been discussed since these would tend to vary from situation to situation though an indication was given that the phenomena studied might be on a local, national and international scale. The criteria for selecting particular items for teaching are to some extent internal to the subject or depend on value judgements which need to be exercised over the whole field of the content of education.

### References and notes

1. This statement is made with qualifications such as those developed in our first report published as Schools Council Working Paper 42, *Education in the Middle Years* (Evans/Methuen Educational, 1972), see chapter III. Some children will reach the formal stage of operations later than others and some not at all. Evolution from one stage to the next is gradual and in the process two ways of thinking may be used concurrently, i.e. in the concrete stage children may think intuitively, or guess about certain relationships, and in the stage of formal operations they may resort to thinking in concrete terms.

101

2. N. J. GRAVES, *Geography in Secondary Education* (Geographical Association, 1971).
3. Geographical Association, *Geography in Primary Schools* (Geographical Association, 1970).
4. *Geography in Secondary Education.*
5. *Geography in Primary Schools*, p. 23.
6. See JOHN PETER COLE and N. J. BEYNON, *New Ways in Geography* (Blackwell, 1969), and REX WALFORD, *Games in Geography*, Education Today (Longman, 1970).
7. For a full and detailed description see *Geography in Primary Schools*, and *New Ways in Geography.*

# VI. History

This chapter is derived from a paper written by a working party of the Schools Council History Committee. In order of presentation, it offers a brief opinion of what history as a discipline and as a school activity should be taken to be; relates the teaching of history to a theory of child development; sketches an outline for history content and method in the middle years; and indicates how history might be 'structured' for children between the ages of 8 and 13, both as a discipline and in relation to other aspects of the curriculum. The Middle Years of Schooling Project has punctuated the chapter with what is hoped will be a useful series of references. Readers may wish to be reminded of the work of the Schools Council Project, History, Geography and Social Science 8–13 (1971–75).[1]

Before the chapter proper begins it might be useful to consider why it is sometimes held that history is not an easy subject for children to learn. J. B. Coltham[2] has suggested reasons for this which fall under four headings, and which essentially are as follows:

1    Learners cannot experience history directly. They can meet it only through partial and biased evidence.
2    History is concerned mainly with the thoughts and actions of adults, which means there is what might be called a generation gap built into the subject.
3    The language necessary to describe historical ideas is often highly abstract (for example, in notions of power and justice), and often presupposes a capacity for deductive, inferential thinking which a child may not possess.
4    The problem of chronology. Children generally experience difficulty in grasping the concept of time and this is particularly so in the context of historical ideas and events.

## History – a conception

History is the study of humanity – of the events and forces which at any particular period have created the social condition. The study of history is regarded by many as an indispensable element of any educative process.[3] A knowledge of history provides an added dimension to all thinking on human affairs; it establishes historical concepts of time and cause and effect, and awakens an appreciation of endeavour and achievement. Through it the pupil is helped

103

to form value judgements, realizing that there are not just heroes and villains but many different aspects of human conduct. Furthermore, the study of history affords points of reference outside our own society and time, and because the study of man's development has ethical implications, it affords an exercise in the development of a moral sense.[4] Through an awareness that there are many sides to an argument, critical judgement and a respect for truth may be acquired, and the capacity to separate fact from fiction. The study of the past, because it is a study of different societies and the process of their change, gives an added awareness of the present.

The study of man in society and the process of social change entails not merely the acquisition of an accurate body of knowledge, but also the practice of a specific discipline which is peculiar to the subject and unique in itself. This discipline may be termed the historical method. It involves the collection and scrutiny of historical material and the ability to distinguish between the partial and the unbiased, and between what is suspect and what is incontrovertible. It necessitates an exercise of the imagination – enlivened but disciplined by the study of evidence – in order to reconstruct a vivid account of what life was like in the past and to engender an intellectual appreciation of the cause and effect of change in human society.

## History in school

It would be unduly ambitious to expect younger children to gain historical experience solely by studying source material. Nevertheless at some time during the middle years, depending on age and ability, pupils must be given the opportunity of gaining experience in using at first hand direct historical evidence. They should begin to learn the skills of assembling and interpreting this material, learn to record their own conclusions and to reconstruct history for themselves. As they grow older and acquire more skills, this practice will be extended and become more sophisticated; but it will never change its nature. It is through the critical appraisal of historical material, as a preliminary to imaginative reconstruction, that history has a unique contribution to make to the education of the young pupil.

In many schools historical method and choice of material has fallen far short of what at best is possible. Where this is so, pupils identify the source of historical material with the textbook and the teacher, and often history for them is a confused amalgam of unrelated facts about kings and queens, battles, dates, etc. Perhaps for these reasons, history has tended in some quarters to become a devalued subject, to be superseded by newer disciplines that are making increasing demands for time in the curriculum. There is certainly a tendency to contract the subject so that it becomes a minor ingredient of a general studies programme, in which the historical content is so reduced that it loses any real meaning. Perhaps the most significant factor in some school situations is that techniques involving the pupil in active participation and inquiry, which have been widely adopted in other subjects, have not been applied to the study of history. History is then considered to be simply an information subject – a digested set of historical data provided by the teacher or culled from an encyclopedic textbook. Material may be skilfully presented and if the interest of the young is aroused, if his imagination is stimulated, then a useful purpose is served. Indeed, interest and enjoyment are essential prerequisites to a more disciplined study and should be the prime objective of the earlier years, but an entirely passive role of listening and remembering cannot be defended. Unfortunately, the ability to memorize and reproduce facts is still considered in many schools to be the sole criterion of historical scholarship. Many teachers will say that this is an overstatement; it may well be so against the background of much enlightened teaching in schools still unfettered by the demands of an examination system. Nevertheless, there is substantial evidence of a need to review the traditional methods of history teaching and to explore a more active approach by the pupil through the collection, investigation and evaluation of historical evidence. This does not imply that the best traditional methods should be wholly abandoned. Good secondary material, including the use of books for reference, comparison and stimulation, cannot be dispensed with. There is also a place for enlightened discourse by the teacher – a discourse supported by good teaching aids[5] designed to inform, to stimulate imagination and activity, and to foster a real and intelligent interest in the subject. It should, however, be appreciated that these methods, even when practised well, do not satisfy the aim and justify the study of history. Its real value is as a discovery subject, more precious for its methods, materials and discipline than for its mere content.

## History and children in the middle years

It is self-evident that any consideration of the teaching of history in the middle years must take into account not only the nature of the subject but also the characteristics of the pupils concerned.[6] It is also true to say that any theoretical statement concerned with the intellectual development of children during the period must be general in nature and that for individual children departure from the theoretical norms will occur. Piaget's theories of developmental psychology are relevant to the teaching of history in the middle years. The middle years are the period when children pass from the 'concrete' stage of intellectual development to the 'formal' stage of thought. In the former, thinking is considered to be largely governed by the logic of classes and relations, reasoning to be inductive in nature, and conceptualization to arise from experience with concrete materials. In the latter, systematic isolation of variables is thought possible, inference may take place and both the inductive and deductive methods of thinking may be employed. At the concrete stage, the conceptual structures are considered essential for the later development of formal thought. At the formal stage, the child's thinking is considered to be no longer limited by concrete experience or the memory of such experience, and is becoming increasingly adult in nature. The change in type of thinking is said to occur somewhere between 11 and 13 years of age – figures which should be interpreted in terms of mental and not chronological age. If these figures are used as guides and the criterion of mental age is taken, then it is clear that while some children will be capable of reasoning 'formally', for the majority thinking in the middle years will be chiefly 'concrete' in nature. For the teacher this conclusion is of the utmost importance, for it follows that the most successful teaching will be that which allows conceptualization to develop from numerous experiences of a concrete nature.

The importance of the nature of the experiences given by the teacher is also stressed by this theory. Thinking develops as a result of the child's accommodation to the demands of the environment, and of his developing for himself the necessary conceptual structures which will enable him to deal with similar experiences in the future. With history – which deals with things remote in time, with increasingly mature judgements on evidence gained from the past and with language which uses the meanings of today to explain remote phenomena – it is vital that the concrete experiences given in its teaching should be those which permit adequate conceptual development within these areas. Here lies the chief challenge to the history teacher.

The following example may help to illustrate the development that has just been described. A child of 8 could enjoy a narrative of the sailing and settlement of the Pilgrim Fathers. A child of 10 could discuss some of the reasons for people leaving England to settle in a strange land, the practical difficulties they faced there, the danger from the Indians, the need for some skilled workers in the colony, the importance of team-work and the handicap of having shirkers in the colony. By 12 or 13 years of age other questions could be discussed – the wider opportunities opening to the colonists, the ethics of dispossessing the Indians, the nature of trade with England and the profitability of the colonies. Up to this point the pattern of thought would be inductive, and based on concrete experiences. Only later could the founding of colonies and their relations with the mother country be dealt with in terms of general economic causes and political differences or of lessons to be learned from the revolt of the Thirteen – all of which would involve not only formal thinking but also deductive processes, that is, the power to argue from abstract principles. Similarly, comparative studies involving formal concepts of causation and identification of variables such as religious motive, social unrest, population pressure, so as to explain the difference between the Thirteen Colonies and Canada, for example, would have to be postponed till well beyond the middle years.

## Content and method

Syllabus content and method must be so contrived as to provide for the acquisition of skills and knowledge valuable not only for their intrinsic merit, but as a preparation for study of a more complex nature. When planning schemes of work, teachers will be concerned to ensure the following:

1    There is the closest liaison between contributory and reception schools in a multi-tier system, in order to co-ordinate 'take-over' points and ensure a developing continuity of method.
2    Subject-matter will be included which reflects in outline or in detail aspects of our heritage which are interesting, relevant and imaginatively fruitful.
3    There is the opportunity at all levels to re-create the past in tangible terms.
4    The pupil is afforded opportunity and incentive to make a personal investigation (depth and complexity relevant to age and ability) of some specific historical subject – the topic, patch or probe. This must involve the pupil in developing and supporting evidence, and the teacher may devise novel methods of presenting the results – for example, the imaginary television interview, the radio commentary, newspaper reporting.
5    The pupil is introduced to the discipline of history through the historical method referred to previously – through the study, evaluation and re-construction of historical evidence and the development of contributory skills so that he may establish a realistic picture of life in the past.

At the beginning of the middle years the teacher should extend and develop the best methods of infant school practice. In this tradition of teaching, specific attempts are usually made to anticipate future techniques. The aim is to foster through interest and enjoyment a growing awareness of the past as distinct from the present. The word 'history' is unlikely to be used, but stories of long ago are told, supported by pictures or models of the past – castles, costumes, knights in armour – and in the process of listening, talking, drawing and making things, the children become increasingly conscious of a difference between past and present. It is not realistic to suppose that the 8- or 9-year-old can fruitfully pursue a disciplined historical investigation, though the introduction of suitable historical exhibits will be a valuable aid in focusing interest and introducing

107

concrete experience. The attitude to be fostered should be one of frank curiosity and enjoyment. Pupils should acquire a more refined awareness of the past – its reality and yet its difference from the present. It should be made to live again in the imagination – the greatness, the colour, the pageantry, the squalor or the hardship of life as it really was, the character of men who actually lived, the feeling for events that really took place. A judicious choice of stories, supported by visual aids, will help to meet this need. These may be chronicles of real life and adventure, stories of great men and everyday affairs, imaginative description or good historical fiction of the kind which faithfully portrays the atmosphere and conditions of the age.[7]

It has been a traditional practice to commence with early history – cavemen, Greeks, Romans, etc. – for younger juniors and to proceed in chronological order as the children grow older. It is debatable whether there is any intrinsic merit in this progression. Some teachers will feel a need to identify forms of society and institution which are sufficiently small and uncomplicated for study by younger children. In this context it may be argued that the bonds, inter-relationships and behaviour of more primitive societies – the tribe, the city state, the medieval manor or feudal army – are simple enough to fit within the younger child's concepts and experience. These will tend to be areas of the past for which evidence is inevitably secondary but nevertheless acceptable for its story content and imaginative appeal. Other teachers may prefer to select more recent periods of history in which the influence on present-day life is more apparent.

At this stage it is probable and certainly desirable that the teacher will have responsibility for general class subjects. An integration of subject interests properly contrived will not detract from the historical values – the stimulus of relevant literature, poetry, music and drama will open up another dimension and lead to a deeper appreciation and wider perspective.[8] At all stages it must be stressed that the children should play their part in re-creating in tangible form their own version of history. Their skills, such as creative writing and self-expression through mime, painting and modelling, will be developing. These should be harnessed to the full, translating the past through the exercise of the child's imagination into a visible form of his own creation.

By the age of 11, the child should have acquired some proficiency in the basic skills – in reading with understanding, writing, and recording. History will still be associated with other subject interests: the role of the pupil in re-creating the past through different media will not be diminished but increasingly it will be a past 'revived' by the pupil and the subject will become more defined and acquire more specific objectives.[9] Emphasis will be placed on the investigation of a particular aspect or period of historical significance which is meaningful to the child. The teacher will obviously make a substantial contribution to the subject-

108

matter in a variety of ways, but under this guidance inquiry will be carried out through the children's own discovery, governed by such considerations as:

What do we want to find out?
How can we find out?
What source of original evidence can be explored?
What conclusions can be reached?
How can they be recorded?
What use can be made of our discoveries?

Whether the exercise is called project, topic, or probe, the child has arrived at the threshold of a disciplined study. It would be unwise to prescribe here specific topics. Their suitability must be considered in relationship to the complete scheme of work in history, the child's age, ability and interest, and in the opportunities afforded by the neighbourhood to relate local and national history. Some general considerations in the choice of subject to be investigated are:

1   The standard textbook should not be the main support of teacher or pupil, nor should it exert significant influence in the selection of syllabus content.
2   The subject should have a natural appeal and a relevance obvious to the pupil; it should involve historical concepts which are comprehensible to the age-group.
3   The study should include a scrutiny of first-hand evidence. This must be readily available and provide the opportunity for activity by the pupil in assessing the value of the material and reconstructing its historical significance.
4   Provision must be made for suitable reference material to promote techniques of personal discovery, i.e. reference books for research, pictures for interpretation, materials for speculation, tapes, transparencies.[10]
5   Possible ways must be explored by which the pupil may assemble the results of his own investigation.

## Local history and the concentric syllabus

An obvious area for historical investigation is in the field of local history.[11] Here the pupil is presented with material from his own experience and environment; opportunity is provided for a precise and disciplined exercise of the historical method. Material is conveniently available and offers strong incentives for real pupil participation in collecting, sorting and assessing first-hand historical evidence. It should not be imagined that primary source material is always of such an abstruse nature as to require professional expertise in its interpretation. In its simpler forms it may be:

109

1   Oral evidence – first-hand accounts from elderly citizens of life and conditions during the early part of this century.
2   Documentary evidence – family history, through details discovered from the family Bible, birth certificates, work certificates, school records, reports, letters, registers, etc.
3   Commercial evidence – old catalogues, ledgers, advertisements, price lists.
4   Pictorial evidence – from newspapers and albums.
5   Material evidence – relics of the past: dress, utensils, tools.
6   Professional evidence – photostat copies of documents, maps and statistical information from the county archivist and supporting material from a museum. In some areas, museums provide a lending service of historical material to schools, in the same way that the local library provides books.[12]

The study of local history lends itself to a natural co-ordination with other subjects. Local study may involve ingredients of geography, architecture, population study, industry and occupations, social studies, etc., and will require associated skills in English, mathematics, art and craft in compiling the final account. Neither can local history be separated from national or European history. A study of the development of the small local community will reflect in microcosm, and be associated with, the wider perspective of world history. There is no traditional community in town or village that has remained unaffected by national and international movements – the impact of war, the quest for freedom, the struggle for material needs or social reform. Thus local history may become the basis of a concentric syllabus embracing historical matters of national and international significance, which could engage the pupil's attention during the latter years of the middle school.

Local history may be approached in a variety of ways. Much will depend on the nature of the locality, but wherever children live they have one common link with the past – through their own forefathers. This may be termed history through the family,[13] and one has only to trace back three or four generations to span a century of change. The 11+ age-group has proved a convenient starting point for such projects. Using the historical source material referred to above, the children reconstruct the historical chain and add in all the details to illuminate conditions of life in the not too remote past. In this way, they are concerned to revive a memory of the past by assembling all the evidence as witness of the times. Their conclusions are made and their findings reproduced in various ways. The emphasis is on social history, with special reference to the cause and effect of changing social conditions – for example, with reference to the concepts of sequence and time. Gradually a picture of local life in the last century emerges, which leads naturally to an inquiry on a broader front, from local to national to international conceptions of history, broadening and changing the child's perspectives in the process. The influence of great national figures and events has had repercussions in the smallest community. Interesting and illuminating facts may emerge from cross-cultural comparisons, and this is an ever-widening field for further research.[14]

A study conducted in this manner requires certain skills – in interpretation, in research through reading, in descriptive writing and documentation, and in the allied fields of inquiry through geography and mathematics. Above all, it calls for the ability to make an objective judgement, to form a conclusion, and to re-create the past through imaginative experience. This, it may be claimed, is the essential element of a *disciplined* historical study. This discipline having been once established will be applied to all future study. Undoubtedly it will involve subject-matter of increasing complexity, requiring more sophisticated techniques. The use of the film projector, radio, television, tape-recorder and record-player are standard procedures. To these audio and visual aids there must be added the resources and the 'know-how' for teachers to operate the overhead projector, the photocopier and the videotape. At the present time, it is often beyond the competence of the teacher and the resources of the school to assemble primary source material of a sophisticated and complex nature.

As a rule the successful production of teaching materials from local sources requires carefully organized team effort. In many cases the preparatory search and production of units already involves the close co-operation of local authority advisers, working parties of teachers, county record office staff, colleges of education, university institutes and schools museum services. The routine tasks of selection, editing, transcribing or copying, duplicating, and packaging sets of primary materials for use in schools certainly calls for the full material and financial support of the local authority, preferably through the services of a well-equipped teachers' centre. In its most complex and sophisticated form, the result will be a series of archive teaching units of primary visual and written source material, supported by adequate notes and auxiliary published materials, adaptable for use with all ages of children within the 8 to 13 age-range. In some cases, these units take the format of the *Jackdaw* type of wallet-folder of materials, while other groups produce booklets of documents and notes stapled together. Some prefer the larger 'Pandora's box' type of collection from which the teacher draws a selection of his own choice. The common aim of all these different forms of collection is the individual document or article, held as evidence in the pupil's hand.

For this task, a centre should have adequate equipment for the copying and duplicating of documents – print, diagrams and pictures – in the many different forms which are necessary for display and use in the modern classroom. Written

111

and printed materials must be capable of reproduction either as single copies or in multiple sets. This demands the use not only of a photocopier but also of an electronic stencil-cutting machine and a duplicator. For pictures, cameras and enlargers capable of producing slides or printed enlargements are essential. Many schools will prefer maps, diagrams and some printed material to be made available as transparencies for the overhead projector. Equipment must be capable of producing large quantities of material* so that, for example, an entire enumerator's book for the Census of 1851 can be reproduced in full (with prior permission from the Public Record Office). The availability of a microfilm camera at a local library or record office is very desirable for teachers who wish to select large quantities of records for future copying and duplication. (The purchase of a microfilm reader is not essential, as microfilm can be shown on a standard filmstrip projector, and is better used as a negative film for reprinting.) Negatives obtained in this way may need to be processed as prints on photographic paper, to act as master copies for stencils, or to be enlarged as wall pictures. The complete package or unit of historical materials for schools should comprise facsimile copies of individual documents, transcripts or abstracts of statistics or other data, pictures both large and small, filmstrip, or slides of visual material, off-prints of small books, diaries, directories, etc., which are out of copyright, with adequate provision of teachers' explanatory notes and guides as to the use of the materials, captions for pictures and background information for the topic to be studied. The unit should also include, if possible, specimen copies of useful textbooks.

It soon becomes evident, however, that apart from the necessary technical equipment and material resources, the essential feature of this process is the recruitment and organization of a teachers' working party, preferably with access to clerical help. The considerable amount of work involved in selection, trial and development of teaching materials is essentially a professional commitment.

Specialist assistance may well be necessary to meet the growing need for direction and guidance on the types of materials for use in schools of a given locality, and on the types of inquiry which might be most rewarding. It will be found that, in an authority as in an individual school, there is a strong case for leadership by specialist history teachers. In the local education authority there should be an adviser or group of leader-teachers whose qualifications and enthusiasm enable them to advise less experienced colleagues on the materials and methods of historical investigation. In the individual school there is probably a growing need for a specialist or semi-specialist head of department responsible

* Teachers should bear in mind the present legal position concerning copyright material. A useful summary is contained in the Publishers Association's booklet, *Photocopying and the Law* (Publishers Association, 1965, rev. edn, 1970).

for advice and co-ordination of studies; this type of teacher should also be a member of the authority's team of teachers working in the centre.

The position of the average middle-school teacher who is not a history specialist certainly calls for review and support in the present situation, as increasing demands are made upon his knowledge of wider and wider areas of inquiry in many different subjects. The increasing mobility of teachers must also be taken into account, as this will tend to militate against a long-term accumulation of first-hand personal experience and knowledge of the history of a local area. The individual teacher cannot be blamed if his response to these problems, unsupported at a professional level by other resources, is to turn to an outworn textbook approach which is safe and relatively undemanding. The average teacher will therefore need advice on the types of historical inquiry in which the pupils could most profitably be engaged and he will need to be made aware of the scope and range of materials which can most readily be made available to him and of the measure of support which his teachers' centre can offer.

When the proper facilities are available, the middle years, unhampered by the demands of any examination, formative in the deepest sense, assisted by lively curiosity, inventiveness and an increasing awareness of growing skills, must surely provide the most ample opportunity for the discovery and development of a sense of history.

## References and notes

1. Schools Council History, Geography and Social Science 8–13 Project (1971–75), based at the School of Education, University of Liverpool and directed by Professor W. A. L. Blyth and R. Derricott. Publishers: Collins and E.S.L.
2. J. B. COLTHAM, *The Development of Thinking and the Learning of History* (Historical Association, 1971).
3. For an optimistic reassessment of the role of history in the curriculum see JOHN FINES, *The History Teacher and Other Disciplines* (Historical Association, 1970).
4. For a discussion of and guide to specifying objectives for history as opposed to broad aims, see J. B. COLTHAM and J. FINES, *Educational Objectives for the Study of History: a Suggested Framework* (Historical Association, 1971).
5. See, for example, G. A. BROOKS, *A Select List of Aids of Use in the Teaching of Recent History* (Historical Association, 1971).
6. See J. B. COLTHAM, *The Development of Thinking and the Learning of History* (Historical Association, 1971).
7. Substantial guides to publications are: M. BARTON and K. DAVIES, *A Junior*

*History Book List* (Historical Association, 1968); and HELEN CAM, *Historical Novels* (Historical Association, 1961).

8. See J. FINES, *The History Teacher and Other Disciplines* (Historical Association, 1970).

9. See J. B. COLTHAM and J. FINES, *Educational Objectives for the Study of History: a Suggested Framework* (Historical Association, 1971).

10. For a recent overview of available sources, see MARGARET BRYANT, 'Documentary and study materials for teachers and pupils, Part I: Survey', *Teaching History*, I (May 1970), 194–202; also J. D. FINES, *The Teaching of History in the United Kingdom: a Select Bibliography* (Historical Association, 1969), and KENNETH CHARLTON, *Recent Historical Fiction for Secondary School Children* (Historical Association, rev. edn, 1969).

11. For example, see G. A. CHINNERY, *Studying Urban History in Schools* (Historical Association, 1971).

12. See *Guide to Illustrative Material for Use in Teaching History* compiled by G. A. WILLIAMS (Historical Association, 1962).

13. See B. J. MURPHY, 'History through the family', *Teaching History*, II (May 1971), and for a relatively sophisticated approach, D. TURNER, *Historical Demography in Schools* (Historical Association, 1971). The author believes that 'historical demography has been successfully tackled by pupils of all ages from 10 upwards' (p. 13).

14. For history in relation to the establishment of national and religious values see HENRI TAIFEL and GUSTAV JAHODA, 'The development in children of ideas about their own and other countries', *New Era*, **48** (May 1967), 87.

# VII. Mathematics

Mathematics has occupied a dominant place in curriculum development over the past decade. It was the first subject to have a middle-years curriculum development project, the Nuffield Mathematics Project 5–13 (1964–71).[1] The first Schools Council Field Report dealt with new developments in mathematics teaching,[2] and Schools Council Curriculum Bulletin No. 1 was entitled *Mathematics in Primary Schools*.[3] The Plowden Report, *Children and their Primary Schools*,[4] referred to a revolution taking place in the teaching of this subject and Professor G. Matthews, of the Nuffield Mathematics Project (5–13), went further and identified two revolutions.[5] At the secondary level, two other revolutions are claimed to have occurred. As far back as 1959 the then Ministry of Education stated in *Primary Education*:

> There is no subject in the primary-school curriculum which gives rise to more thought at the present time than mathematics . . . it is the theme of discussions and conferences in all parts of the country . . . and mathematicians are increasingly giving thought and attention to the development of this subject in the minds of young children.[6]

No other subject appears to have had as much attention as mathematics; no other subject appears to have aroused such strong feelings in the minds of both pupils and teachers, or has been a matter of greater controversy. 'It is widely agreed', said Dr John Biggs in a BBC broadcast, 'that with the exception of the gifted few, all the world seems to loathe mathematics, and particularly arithmetic, with a peculiar intensity. Something has definitely gone wrong somewhere: the question is, what?'[7]

The Nuffield Mathematics Project's introductory text, *I Do, and I Understand*, recognized that mathematics was possibly not the most popular of studies and suggested that 'in order to prevent the continuation of certain attitudes prevalent today which manifest themselves in such remarks as "I was never any good at maths", "I hated arithmetic", "Maths always terrified me", care must be taken to prevent the possibility of their early establishment.' A claim was made for 'understanding' as the solution to the problem – for children to make their own discoveries and achieve understanding. 'In this way the whole attitude to the subject can be changed and "Ugh, no, I didn't like maths" will be heard no more.'[8]

115

The prominent place of mathematics in the middle-years curriculum has seldom been challenged and despite the fact that changes in some schools over the past decade have virtually replaced the old syllabus with something quite new, it has invariably been assumed that this new curriculum has the right of accession to a place of major importance in the school.

The utilitarian objectives for teaching mathematics are clear, soundly based and of long standing. The three Rs, reading, writing and arithmetic, were dominant in the curriculum of the early elementary schools and despite the changes in society which are, to some extent, reflected by changes in the curriculum, it is still true to say that those who remain illiterate and innumerate are disadvantaged. 'How many?' and 'how much?' are two recurring questions which call for some mathematical understanding on the part of both children and adults. In more recent years there has been a move towards adopting a number of more broadly based objectives in the learning of mathematics and many of the reformers have clearly felt that one of the first steps towards change was to discredit teaching methods which placed an over-emphasis on drills and rote learning. Schools Council Curriculum Bulletin No. 1, *Mathematics in Primary Schools*, puts forward three objectives for mathematics teaching in the 8 to 11 age-range:

1   To make children think for themselves.
2   To give knowledge and appreciation of mathematics as a creative subject; of its order and pattern (in number as well as in geometrical form); of its vital presence in everyday life and in the environment, not only in man-made things, but in natural forms as well.
3   To give children a facility with number and quantity relationships or, more briefly, to give them skill in computation.[9]

The Nuffield Mathematics Project aimed to devise a contemporary course for children from 5 to 13, and put forward certain basic ideas which, if not identical, are certainly closely parallel to those given above:

Running through all the work is the central notion that the children must be set free to make their own discoveries and think for themselves, and so achieve understanding, instead of learning off mysterious drills.

The justification for including mathematics in the curriculum of the primary school would seem to lie in this notion of pattern and relationships, for this is how mathematics has enabled man to discover something of the shape and pattern of the universe, and so move towards the gradual mastery of his environment.

116

This empirical approach is the natural approach of a primary-school child to his environment. It might be summarised as follows:

(a) free experimentation with material
(b) the formation of a hypothesis
(c) the testing of the hypothesis
(d) the communication of findings.[10]

Although Nuffield Mathematics (5–13) has been the only major project to cover the whole middle years age-range, there have been several other secondary-school projects which have included the 11- to 13-year-old children in their programmes. Probably the most widely known of these are the Midland Mathematics Experiment,[11] and the School Mathematics Project.[12] The radical nature of these projects forms part of an international reappraisal of mathematics teaching, but in this country primary and secondary developments have taken on a character of their own, and to start with it is necessary to look at them separately.

At the primary level a convenient starting point is the publication in 1953 of L. D. Adam's *Background to Primary School Mathematics*,[13] a text which sets out in straightforward language an approach to the teaching of elementary mathematics based on children's understanding, and advocates a practical or 'concrete' approach to the subject. This was followed in 1956 by the Mathematical Association's *Teaching of Mathematics in the Primary School*.[14] These two texts probably more than any others served to familiarize teachers with the possibility of including in the curriculum something more than the traditional, rather arid diet of arithmetic, and both serve as excellent examples of the new wave of thinking which was to influence the work of some primary schools throughout the 1950s and early 1960s. They show quite clearly that at this period the initiators of change were emphasizing the need for a new approach in methodology. They stress the importance of children having a conceptual understanding of arithmetical processes, rather than the more common practice of teaching them how to do sums. They point out the 'delicate nature of the teacher's task in keeping a balance between the two aspects of mathematical learning, namely a growth of understanding on the one hand, and the development of habits of thought on the other.'[15]

There is much evidence to show that there was by no means a rapid acceptance of this approach throughout the majority of junior schools. At the beginning of the 1960s a deliberate attempt was made to 'accelerate the pace of reform, and particularly, to increase the confidence of that great majority of primary-school teachers who had to teach mathematics while disclaiming any expertise for, or even liking of, the subject. Miss E. E. Biggs, HMI, was commissioned to mobilise all the available forces up and down the country that could help to spread and consolidate liberal ideas on the learning of mathematics by primary school children.'[16] In 1966 Miss Biggs wrote, 'During the numerous local in-service courses in the past seven years efforts have been concentrated on a change of approach rather than the introduction of "modern" material.'[17]

Publishers and suppliers of educational equipment were quick to produce a flow of new textbooks and a wide range of structured and incidental apparatus. By 1968 the shelves of the National Textbook Library, at London University Institute of Education, contained well over seven hundred primary mathematics textbooks currently in print. Throughout the whole of the 1960s both BBC and Independent Television transmitted a continuous series of primary mathematics programmes for schools; courses and conferences for primary teachers dominated the in-service training programmes of the majority of LEAs. There can be no doubt that the machinery for change established during this decade was far more extensive than had ever before been attempted for any other aspect of the curriculum.

All the schools visited by the Middle Years Project team have seen fit to make considerable changes in the traditional arithmetic course, but they do not appear to have changed from a given 'A' to a given 'B'. Today there is much greater diversity to be seen than in the past, and this has been welcomed by Professor Matthews, organizer of the Nuffield Mathematics Project 5–13. Professor Matthews has expressed with some force his view of the danger of a 'package deal' and of an approved syllabus. He has written of 'Two [junior] schools . . . in the same street, or very close – in one of which you can't at first see whether the children are learning anything at all, but they certainly are, integrating maths and science in the most purposeful way. Just down the street there's the other school where they have more directed maths, but still good stuff. A visitor coming from abroad wouldn't know that these two schools were in the same country, let alone in the same project. But they are in the same project and I am glad that they should be.'[18] The differences observed by the Middle Years Project team would seem, at least to Professor Matthews, to be one of the expected outcomes of this stage of the mathematics revolution. But it must obviously cause us to question what the work of these two schools had in common.

So far we have been concerned with the nature of change at the junior level where it has frequently formed part of a more general pattern of change which has radically affected the work of non-specialist teachers and has involved the whole of the school curriculum. By contrast, the changes at secondary level initially appear less dramatic and more controlled, especially at the middle-years level. The authors of Schools Council Field Report No. 1,[19] however, once again

118

chose to introduce the word 'revolution' when describing the changes which had taken place. Pointing out that there had been a steady liberalizing of secondary-school mathematics over the past forty years, they go on to state that, 'in the last few years two revolutionary impacts have been made on the evolving shape of secondary school mathematics; one the introduction of new topics and branches, conventionally styled "modern mathematics", has reached the schools from the universities and has concerned mainly, but by no means exclusively, the more able pupils in the grammar schools; the other has been the new thinking and the new ways of examination involved in the Certificate of Secondary Education and directed mainly, but again by no means exclusively, toward pupils of average, or even below average, ability.' The Field Report then asks, 'What was the effect of this fermenting of the secondary mathematical lump on the primary schools?' And concludes, 'Very little; for the hopes and expectations of those shortly to teach mathematics to these pupils at the secondary stage were almost entirely confined to performances of skills in computation.'

There is an interesting comparison to be made between the visible products of the School Mathematics Project which might be taken as a representative secondary-school project, and the Nuffield Mathematics Project 5–13. The School Mathematics Project has produced for the use of the 11- to 13-year-old children two sets of carefully planned course books which, however different in content from traditional texts, are nevertheless part of a textbook course. By contrast the Nuffield Project offers no textbooks, but a series of guides for teachers which give an outline of content thought to be desirable and suggest certain methodological approaches to the work. A great deal has been left to the imagination and initiative of the teachers. Behind these visible products from the two projects there would appear to have been somewhat different objectives in mind, or if not different objectives then certainly different ways of achieving the same objectives. This contrast between the two projects illustrates a larger question – that of structure – which constantly recurs in discussions on curriculum development. The School Mathematics Project scheme tends towards the directive, the Nuffield towards the non-directive. As so often in these matters there is no 'right' or 'wrong'; one teacher or one school may prefer direction, another not. It may be that a school might wish to start with a directive scheme and then move gradually to a less directive one. This is a question of means; ends, in all probability, remain the same and are concerned with the network of understandings, the development of attitudes and interests and the overlapping of skills which lie behind competence in the field of mathematics.

The Nuffield Project links very closely together both content and method and claims that 'at the very heart of the matter, it is impossible to reform *what* (what

119

to teach, the new content), without also considering *how* (how do children learn?).' This emphasis is less easy to discern in the majority of textbooks produced for the 11- to 13-year-old child.

In many parts of the country working parties of teachers have produced reports and handbooks on the teaching of mathematics which clearly indicate the spread of new ideas. Early in the field in the 1960s was the Essex publication *Suggested Outline of Primary Mathematics*. The working party report published by the Berkshire Education Committee contains well illustrated and carefully presented suggestions for teachers, with selected bibliographies for further reading after each chapter. It is interesting to observe that this working party has a majority of members who were actively engaged in teaching mathematics at the secondary level, but the document which they produced (also in the 1960s) is entitled *Mathematics in the Primary School*. It contains no guidance on ways in which any follow-up to the primary work might be attempted at the secondary level. This is not intended as a criticism of the Berkshire guide, but simply illustrates the compartmentalized approach to curriculum development in this area which was common throughout the country until relatively recently. Some of the more recent working party reports which we have received have been planned to cover the whole range of the middle years, and several are in loose-leaf folders, making it clear that the originators regard curriculum development as a continuous process and that further papers will be produced in the future for inclusion in the folders.

Some of the secondary schools visited by the project team had established mathematics workshops well supplied with materials and equipment, where children of different ability levels were working on assignments covering a range of topics. We were told by the teachers of the high level of interest and enthusiasm engendered in both academic and non-academic pupils. Some of these teachers were already seeking to carry their work further and were looking for ways in which the school timetable might be modified to provide them with greater flexibility in their working methods so as to ensure that the kind of investigation being undertaken had a natural lease of life. The range of work to be observed in some junior schools has been well documented in other publications, and some of what has been observed by the members of the project team seems to indicate that a number of receiving secondary schools are both aware of, and satisfied with, the work in mathematics being undertaken by their contributory schools. There is obviously much more that could be written on the credit side of the account, but few would claim that there are grounds for complacency at present.

From the evidence collected by the project team we feel that it is wrong to talk of the 'mathematics revolution' in the middle years of schooling as being in
120

the past tense. The concept of 'continuous revolution' seems more appropriate. A high proportion of the heads and class teachers we interviewed expressed uncertainty, concern, and often anxiety, over the teaching of mathematics at the upper junior level. While many showed satisfaction over their achievements in other aspects of the curriculum it was only in isolated cases that we met teachers who expressed similar satisfaction over their work in mathematics. 'We have not arrived, we are just setting out on the journey' is a fair summary of the feelings of most of the teachers we met. The Nuffield Project has stated that 'the hope for the future lies in the possibility of a gradually developing syllabus rather than one which will fossilise for half a century and need another revolution like the present one to change it.'[20] Perhaps this concept of continuous development needs to be given greater emphasis so that teachers can adjust to the certainty of continued uncertainty.

There is also a need to emphasize the importance of close liaison between schools as the work in mathematics develops. It seems unwise to interpret 'gradually developing syllabus' as indicating a policy of teachers and schools developing new approaches to mathematics in complete isolation. While separate institutions exist and children transfer from one to another a need for continuity will remain. In the past this was partly achieved by the provision of a limited number of textbooks offering similar content, and by the pressures of the external examination at 11-plus. Today much more depends on the initiative shown by primary and secondary teachers in finding ways of working together to ensure that the curriculum, as experienced by the child, represents a sequence of related and interconnected experiences and not a random hotchpotch.

It is on mathematics more than any other aspect of the curriculum that we have faced probing questions from teachers, and many appear to be looking for more guidance on what to do. The dissemination of ideas takes a considerable time and in some schools development has followed a gradual and logical sequence over the past decade. For other schools – perhaps the majority at the primary level – there is a considerable time-lag and the further they are away from the mainstream of communication, the greater the chance of new ideas reaching them in clusters, out of sequence, or somewhat distorted in the dissemination process. The Plowden Report estimated that about 15 per cent of all primary teachers in England had, by 1967, attended courses and conferences organized by HM Inspectorate.[21] Without attempting in any way to belittle the magnitude of this achievement, we have to bear in mind that the great majority of these courses were of short duration, and even so, some 85 per cent of the teachers had not attended one. In 1971 eight primary schools visited by the project team were participating in the Nuffield Mathematics Project; of the seventy-six teachers working in these schools thirty-five had not participated in

121

any refresher courses, conferences or teachers' centre work since leaving college. Thirty-seven had attended some form of short course either at the local teachers' centre or a college of education, two had attended a course of two weeks' duration and two others had been released for a one-term course.

It seems clear that the massive operation mounted to effect changes in mathematics teaching at the primary level became more complicated as it got under way. Initially, it was chiefly confined to changes in methodology, but later other variables arose. The spreading upwards of new methods met with the spreading downwards of new content and it has been in the middle years, especially the lower middle years, that these two movements have converged. During the same period of time, teachers 'disclaiming any expertise for, or even liking of, the subject' have been dealing with some additional changes brought about by the decimalization of our currency and the move towards metrication.

It appears that the heart of the difficulty faced by many conscientious teachers is that of insecurity; it is an insecurity brought about by the rapidity and complexity of current changes and, frequently, uncertainty about the rightness of those changes. From the slow evolutionary development which let farthings slip away to join the rods, poles and perches, teachers have been faced in quick succession with a number of possible options, none of which carries that reassuring hallmark of established tradition. Teachers who make no claim to being specialists in the teaching of mathematics feel they are being asked to make carefully considered curriculum choices in an area in which even the experts appear uncertain, if not in conflict. In some cases we found teachers working together in the same school who had attended courses covering the work of children in the same age-range; but these courses had been using two different types of language and advocating two different types of content. It is not simply a problem of new maths or old maths but also the difficulty of organizing the learning experiences of children which causes concern. Professor Doris Lee has stressed the sequential approach in learning mathematics:

> Consideration of the logical structure of the subject concerns the arrangement of each topic or process in the mathematical stages so that every step leads on to the next, and can therefore be approached in its rightful place in the mathematical sequence. This arrangement of steps in a logical order is indispensable since in any branch of mathematics this order is essential to the acquisition of tools and techniques for each successive stage as it occurs.[22]

The text published by the Association of Teachers of Mathematics seems to suggest a somewhat different approach:

If mathematics is not seen as restricted to a few conventionally accepted areas of experience, or constrained to follow a simple linear development, the teacher can encourage the pupils to range far and wide in their mathematical activity. They can explore situations which are incredibly rich in their mathematical yield. There are situations, some of which we mention, which are direct enough to be grasped by all children, and yet which provide such a wealth of possibilities that they are difficult to exhaust. Faced with the responses of children to such situations, confident judgements about the mathematics appropriate for a particular age, or the precedence of some piece of mathematics over another, have to be abandoned. It becomes obvious that the learning of mathematics is a complex activity and the children can work happily within that complexity.[23]

When we come to look at the content of the mathematics curriculum in the middle years it certainly appears to be a 'complex activity'. In part we must be influenced by its utilitarian role and in part by its position as the science of number and space. To a lesser extent, we must have in mind that at a more advanced stage it provides a structure of clear, logical argument. Perhaps the two basic considerations in planning the curriculum are the nature of cognitive development in children throughout the middle years, and the nature of mathematical concepts and skills. In neither case can simple, rule-of-thumb answers be given. We recognize individual differences in children, their capabilities, rates and modes of learning, their varying levels of interest and motivation. There are also current disagreements over the nature of mathematics as a discipline, the nature and structure of mathematical concepts, their relative independence or interdependence, their variable or invariable sequence. These psychological and mathematical issues are further complicated by: **a** the variable context in which learning is expected to take place; **b** the influence of past tradition and experience; and **c** the requirements and pressures of contemporary society. Under the first heading, middle-years children are learning mathematics in first schools, junior and middle schools and in the range of different types of secondary schools. While this chapter is concerned with mathematics in the middle years, we have to recognize that for most children the curriculum is at present planned in two isolated sections, as the concluding section of a whole six-year primary course, and the first years of a complete secondary course.

The schools in which the learning takes place vary in their location and resources, in their staff–pupil ratios, in staff training, expertise and experience, in their institutional objectives – in fact in the many social, administrative and professional variables which are the context of education in the middle years in

123

this country. It is within this highly complex network of a school environment that the final selection of the work in mathematics takes place. The emphasis, bias or direction which the programme is given depends to a considerable extent on the previous experiences of the teachers planning the programmes and the extent to which they are affected by both the influence of the past and by the contemporary pressures of society. There may be a desire to maintain the level of computational skills which were common when a simple arithmetical course was being followed, for example, or a feeling of urgency to prepare children for external examination. The effectiveness of the curriculum planned will depend on its appropriateness for the children attending the school, the extent to which it is understood and accepted by the teachers who have to implement it, their skill in presenting the material to the children, and the provision of adequate resources.

The teacher of mathematics will be aware that mathematics is a mental activity and that writing on paper is merely an aid, as also is the provision of concrete materials in the form of structured and incidental apparatus. These are no more than the vehicles used by the teacher and pupil as part of the process leading to the eventual understanding of an abstraction. The understanding of one cluster of abstractions by a child does not necessarily imply that he is now 'ready' for abstract learning and that the further use of materials is unnecessary. Indeed many adults still find the need to create some visual aid when faced with a mathematical solution with which they are not familiar. Furthermore, there are whole systems of concepts involved in mathematics, and the understanding of one may depend on a child's ability to utilize his grasp of several others in order to comprehend a new concept. At this stage there is frequently a need to revert to the manipulation of objects or models to ensure a sound grasp of the new learning.

Once children have started to learn mathematics, there comes a need for them to have some grasp of the language so that they can organize their own thinking and also communicate their ideas to others. However, grasping mathematical concepts is not the beginning and end of mathematical ability. To develop the ability, a knowledge of mathematical symbols, methods and proofs is needed. Some of these have to be learned, retained and reproduced; they have to be combined with others to form the basis for the understanding of some further piece of mathematics and for the solving of mathematical problems. For example, a child at the beginning of the middle years may well be able to undertake the physical classification of a number of cardboard shapes into sets of triangles, squares and circles. He may also be in a position to ascribe to each set a given name, but he may still be some way from being able consciously to identify their different characteristics, or to express these in verbal terms. He may be even further removed from, say, the ability to classify the different sets of quadrilaterals. To do this would depend on further knowledge which is not yet within his grasp and before such a task can be done he will need both additional experience and the language associated with that experience.

It is at this level that we can see the value of both Professor Lee's emphasis on the importance of sequential learning and the Association of Teachers of Mathematics' claim for encouraging the children 'to range far and wide in their mathematical activity'. There are many areas of mathematics that can profitably be explored by children in the middle years, but whatever areas are chosen the work will inevitably depend for progression on an understanding of the language and concepts associated with those areas; there will exist sequences one or other of which must be followed. This is far from saying that such a sequence can only be taught by a series of formal lessons. Indeed individual studies, group work or the adoption of learning techniques commonly described as discovery methods are likely to prove much more suitable. Nevertheless, irrespective of the topics chosen or the methodology used, children's learning will depend upon a certain sequential approach. Measurement of length, for example, implies a vocabulary which includes longer, shorter, taller, etc., the ability to compare and order lengths, and the recognition of the need for some unit of length as a measuring device. If the child is expected to *start* with a ruler, metrestick, click-wheel, or some other standardized unit, then the earlier stages of experience which would establish the justification for such behaviour has been ignored. It is the omission of important steps in the development of understanding which appears to be responsible for much failure at the later stages of learning mathematics. Children will enter the middle years of schooling with different levels of mathematical understanding and ability, and as their learning continues, so the differences are likely to increase. In order to allow the more able child to reach his potential and the slower learner to make sound progress at a more limited rate, much individual and group work will be needed. Even when it seems desirable to introduce new work to a class or to a large group of children, there still seems to be a need to take account not only of the different rates of learning but also of the different levels of thinking. Throughout the whole of the middle years apparatus and material must be provided. For some children these will be important for the bulk of the time; for the more able, their use will decline as understanding grows, but it is important to recognize that every new concept is likely to require an exploratory stage. This is likely to be facilitated by discussion and by the provision of materials which enable it to be visualized in a concrete form before attempting to comprehend the abstraction.

When this chapter was originally circulated in draft form to teachers' centres throughout the country it was discussed by numbers of teachers who were already active members of mathematics panels, working parties or study groups which had previously been established in their localities. A number of these groups commented adversely on the chapter. The chief criticism was that it 'contained little that is not well known already', and that 'it offers no clear and positive lead'. From what has been said earlier about the variable nature of mathematics teaching in the middle-years institutions, the different viewpoints of teachers and the range of possible content, it is clear that there are no certain grounds for positive and specific directives. However, whatever aspects of mathematics are included in the curriculum, certain basic elements seem essential, either because of their importance in the growth of mathematical understanding, or because of their utilitarian role in our society. These essentials may be expressed in the terminology of modern mathematics or the language used may be more familiar to the non-specialist. For example:

1   Elements: things or objects which can be thought of as distinct. The foundation of all mathematics is the theory of sets.
2   Relations between elements of the same or different sets.
3   Operations which, starting from elements of a set, produce others which are found to be elements of the original set, or elements created by the operation. In the second case, the new elements form an extension of the original set.
4   Functions, which are particular kinds of operations.
5   Quantifiers, which specify the elements to which any statement applies.
6   The idea of a neighbourhood, which in pure mathematics leads us to the idea of continuity, and in applied mathematics to the idea of approximation and mean.[24]

From the reports received by the Middle Years Project and from visits made by the project team to schools and teachers' centres, it seems clear that such statements are meaningful and represent a clear and useful outline of some of the essentials to groups of teachers working in certain parts of the country. It is equally clear that such language conveys little to other teachers working in other parts of the country – they are likely to find more acceptable an approach elaborated under headings such as:

1   number and the operations of number
2   aspects of measurement (money, time, mass, length, capacity, area and volume)
3   shape
4   visual representation.

126

It would seem that whatever the form of language used, there are likely to be many areas of overlap and these forms of global headings are all capable of enormous expansion. Certainly there is no shortage of published material giving guidance on how this might be done. Some of the texts have been written with an emphasis on methodology, others stress content, but whatever else may be included or omitted, and whether the language is that of traditional or modern mathematics, some expansion of the work involving the second list of headings will almost certainly be present.

An examination of many publications dealing with the teaching of mathematics reveals something of the range of possible material for inclusion in the curriculum. This is so extensive that there would seem little value in producing a catalogue of all that has been suggested. It would also call for a highly experienced team of teachers and mathematicians to identify and classify what mathematical learning the writers might be including under their range of headings, for some of them are almost certainly unfamiliar to the non-specialist teacher. Since mathematics is one of the critical areas of the curriculum where there is not only a wide divergence to be found in both content and methodology, but also in the language used to describe content, there seems to be an urgent need for some agreement to be reached between contributory and receiving schools regarding the teaching of mathematics. A number of useful possible starting points might be used when beginning a liaison to achieve this. Schools Council Curriculum Bulletin No. 1 *Mathematics in Primary Schools* might be taken as a basis from which work for the older middle-years children might be developed. The output of the Nuffield Mathematics Project 5–13 offers another useful source. At the time of writing it appears that the School Mathematics Project has plans to extend its operations to a lower age-range (see note 12) and, in response to the requests from many teachers who read this chapter in draft form, the project team has added as an appendix to this chapter one possible outline of content for the middle years prepared for the Middle Years Project by Miss E. E. Biggs, HMI. (See pages 131–42.) The terminology used takes account of the fact that the majority of those teaching mathematics in the middle years are not specialists.

In suggesting the need for an agreement between local schools the project team is aware of the danger that this could be misinterpreted as suggesting the acceptance of a minimum standard to be reached by all pupils at the time of transfer. The failure of such an approach was manifest when primary schools operated with a common syllabus imposed by the 11-plus examination. What is needed now is something quite different. Efficient ways need to be devised in which the teacher in one school can communicate to the teacher in another school the kind of mathematical understanding which individual children are

127

likely to have, and the receiving school needs to ensure that this mathematical development continues with the minimum of dislocation. One of the essentials would be the design of realistic record folders which would allow contributory schools to provide information they regard as important, and also contain some standardized elements enabling the receiving teachers to understand clearly what information is being communicated.

So far, this chapter has made no mention of the time allocated to mathematics. This seems quite arbitrary when any attempt is made to justify mathematics. Tradition has largely determined that it has far more time than subjects such as history, geography, and often science. The subject seems to obey some kind of Parkinson's Law, whereby mathematical content expands to fill the time available. If given half a week, there is little doubt that there would be a growth of mathematical activity to fill it. Much depends on what the curriculum includes under mathematics in the middle years and what objectives have been set. If the emphasis is placed on the purely utilitarian aspect of mathematics it would seem that the advent of decimalization and metrication coupled with improved teaching methods and the use of simple calculating machines might well result in considerably less time being spent learning mathematics than in the past. Such an emphasis would be resisted by the great majority of teachers and others whose view of the subject extends beyond this basic level of thinking. They would claim that over and above the purely utilitarian purpose of mathematics it is a powerful tool for clear and logical thinking; that an understanding of mathematics is essential for an appreciation of the order and pattern in both the natural world and the man-made environment; that mathematics is 'the queen and servant of all the sciences', and that the further education of many children has, in the past, been impeded by a lack of mathematical understanding. They would point out that in the middle years mathematics should offer far more than teaching the end-products of other people's discoveries, and that the subject offers considerable scope for creativity.

When these claims are well presented, they undoubtedly represent a powerful argument for more and better mathematics, but such claims place a heavy responsibility on the shoulders of teachers and those responsible for the training of teachers. We are living through a transitional period when many teachers, trained and experienced in an earlier tradition, are having to develop a new mathematical awareness and understanding. To some extent, the length of this transitional period will depend on the speed with which we undertake the retraining of teachers, both in the new mathematical knowledge and in the skills and techniques for organizing new and effective teaching in the middle years. It would be wrong to assume that this process is now almost completed, for much still remains to be done. From discussions with many teachers and advisers it

128

would seem that at present many, perhaps most, are well aware of the weaknesses of past teaching and of the need for change. The language associated with new developments in mathematics has been well disseminated, but this does not permit us to claim that those responsible for teaching mathematics in the middle years are satisfied with their own knowledge of the subject, nor that they know the best ways of organizing the learning, and of deciding the mathematical content which should be included.

At present, many teachers are finding that more active learning on the part of their pupils, the use of much apparatus and equipment and the adoption of the 'discovery' approach, calls for more time than was previously spent when using direct teaching methods. If they include some of the new topics and branches of mathematics, then even more time is called for.

Some schools have resolved this difficulty by producing schemes of work which outline part of the mathematics course in an ordered sequence thus giving to the work some basic structure. For the remainder of the time they suggest a wide range of suitable topics or areas of study from which selections can be made. This latter part is designed both to increase the children's understanding of mathematics and to foster desirable attitudes towards the subject. This dual approach – partly structured, partly unstructured – can be far more than the traditional arithmetic course plus a few optional extras, and it certainly does not imply that teachers are encouraged to treat part of the work formally and part informally. It seems to offer considerable scope and freedom to both teachers and pupils, but it also ensures that there is some regular progression, a highly desirable feature in schools where there are frequent changes in teaching staff, or where there are teachers who may be inexperienced or feel insecure about the mathematical experiences they should be offering to their pupils.

The record of the past has shown that 'maths every day' for over a century has not guaranteed a numerate, maths-delighting majority, but there are sufficient growing-points in schools to suggest that more pupils are now finding delight in the subject and that mathematics can enrich work in music, geography, art, biology, and other aspects of the curriculum. There are, at present, no rules but precedent. 'Teachers cannot know with certainty what the future needs of their pupils are. It is doubtful if it is possible to predict ten years ahead precisely what mathematics they should know . . . There is no absolute guide to right decisions; there can only be informed and sensitive guess-work', wrote L. Felix in *Modern Mathematics and the Teacher*.[25] For children in the middle years, she writes, 'The teacher must have taken every opportunity to open the children's minds and to offer them a mathematical language, in written and verbal form, that is good enough to be used in the future.'[26] Within the middle years of schooling there appears to be universal agreement that mathematics should form an important study for every child, and a general desire that such studies should offer rewarding and interesting activities, sufficient to give many middle-years children a desire to continue this work in their future education.

## References and notes

1. Nuffield Mathematics Project 5–13 (1964–71), organizer Professor Geoffrey Matthews. Publishers: W. & R. Chambers and John Murray.
2. Schools Council Field Report No. 1, *New Developments in Mathematics Teaching* (Schools Council, 1966, out of print).
3. Schools Council Curriculum Bulletin No. 1, *Mathematics in Primary Schools* (HMSO, 1965; 4th edn, 1972).
4. Central Advisory Council for Education (England), *Children and their Primary Schools* (HMSO, 1967), Vol. 1, para. 647.
5. Schools Council Working Paper No. 22, *The Middle Years of Schooling from 8 to 13* (HMSO, 1969), p. 64.
6. Ministry of Education, *Primary Education* (HMSO, 1959), p. 179.
7. See JOHN BIGGS, 'The psychopathology of arithmetic', *The Listener* (19 April 1962), 681–3.
8. Nuffield Mathematics Project, *I Do, and I Understand* (W. & R. Chambers and John Murray, 1969), p. 5 and General Introduction.
9. Schools Council Curriculum Bulletin No. 1, *Mathematics in Primary Schools* (HMSO, 1965; 4th edn, 1972), see page 10.
10. Nuffield Mathematics Project, *I Do, and I Understand* (W. & R. Chambers and John Murray, 1969), General Introduction and page 4.
11. The Midland Mathematics Experiment, a privately sponsored project, began in 1961. It has been directed by R. M. Stokes, at Coventry College of Education, since April 1972. Publisher: George Harrap.
12. The School Mathematics Project, director Dr Bryan Thwaites, was set up in 1961. Its original aim was to rewrite and modernize the GCE O- and A-level mathematics syllabuses for pupils aged 13 to 18 (later from 11+ onwards). The project team produced GCE courses, and in 1966 began work on a CSE series, now known as the Main School Course. In 1973 they embarked on a new middle-years project. SMP teaching materials are published by Cambridge University Press.
13. L. D. ADAMS, *Background to Primary School Mathematics* (Oxford University Press, 1953).
14. Mathematical Association, *The Teaching of Mathematics in the Primary School* (Bell, 1956).

15. L. D. ADAMS, *Background to Primary School Mathematics* (Oxford University Press, 1953), p. 2.
16. Schools Council Field Report No. 1, *New Developments in Mathematics Teaching* (Schools Council, 1966, out of print).
17. Schools Council Curriculum Bulletin No. 1, *Mathematics in Primary Schools* (HMSO, 1965; 4th edn, 1972), 2nd edn, 1966, p. xiv.
18. Schools Council Working Paper No. 22, *The Middle Years of Schooling from 8 to 13* (HMSO, 1969), p. 64.
19. Schools Council Field Report No. 1, *New Developments in Mathematics Teaching* (Schools Council, 1966, out of print).
20. Nuffield Mathematics Project, *Into Secondary School* (W. & R. Chambers and John Murray, 1970), p. 3.
21. Central Advisory Council for Education (England), *Children and their Primary Schools* (HMSO, 1967), Vol. I, para. 650.
22. D. M. LEE, *Background to Mathematical Development* (Oldbourne, 1962), p. 208.
23. Association of Teachers of Mathematics, *Notes on the Teaching of Mathematics in Primary Schools* (Cambridge University Press, 1967), p. 3.
24. See L. FELIX, *Modern Mathematics and the Teacher*, trans. Association of Teachers of Mathematics (Cambridge University Press, 1966).
25. Ibid., p. ix.
26. Ibid., p. 1.

**Appendix**  Suggested syllabus for mathematics in the middle years*

There is no doubt that learning mathematics by investigation – the initial stage whenever a new topic is introduced – gives pupils an intense and sometimes lasting interest in the subject as well as an understanding of concepts. I have used the term 'investigation' because this has a wider connotation than practical work. Investigation includes looking for patterns and relations in very varied situations. Awareness of the mathematical potential of the natural and man-made environment, and the ability to generalize and abstract, is one of the most important achievements for the pupil. But we must not forget that the skills of computation are still important. On the whole teachers require more help with computational skills than with the skills in any other field.

* Prepared for the project by Edith Biggs, HMI.

131

Before I consider content let me make several important points. These concern the nature of investigation. There is a good deal of misunderstanding about practical work.

1    It does not mean running about with a measuring tape or trundle wheel 'measuring' a room over and over again at various stages of the pupil's life. Practical work of this nature is time-consuming and the teacher needs to have a very clear mathematical purpose for every activity undertaken.

2    Moreover, one piece of practical work can often be the starting point for a variety of mathematical ideas, provided the teacher has the mathematical imagination to appreciate this.

3    Certain ideas are so important that pupils need to meet them over and over again, each time at a more demanding level and in a different context. Normally one discovery is not enough. This means that, within a flexible framework which allows pupils to make their own investigations when a new topic is introduced, we need to structure the mathematics we want them to learn. Sometimes pupils should be allowed to pursue their own ideas. At other times we would focus attention on certain lines of development we wanted the pupil to follow. This implies that we need to have many ideas available and also that we need to know our subject matter. This does not mean, of course, that we should know the answer to every question our pupils ask. This would rob the work of its spontaneity and of what Professor D. Hawkins describes as the particular relationship established between teacher and child when investigating a common problem to which neither knows the answer.

4    All this implies the need to staff every middle school (and large primary schools for that matter) with at least one teacher who has a special interest in and knowledge of mathematics – for example, a teacher who took mathematics as a main subject at a college of education or one who took a supplementary course later.

ARITHMETIC

This should *not* be dealt with in isolation. Much of the work at present covered in primary schools has a bearing on arithmetic although teachers do not always realize this. The period 8 to 10 years is usually the time when a child meets problems which involve increasingly complicated written calculations. This is the stage when he will come across problems which require techniques of long multiplication and long division for efficient solution. But he must have sufficient oral number knowledge before he is required to do written calculations of this

132

nature. His first methods will normally involve repeated addition or subtraction. The teacher's questions will help him refine these methods.

I believe we try to teach too many number facts. The most important number facts are those which children are delighted to discover for themselves. Perhaps the most important discovery of all is the unending sequence of the counting numbers and the variety of patterns to be discovered.

Of course children need to know some number facts, but once they know the facts concerning the small numbers (for example, those whose sum is not greater than 10) they can quickly build up the others for themselves. At no stage, however, should we try to prevent an able and interested child from learning as many facts as he wishes. On the other hand, all children will benefit from a knowledge of the relationships concerning the small numbers. But this should be an absorbing pastime and not a boring experience.

Some of the important stages in the acquisition of the number facts (not in order) are:

**1** Doubling (and halving) numbers.

**2** Adding (and subtracting) 1 from any starting point.

**3** Adding (and subtracting) 2 from any starting point.

**4** Recognition of odd and even numbers.

**5** Adding pairs of numbers, e.g. 3, 4 as $2 \times 3 + 1$, and $2 \times 4 - 1$.

**6** Experimenting with small numbers, e.g. $3 = 9 - 6 = 8 - 5 = 7 - 4$, etc.; building up tables $1 \times 4 = 4$, $2 \times 4 = 8$, $3 \times 4 = 12$. In how many ways can we build up $4 \times 4$ etc.?

**7** Adding 10, first to numbers less than 10, then in an unending sequence. A number line is invaluable here.

**8** Adding 9, e.g. $9 + 6 = 15$, because 9 is one less than 10 and I know that $10 + 6 = 16$.

**9** $2 + 5 = 5 + 2$ etc., i.e. $a + b = b + a$ is explicit and operational.

**10** $4 \times 3 = 3 \times 4$, i.e. $a \times b = b \times a$ is explicit and operational.

**11** $9 \times 10 = 90$, $10 \times 9 = 90$, $17 \times 10 = 170$, etc.

These facts are particularly important when it comes to long multiplication and long division. The question should frequently be asked: why do these products end in zero? (The response should be: because there are no units, these are all tens.)

**12** Number trios, e.g. 2, 5, 7, often help children to remember the four addition and subtraction facts concerning these numbers: $5 + 2 = 7$; $2 + 5 = 7$, $7 - 5 = 2$, $7 - 2 = 5$.

For multiplication and division: 3, 4, 12. $4 \times 3 = 12$, $3 \times 4 = 12$, $12 \div 4 = 3$, $12 \div 3 = 4$.

*Multiplication and division tables*

It is an advantage for children to *know* many of the facts (as far as multiplication by 10) once they have discovered and worked with patterns from the 100 square and multiplication square. But a few children find the learning such a labour that they are put off mathematics for ever! For these children it is better to let them make a section of the multiplication square and use it for the facts they do know.

The 2, 4, 8 multiplication facts are quickly built by successive doubling.

For example:

| 1 | 2 | 4 | 8 |
|---|---|---|---|
| 0 | 0 | 0 | 0 |
| 1 | 2 | 4 | 8 |
| 2 | 4 | 8 | 16 |
| 4 | 8 | 16 | 32 |
| 5 | 10 | 20 | 40 |

Multiplication by 10 is essential; multiplication by 5 can be obtained by halving the result. The 3, 6, 9 tables can be grouped although the table of 9s has a special attractive pattern 9, 18, 27, 36, 45, etc. which makes it easy to memorize. Once a pupil has discovered the sum of the digits 'pattern', he has no difficulty. The table of 7s with its association with the calendar is worth investigating.* Pupils should also be encouraged to know the squares of the whole numbers as far as $10^2$.

There are various ways in which we can help children to learn tables, for example, by taking a ceiling such as 24, and learning all the number facts (plus and minus as well as multiplication and division) from 1 to 24, then raising the ceiling to 36, etc. This has been found useful by many teachers. Knowledge of long multiplication and long division implies a knowledge of:

**1**	the commutative laws;
**2**	the associative laws (e.g. $2 + 13 + 8 = 2 + 8 + 13$);
**3**	the distributive law (e.g. $57 \times 29 = 57 \times 20 + 57 \times 9$).

These laws should be made explicit at this stage.

*Long multiplication*

Consider the example: how many tiles are there on a classroom floor with 37 tiles one way and 36 the other way?

* See Association of Teachers of Mathematics, *Notes on the Teaching of Mathematics in Primary Schools* (Cambridge University Press, 1967).

134

*First effort*

$$30 \times 30 = 900$$
$$7 \times 6 = 42$$
$$\overline{\phantom{00}}$$
$$942 \text{ total}$$

The picture showed that this was wrong (but this can lead to an efficient solution).

*Second effort*

37

| | 10 | 10 | 10 | 7 |
|---|---|---|---|---|
| 36 | 360 | 360 | 360 | 252 |
| | | | | |

| *Recorded* (1) | *Recorded* (2) |
|---|---|
| 360 = 10 times | 36 |
| 360 = 10 times | 37 |
| 360 = 10 times | 1080 = 30 times |
| 252 = 7 times | 252 = 7 times |
| 1332 = 37 times | 1332 = 37 times |

The room was divided into 3 strips of 10 and a strip of 7. This was eventually recorded by the children themselves in the traditional way. Variety of methods is to be encouraged, but every child should have one efficient method and should practise this.

### Division

'Maximum load 2000 kilograms' is the notice Mr Short reads as he steps into the lift. Find out how many men each weighing 85 kilograms could be carried in the lift.

*First method*

| 2000 kg | |
|---|---|
| 850 | (10 men) |
| 1150 | |
| 850 | (10 men) |
| 300 | |
| 170 | ( 2 men) |
| 130 | |
| 85 | ( 1 man) |
| 45 kg | 23 men |

*Second method*

| 2000 kg | |
|---|---|
| 1700 | (20 men) |
| 300 | |
| 255 | ( 3 men) |
| 45 kg | 23 men |

135

Practice is essential. From time to time teachers need to give a piece of practice and to ask the pupils to write a problem (story sum) to fit the practice to see if the pupils understand when to use the operation.

## NOTATION

The use of Dienes' multi-base arithmetic blocks gives the best introduction if it is desired to introduce this topic at 7 or 8 years. The binary system can also be introduced by using imperial kitchen weights or structural material between the ages of 8 and 10 years. The pattern is easily recognized. Practice with the abacus using different bases (perhaps playing a dice game) will give groups of two or three children the experience they need. Many children of the ages 9 and 10 enjoy working in bases other than 10, especially when they realize the need to invent new symbols for base 12, etc. The sequence should emerge at this stage and should be extended to include decimals.

| | | | | | | |
|---|---|---|---|---|---|---|
| *10 000* | *1000* | *100* | *10* | *1* | $\frac{1}{10}$ | ? |
| $10^4$ | $10^3$ | $10^2$ | ? | ? | ? | ? |
| or 10 000 | 1000 | 100 | 10 | 1 | 0.1 | ? |

*Extension of number system*
*Fractions and decimals.* $\frac{1}{2}$, $\frac{1}{4}$ and $\frac{3}{4}$ will still be needed in everyday life and the idea of equivalence (a half being equal to two quarters, etc.), which is the only knowledge required for operations ($+$, $-$, $\times$, $\div$) on fractions, will arise naturally. Fractions will later be met as rational numbers when the question is asked: does the commutative law apply to division? For an understanding of decimals, children will need to know about the fractions, or: tenths and hundredths, etc. Decimal fractions are a convenient way of writing these fractions. The use of decimal currency and of measuring in international units should help young children to an earlier understanding of decimals. It is of first importance that children should know, for example, which is greater, 0.7 or 0.15, before they are given practice in calculations using decimals.

*Directed numbers.* Similarly negative numbers will first arise when a negative number line is introduced. (This might first be introduced with its numbers in a different colour from the numbers on the positive number line.) The question of negative numbers often arises when graphs are drawn – for example, graphs of the multiplication tables or the squares, when children ask, 'What happens next?' The 'application' of the commutative law to subtraction also leads to the introduction of negative numbers. (Writing directed numbers as $^-1$, $^-2$, $^-3$, etc.

136

to distinguish these from the operations of $+$ and $-$ is very helpful in the early stages.)

MEASURING – length, weight and density, time and rate, volume, area

Once young children have realized the need for standard units of measurement (by the use of arbitrary units such as the lengths of feet and hands and the weights of acorns and marbles, etc.), they should be given substantial experience using a wide variety of metric measures to enable them to 'think metric'. When at a later stage they mention other units they have seen at home or in shops, teachers will want to introduce them to imperial units. Provided children have had sufficient early experience using arbitrary units they will not be troubled by the existence of two sets of units. Rarely, if ever, will there be need for conversion from one set of units to the other. (At the later secondary stages this may sometimes be necessary in the use of machinery in crafts, but tables of conversion can then be used.)

Some teachers may want to introduce units of force and to let pupils know that kilograms are units of mass. Force is measured in newtons. Children can find their pulling force using extension scales. They can find their 'squeeze' using bathroom scales graduated in newtons instead of kilograms. They can find the approximate equivalent in newtons of the force of gravity exerted on a kilogram mass by hanging this on extension scales calibrated in newtons.

At the top of the junior stage some children will be measuring forces. From viewing moon explorations on television, children are aware that objects weigh less when outside the earth's gravitational field. The farther we are from the centre of the earth, the weaker the earth's pull is. Many children will know that our weight (the result of the pull of gravity) would be slightly more at the flattened poles than at the equator. Many also know that the gravitational pull of the moon is far less than that of the earth. At the same time children are also prepared to accept that astronauts do not disappear when in space! When we use a compression scale to weigh ourselves, we are finding the gravitational pull (a force) and should give our answer in newtons. The unit of weight (a force) is a newton. The unit of mass is a kilogram. There is a simple approximate numerical relation between these two units.

Historically, the kilogram has been used as if it were a unit of force. When we are balancing masses it does not matter whether we use kilograms or newtons because at any one place mass is proportional to weight. However, as soon as children begin to measure force (top junior or lower secondary) it is better to use the correct units and vocabulary.

137

Certain important topics will arise at different levels, e.g. the circumference/diameter relationship of a circle.

Various mathematical concepts are common to all types of measurement (including temperature and angles) and also to number and shape:

Comparison (subtraction and division)
Classification and sorting leading to conservation and equivalence
Inequalities and ordering
Approximation, averages, estimation
Ideas of a variable generalization
Patterns and relations
Operations
Ratio and proportion
Limits (maximum and minimum).

STATISTICS AND PROBABILITY

*Statistics*
These subjects have already been introduced into primary schools and graphical representation of various kinds is now common. Not enough attention has been paid to the *ordering* of information. This may well be because this topic does not receive due attention in the earlier stages (for example, Piaget's seriation). Children soon begin to look for opportunities of ordering once they have experience of this. (For example, 'Order containers in as many ways as you can'.) From the age of 10 to about 12 pupils will order information, *group* it and also appreciate the effect of taking a larger and larger sample (for example, the weights of children in one age group in all schools in Nottingham – the children were able to recognize the pattern which emerged). Older pupils (possibly 11 to 13) will be able to find the relationship between the two variables – for example, using a scattergram of *height* and *reach* in answer to the question, 'Are you a square?'

A knowledge of the *mean* and *mode* and the relevance of each. (This may be introduced through measurement – for example, 'Find the length of your average pace'.) For some pupils a *cumulative* graph will have interest and relevance. For example, 'How many of this sample have weights less than 50 kg? What is the median value?'

*Probability*
Experiences such as recording remainders when different samples are divided by 2 (or 3, 4, etc.), coin tossing, drawing cards from a pack, spinning a top,
138

throwing 1 die, 2 dice, etc., leading to ideas of 'expected' frequency. (Operation tables in the four operations are useful and can be associated with these experiments.)

SHAPES – conservation, symmetry, and congruence, similarity (transformation geometry)

In children's experience, three-dimensional shapes precede two-dimensional shapes. Children abstract their knowledge of two-dimensional shapes from handling three-dimensional shapes in the first instance.

*Three-dimensional shapes and symmetry – mirror and rotational*

i   *Knowledge of the properties* of cubes, cuboids, cylinders, cones, balls (now spheres?), pyramids. Also squares, rectangles, circles, ellipses, triangles, using three-dimensional shapes to link three and two dimensions. (An acid test of whether a child understands squares is to give him a number of identical squares and ask him to build the largest square he can manage with these. A similar exercise can be given with cubes.)

ii  *Similarity and scale.* Properties of cubes made from identical unit cubes. Sequences such as perimeter and area of one face, volume, total skin area, skin area/volume relationship. The *n*th term (and those preceding and succeeding the *n*th term) is useful for those who are able to give this. Graphs can be made from these using:

a   Unit cubes (discontinuous graphs).
b   A continuous graph. The drawing of a continuous line must always be justified. Do intermediate points have a meaning?

This often encourages children to look for the different patterns in the number sequences. Applications: biology, geography, physics (bridges and girders).

*Two-dimensional shapes and symmetry – mirror and rotational*

i   *Regular two-dimensional shapes and their properties.* Triangles (angle sum), squares, pentagons, hexagons, octagons, etc. Tessellations (using triangles to discover parallel properties as well as the angle sum properties). Tessellations with identical irregular triangles and quadrilaterals. Reasons for standard unit in area.

139

**ii** *Properties of the quadrilaterals* through paper folding, paper cutting, geoboards.

**iii** *Transformations* – translations, reflections, rotation.

**iv** *Symmetrical polygons.* Relationships such as angles at centre/number of edges (constant product), interior angle/number of edges, exterior angle/number of edges.

**v** *Rigidity of framework* using Meccano strips. Relationships of the sequence of polygons (number of edges, number of struts, number of triangles, angle sum, interior angle). Algebraic relationships.

**vi** *Conservation of perimeter.* Investigation of area of any shape, regular polygons, rectangles, triangles, etc. Algebraic relationships, graphs. Sets of triangles with constant perimeter also make an interesting problem. Reverse problem, conservation of area, relationship perimeters. This can be done using identical unit squares, pupils to make their own rules. Finally a set of rectangles with constant area can be studied, cut out and 'patterned', graphed, etc.

RELATIONSHIPS GRAPHS

This work can be linked with operation tables of addition and multiplication for the numbers 1 to 10, for example.

*Co-ordinates*
This may be introduced through activities such as birthday day and month of all the pupils in the class, height and reach measures for every pupil in the class. Or at a younger stage the salient points on a pupil's treasure island can be drawn on squared paper and the positions defined with compass directions and distances.

*Proportion*
Direct proportion. Pupils from about the age of 11 should be able to recognize examples of direct proportion at a glance and to know immediately what the graph will look like. For example, the multiplication tables, perimeter/edge relationships for a square, the circumference/diameter relationship for a circle. Ready reckoner graphs – for example, prices at petrol pumps, air and rail fares. Prices of articles and materials bought in bulk can be compared with prices of individual articles. Conversion graphs – for example, the number of kilometres travelled per litre of petrol.

*Inverse proportion*
For example, rectangles of constant area; the operation table for multiplication; angle at centre of regular polygon/number of edges, exterior angle/number of edges; angle between two hinged mirrors and number of images (plus object) seen; on a see-saw – weight and distance from a fulcrum. Pupils should know what the graphs of these examples of inverse proportion should look like. Able pupils would be interested to make a three-dimensional graph having the dimensions of cuboids (volume, for example, 64 cubes).

*Other functions*
Graph of squares and of cubes and of growth relationships. The question, 'What happens next?' could be an introduction to negative integers. Children who compare the graph of squares with the area graph of rectangles with constant perimeter sometimes ask where the other half of the graph of the squares is, especially if they have seen the similarity of the number patterns. This can sometimes be an introduction to the multiplication of negative integers.

*Inequalities* (see section on statistics) leading to linear programming
Gradients can be introduced from the multiplication tables; simple vectors; limits. These will arise in a number of the examples already mentioned. For example, if the width of rectangles with constant area is repeatedly halved pupils often say that the rectangle becomes as thin as a piece of tracing paper but will never disappear altogether.

Ideas of similarity (three dimensions and two dimensions) should now be explicit. Applications: surveying and trigonometry.

*Introduction of algebra*
Algebra can be introduced in a natural way through work on number patterns – for example, in the sequences made with unit squares or cubes, perimeter of squares, area of squares, volume of cubes, skin (total) area of cubes, the $n$th term can be formed (and the terms preceding and succeeding the $n$th term). Pupils can also be encouraged to obtain the algebraic relations of the graphs they draw and to study the symmetries.

True, false and open sentences are a sound introduction to the solution of equations and can be related to the work on graphical relationships (for example, intersection of the graphs showing the areas of squares and the areas of rectangles of perimeter 20 cm).

141

I foresee an exciting future for middle schools given one leader teacher with mathematical imagination in each school. Team teaching might help to extend such methods and ideas.

# VIII. Music

Music makes its principal contribution to the curriculum in the aesthetic area but, like many other subjects, it has significant contributions to make elsewhere as well. The learning experiences afforded by music run through the whole range of cognitive, affective and psycho-motor skills. It can be shown to be worth pursuing for its own sake and in isolation from other pursuits but also in combination with other activities as a means of heightening the quality of the experience. It has a certain utilitarian function in the formal occasions which make up part of school life and which provide a child with experiences needed for help in adjustment to life, but its main justification stems from its unique nature as an art form and as a means of creative expression without which many children would not be able properly to fulfil themselves. Musicians can therefore make substantial claims upon the time and other resources available and, as in many other cases, a particularly strong case can be made out for generous treatment in the middle years. The project team has been able to draw upon the valuable paper written for the project by a working party set up by the Schools Council Music Committee, and upon the comments teachers made on this paper. Further development work is being done by the Schools Council's Music Education for Young Children Project (3–11) (1970–76), based at the University of Reading and directed by Dr A. Bentley.

The working party's paper begins by pointing out that 'from the age of 8 or so, many children are ready both mentally and physically to enjoy making music with their voices or with instruments'. The acquisition of language makes it possible for children to notice and enjoy the rhythms and intonations of words. Music can indeed be thought of as an additional language, a means of communication as well as creative expression and with its own form of reading and writing. Just as reading and writing of words go forward in these years so can those similar skills appropriate to musical expression be developed.

In music there are important considerations concerned with the physical equipment needed for the development of skills. By the age of 8, the singing voice has, in many cases, attained a considerable degree of flexibility and control though there are, of course, the usual variations in attainment. When vocal control has been established early – exemplified perhaps most markedly in the voices of those admitted at 8 to a cathedral choir – it makes possible the production of a unique quality of sound which composers of all periods have recognized. The final physical control needed for singing is needed in other forms of music-making. The working party's paper writes of the development

143

of the muscular co-ordination and mental concentration needed to acquire the complex techniques of playing instruments such as the recorder, the violin and the piano. These psycho-motor skills are capable of being developed at a more rapid rate in the middle years than at any other period and it is well known that, for the highly gifted, intensive development in these years is necessary if the full potential is to be achieved. It would be wrong, of course, to think of music in the middle years in terms of the highly gifted individuals for whom a specialized education is required. The development achieved by individual children in the years 8 to 13 will certainly depend upon natural aptitude but it will depend also upon the quality and range of the experiences available in school, at home and elsewhere in the middle and the preceding years. Just as language skills depend upon early experience so too do musical skills. Though nursery- and first-school programmes can do much, it is the totality of the child's experience which forms the basis of the development of musical as well as linguistic skills.

The working party speaks of conditions in the school being 'not unpropitious'. This somewhat guarded judgement no doubt reflects the fact that development is extremely uneven. Specialists are, of course, able to make particularly valuable contributions, but the general level of musicality in primary schools depends to a large extent upon the initiative and enterprise of non-specialist teachers. The BBC film, *Our Own Music*,[1] demonstrates what such teachers are capable of achieving. The Plowden Report, *Children and their Primary Schools*, spoke of a climate in junior school 'more favourable to music education than ever before'.[2] Awareness of the individual differences in rates of development, here as elsewhere, has led to much greater emphasis upon individual and group methods and less upon mass instruction which, the working party suggests, 'too often in the past caused frustration to the talented and sensitive while submerging the average or below-average pupil in an outwardly impressive but educationally deceptive body of unison singing or percussion playing.' The Plowden Report also commented upon the tendency to make music in school an occasion for mass rather than individual or group activities.[3]

The working party points out that there is still some way to go before a liberal and progressive scheme of education is available to every child. A principal difficulty is that imaginative teaching talent is very unevenly spread over the schools. Too many children 'pass through their primary years without coming into contact with a musical personality or do so only for brief periods.' Even when the situation is more favourable there is an insufficiently articulated programme of development. Lack of continuity at the 11-plus transfer is also blamed for failure to develop a coherent programme. Finally there are the points which occur in most comments – shortage of specialist accommodation, of equipment and of time ('daily opportunities') on the timetable.

144

The working party suggests that there is particular advantage for musical education in seeing the development across the 8 to 13 period as one span, and refers to a passage in the Department of Education and Science pamphlet, *Music in Schools*, pointing out that the musical achievements of some independent boys' preparatory schools may well be related to this: 'Vocally these middle years span the average boy's greatest ability to sing whilst instrumentally they enable uninterrupted progress to be made during a period in which he is best able to lay the foundations of a sound technique.'[4]

In the light of the primary-school background and the potentialities of the age-range concerned, what then could reasonably be attempted in the middle years? The working party's list of aims is as follows:

1   To give children access to a mode of experience which is unique in the kind of education it provides for the senses, the emotions, and the intellect and at the same time is almost universal in its appeal.
2   To offer a medium through which creative expression can be achieved, both individually and in groups.
3   To demonstrate the social as well as the individual satisfaction of practising an art in which disciplined team-work is an important factor.
4   To lay the foundations of musical discrimination and performing skills on which further enjoyable experience as listener, performer, or creator can be built at later stages of school education and in adult life.
5   To ensure that during these middle years as many children as possible become musically literate by acquiring a working knowledge of reading and writing musical notation.

The working party then translates these aims into practical objectives and suggests that the school might attempt to give every child, according to his aptitude and interest, opportunities for musical experience of the following kinds:

1   All should have help and encouragement in using their singing voices, easily and unselfconsciously, from an early age.
2   All should be introduced to forms of non-vocal performance, ranging according to natural abilities from the simplest clapping, stamping and percussion playing to playing instruments requiring complex techniques. It is probably true to say that in the broadest sense there is an instrument suitable for every child.
3   Making music involves listening to oneself and to others, and should lead on to the enjoyment of listening, at first for very short spells, without active participation. In this process some of the terms used in describing

145

musical forms and textures, as well as the names of composers and executants, can be picked up incidentally.

4  Through singing, playing instruments, and listening, the children will form concepts of the various elements that make up music, such as pitch, timbre, dynamics, speed, and duration of sounds – all of which can be expressed visually in musical notation of one kind or another. The formation and strengthening of musical concepts, and the systematic development of ability to understand and use musical notation, will be among the most important tasks of the teacher of music during the middle years, and the extent of his success in this direction may well be decisive for the child's future enjoyment and pursuit of music.

5  The processes of teaching and learning should reveal the value of using selectively the mechanical aids – radio, television, sound-film, tape-recorder, and record.

6  Every child should have opportunities for expressing musical ideas of his own, using his voice and any instruments available. In the words of the Gittins Report: 'The phase which is still missing for most children is exploration and first-hand experience.'[5] The ability to record one's discoveries in musical notation often enhances the satisfaction derived from the creative process and enables it to be carried further.

7  Musical activities may be interwoven with the use of language and movement in drama, mime, and dance, and there should be constant illustration and illumination of other branches of the curriculum through music.

8  The function of music as one of the arts of mankind, transcending divisions of age and race and helping to bring the past to life, gives it an overwhelming importance in education. 'Rhythm and music are intertwined with social and personal life, as can be clearly seen in primitive cultures.'[6] Music can have a particular value in bringing about a deeper understanding of non-European societies.

The working party then provides some comments on particular elements in a musical education – singing, rhythm and pitch, notation, instrumental music, and listening – which are reproduced below.

## Singing

While welcoming the extension of musical resources made possible through the introduction of classroom and orchestral instruments, there is no reason to depart from the traditional view that the foundations of musical training should rest on the use of the singing voice. This belief is supported not only by an

146

impressive body of teaching experience in England and Wales, but also by twentieth-century continental methods which have attracted much attention internationally. Chief among these are the teachings of Zoltan Kodaly and Carl Orff. The vocal foundations of the Kodaly method are apparent on every page of the literature, but it is too often overlooked that the use of the voice is essential to the Carl Orff methods also, both before and alongside the use of the instruments. In creative music-making the voice is at least as important and effective as instrumental improvisation.

Aural training in school is also most effectively carried out through individual and group singing. The presence in singing groups of 'growlers', 'drones', or (to use the now accepted technical term) 'monotones' is often a source of distress to the teacher and the more musical pupils. Recent scientific research has borne out the conviction, long held by experienced teachers of singing, that monotoning is a form of late development in recognizing and responding to pitch differences, and that its incidence can be greatly reduced, and even eliminated altogether, by plentiful opportunities for listening and by individual or group remedial work.

An understanding of children's voices, and an ability to present good examples of easy, well-placed vocal tone, diction, and intonation, are among the teacher's most useful assets in dealing with the middle years of schooling. Sound vocal habits formed at this period, together with a carefully-planned introduction to part-singing and the use of notation, will be an investment for the development of musical interest throughout school life and afterwards. The middle school age-range could provide excellent opportunities for giving a wide and progressive choral experience. This will have a welcome effect on festival and other more formal occasions where in the past the break of continuity at the age of 11 has been a hindrance.

At the upper end of the age-span the voice of many of the children, especially boys, will be entering upon a period of instability or change. The main responsibility for handling this controversial problem will lie with the secondary school, but it will nevertheless affect the work of the middle years and make it desirable for the teacher to have some knowledge of the adolescent voice and its treatment.

## Rhythm and pitch

Some of the most encouraging recent advances in musical education have come about by establishing links between the innate sense of rhythm, based on regular heart, pulse and breathing rates, and acquired speech rhythms. The Carl Orff and Kodaly methods and their derivatives use this connexion from their earliest

147

stages, and make it the foundation of creative techniques. 'This approach exploits the close relationship between language and musical rhythm and provides a situation in which children can explore, improvise, and create music.'[7]

Any available percussion instruments of good quality are valuable in developing sensitivity to rhythm and timbre and in making both performance and creation accessible to all. Pitched or tuned percussion instruments are of particular help in integrating rhythm and pitch training and enriching the creative media. It is worth observing that the increased use of these instruments in the classroom has coincided with the heightened importance of percussion in all kinds of serious and popular twentieth-century music.

Young children normally have a remarkable facility for picking up sounds by vocal imitation. The most familiar illustration of this is the acquisition of the mother tongue, but studies of bilingualism have shown that a second language can be learnt at the same time if undertaken before the imitative faculties begin to wane. There seems to be an obvious application here to learning music by ear.

Early vocal explorations can include the imitation of indefinite sounds, such as those of animals and machines, accompanied by mime or movement. Later musical phrases can be imitated from the teacher's patterning; this is usually much more effective if given by voice rather than by instrument. For this purpose, a quiet well-controlled quality of voice forms the most suitable model: a 'trained' adult voice is not only unnecessary but may be actually undesirable. Many successful teachers are convinced that the practice of using orally the traditional solfa syllables, as adapted to classroom conditions by John Curwen in the nineteenth century and renewed and extended by Kodaly in the twentieth, has proved its value in forming pitch concepts and ensuring accurate vocal (and instrumental) intonation. Solfa can ensure a firm grasp of *relative* pitch; accurately made percussion instruments (and no others should be tolerated) can help to develop a sense of *absolute* pitch, an important factor in understanding and performing the music of the present day.

## Notation

The importance of acquiring a secure basis of musical literacy in the middle years of schooling has already been referred to. The reorganization of the education of the middle years as a continuous whole offers an opportunity almost without precedent for bringing about a much-needed improvement in this aspect of musical education. This may not only increase the depth and quality of musical experience during the middle years themselves, but also do much to prevent the discouragement and loss of interest that often come about in the middle and late

148

teens, largely owing to a lack of substance in the musical fare provided and to an inadequate command of elementary skills.

A great deal of musical communication can be carried on without the aid of notation. Folk music, for example, in its natural state is independent of writing, and in the earliest years of a child's life musical impressions are and should be absorbed directly through the ear. But without some command of notation the older child is as closely restricted in music as he would be in language if he were unable to read and write, or in mathematics if he were unable to interpret and manipulate figures and other basic symbols. While, as with other intellectual skills, there must inevitably be much variation in ability and attainment between one child and another, there is cause for concern if, as happens at present, a large number of children grow up with little or no facility in using musical notation. This disquiet is even more justified when it is realized that musical illiteracy is often only a symptom of a general poverty of musical experience in the earlier years of school life. The difficulty of acquiring music reading ability in adolescence arises not so much from the actual notation itself (after all, many other codes of symbols are readily learnt at this age) or to the pressure of other interests, as from the absence of a stock of musical concepts to which the notation can be referred.

Until recently literacy in music as far as the school is concerned has usually been equated with an ability to translate notation into vocal performance – the 'sight-singing' that was so highly valued, on social and religious as well as artistic grounds, in the formative period of British elementary education. In the present century the introduction of classroom instruments such as the recorder has to a great extent altered the focus of the teaching of notation, though it is an over-simplification to suppose that learning an instrument will in itself produce literacy.

It must now be recognized, however, that with the widening horizons of contemporary music new kinds of literacy are in the ascendant – chord and cadence formulae, tablatures for fretted instruments, novel types of score devised for improvised, indeterminate, and electronic music are among the devices that must be taken into account. Experiments in creative music in school have also shown that a child will sometimes invent his own system for recording his discoveries. Any definition of literacy must be broad enough to cover all these graphic possibilities, together with the traditional notations of western music. A full, varied, and progressive range of active musical experiences will point at every stage to the need for visual symbols of one kind or another. Some children will need only a little notation, others much more. Some of the latter who may be required later on to take external examinations will not find it difficult to assemble and formulate their knowledge if it has been gained by

149

realistic learning through musical experience. In the words of the Plowden Report: 'Literacy must . . . be closely related to active music making; it must be functional, not theoretical.'[8]

## Instrumental music

Specialized instrumental work, as distinct from the use of the simpler 'classroom instruments', is most likely to begin in the middle years, although a good case can be made for starting it even earlier with gifted children. The complex skills of string playing in particular are most readily acquired if begun at the age of 7 or 8, but they should go along with the training of the ear and the use of the singing voice. The success of the Kodaly method in Hungary has demonstrated that not only out-of-tune singing but also out-of-tune violin playing (so often in the past suffered with resignation by parents and teachers) can be avoided if the instrumental teaching is based on the formation of pitch concepts with the aid of solfa.

It should not be assumed that the first instrument to be attempted will represent a child's final choice. This is not so much a question of musicality as of taste and physical aptitude. Some very musical children positively dislike their first attempts at an instrument, and gladly relinquish it for another, on which they then make uninterrupted progress. It is necessary to watch carefully for signs that a change is desirable for either physical or psychological reasons.

It is perhaps worth while mentioning that the piano is still one of the most attractive and useful instruments for many children, and there is no reason why its teaching should always be left to the private sector, especially as several methods of group instruction have been devised and might be adapted to the school situation.

## Listening

The development of attention, concentration, and discrimination is of course implicit in all music teaching, and is required for any success in playing an instrument, however simple:

> Children's capacity to listen can be developed by practice, both as performers and as audience. As performers, they should be trained to listen carefully to themselves, in relation to the performance of the other children in the group.[9]

Listening as an audience, without active participation, can be practised from the earliest years of the course. As far as possible it should be integrated with the rest of the teaching, rather than treated as a separate 'appreciation' lesson in the early stages. Listening to music of various periods and styles may usefully be linked with projects in other subjects of the curriculum, and above all with drama, movement, and dancing. Some of the current styles of popular and light music may well play an enjoyable and valuable part in learning to listen. For example, a great deal of Latin American music is vital and attractive. Folk song and dance, presented in various ways, also offer endless possibilities. At the same time, listening to music will not of course be confined exclusively to folk and dance music of whatever style, level or period. A beginning should be made in helping the older pupils to come to grips with some of those masterpieces whose greater musical complexity and emotional depth demand a greater degree of concentration than will have been asked of them before. Disc and tape recordings are indispensable in the classroom, but often have their greatest effect if they recall a live experience rather than act as substitutes for it.

We return now to the question of resources and, as always, it is better to focus not on provision for the highly gifted nor on schools in which music (perhaps because of a tradition, the head, or some other cause) is a special feature, but on that general provision for all children which might be judged, bearing in mind all the other claims, to be reasonable.

## Staff

It should be said at once that in musical education considerable use is already made of specially qualified staff whose skills are made available to a number of schools. Few local authorities are now without advisers and in many areas there are centres where the range and quality of a child's (and a teacher's) musical experience may be extended. In addition there are the peripatetic and visiting teachers of music and it is apparent that if there is to be less inequality in the provision of musical experience from school to school greater use will have to be made of these teachers. A school catering for middle-years children will, however, require a more readily accessible source of specialist skill. In the case of secondary schools there will be a specialist department so the problem is really that of the primary or middle school. Several speakers at the Schools Council conference on the middle years of schooling (the report of the conference was published as School Council Working Paper No. 22) mentioned semi-specialists[10] and the idea is worked out further in the Department of Education and Science pamphlet, *Towards the Middle School*.[11] *Music in Schools* applies it to music:

> Obviously if there is a musician of parts on the staff he may help in planning and in general act as consultant to colleagues and children. He

151

may form a school choir and orchestra and organise and keep close contact with instrumental work requiring visiting teachers. His room may be a recognised music room suitably sited and equipped for the purpose even though some other kinds of work may have to go on there.[12]

The working party of the Schools Council Music Committee felt it undesirable for a part-time teacher to be in charge of music but that a two-form entry middle school could appoint a music specialist whose time might be spent as follows:

|  | Periods per week |
| --- | --- |
| General class teaching | 17 |
| Teaching music to four classes | 8 |
| Group work and specialist help for the rest of the staff | 6 |
| Free periods for attending to instruments, arranging scores, etc. | 4 |

## Accommodation and equipment

The problem is not entirely one of large spaces though it should be noted that the Department of Education and Science Building Bulletin on Middle Schools[13] provides for accommodation for music and drama in all its examples of middle-school buildings. The Plowden Report pointed out that 'the proliferation of musical activities at this period greatly increases the need for planned accommodation for group and individual tuition and for the storage of instruments.'[14] The working party of the Schools Council Music Committee asks for 'areas of privacy' in which visiting teachers can take small groups of pupils and where children can work on musical projects of their own without disturbing the rest of the school. Such spaces need not be costly in terms of total teaching areas but they should be functional and free from through-traffic and other avoidable interruptions.

It is clear from the statement of objectives above that the requirements in terms of equipment are considerable. A range of instruments and mechanical aids is needed both to give the children the range of experience needed and to permit choice between different modes of creative expression. Quality as well as range must also be stressed even though this will usually add to the cost involved.

There remains one special problem – that of the relationship between school and home, especially in relation to private teaching. The working party of the Schools Council Music Committee pointed out that few school subject areas are as directly influenced by home conditions as music.

152

Without parental interest and support it is difficult to practise an instrument (much more to acquire one), to stay at school after class hours, or to attend concerts and festivals. The through-lounge of the modern house, and the domination of the television set, make practising and concentrated listening a very real problem for many potentially musical children. Parents are usually ready to commend success in subjects with career prospects, or in sport, but comparatively few are in sympathy with the serious pursuit of an art. On the other hand, music is traditionally the one subject for which parents not infrequently pay for private tuition outside the school; and the very fact that a minority of children are thus put in a favoured position gives the school music teacher additional complications to deal with, as the privately taught child (or, for that matter, one receiving individual or group tuition under the aegis of the school) is likely to be ahead of his contemporaries in the music class.

The working party concludes that with the modern approach it is now relatively easy for the teacher to turn the differences in children's level of musical attainment to good account and thus to increase the enjoyment of the whole group.

## References and notes

1. The film, *Our Own Music*, may be bought from the BBC or hired from the Educational Foundation for Visual Aids, 254–56 Belsize Road, London NW6.
2. Central Advisory Council for Education (England), *Children and their Primary Schools* (HMSO, 1967), Vol. 1, para. 689.
3. Ibid., para. 692.
4. Department of Education and Science, *Music in Schools*, Education Pamphlet No. 27 (HMSO, 2nd edn, 1969).
5. Central Advisory Council for Education (Wales), *Primary Education in Wales* (HMSO, 1967), para. 19.9.
6. Ibid., para. 19.2.
7. Ibid., para. 19.9.
8. Central Advisory Council for Education (England), *Children and their Primary Schools* (HMSO, 1967), Vol. 1, para. 692.
9. Department of Education and Science, *Music in Schools*, Education Pamphlet No. 27 (HMSO, 2nd edn, 1969), p. 15.
10. Schools Council Working Paper No. 22, *The Middle Years of Schooling from 8–13* (HMSO, 1969). See, for example, pp. 14, 20, 23, 70, 79.
11. Department of Education and Science, *Towards the Middle School*, Education Pamphlet No. 57 (HMSO, 1970). See pp. 24–5.

12. Department of Education and Science, *Music in Schools*, Education Pamphlet No. 27 (HMSO, 2nd edn, 1969), p. 25.
13. Department of Education and Science, *New Problems in School Design: Middle Schools*, Building Bulletin No. 35 (HMSO, 1966).
14. Central Advisory Council for Education (England), *Children and their Primary Schools* (HMSO, 1967), Vol. 1, para. 695.

# IX. Science

This is a well documented aspect of the curriculum, and throughout the past ten years there has been a series of development projects considering the place of science in the middle years and producing guides and texts for teachers. It would be quite out of place for a small team of non-scientists engaged on a study of the whole curriculum to attempt to produce any radical new thinking in a single chapter such as this. What has been done is to provide a brief review of some recent developments in science teaching. For this we have visited over a hundred schools. We have also considered the publications produced by the Nuffield science projects: Nuffield Chemistry, Physics and Biology Projects (so far as they deal with the 8 to 13 age-range) Nuffield Junior Science, the Nuffield Combined Science Project and – although it falls outside the middle-years age-range – the Nuffield Secondary Science Project. We are indebted to the Oxford Junior Science Project, the Association for Science Education, and most of all to the Science 5–13 Project, sponsored jointly by the Schools Council, Nuffield Foundation and the Scottish Education Department, the only major science project for the entire middle-years age-range.[1]

One of the pleasures in considering the wealth of material which has been produced for science in the middle years has been to observe the positive, vigorous and enthusiastic approach which seems to have characterized the literature – from the earliest days of the old nature study movement up to the present. Science has been canvassed with zest and energy. There was to be a place for it in the learning of all children and it was to be a place unspoilt by much of the dull, routine learning of the past.

The Newsom Report[2] commented that boys were 'usually excited by the prospect of a science course'. Through science the child 'experiences a sense of wonder and sense of power . . . if he cannot produce a sunset, he can change the colour in his test-tube.' Perhaps rather tartly the report adds: 'If he finds this dull his teachers must accept part of the blame.' The report claimed that, though 'girls may come to the science lesson with less eager curiosity than the boys', the work would be useful to them. 'She too will need to feel at home with machinery and will be subject to the prestige which science has in the world . . . Whether science to her is a friend or enemy she will be better equipped by having some inkling of its nature.'

In the Plowden Report, *Children and their Primary Schools*, science received more attention than any other aspect of the curriculum except the composite subject, English. Some indications are given of possible content, but the main emphasis is strongly on methodology: 'The treatment of the subject matter may be summarised in the phrase "learning by discovery".'[3]

During the past decade, science has had a major place in curriculum development. Some projects have covered the primary sector, others the secondary. One, the Science 5–13 Project, cuts across the institutional age-ranges, and is the first major attempt to establish some continuity of learning across the upper primary and lower secondary boundary. The various projects are considered in more detail later but it is evident that, despite their individual characteristics, they all continue to adopt an outlook which has been consistent for over half a century and which is expressed as the principal aim of the first Nuffield science projects, namely 'to develop materials that will help teachers to present science in a lively, exciting and intelligible way.'

Much has been written about the possibilities in middle-years science, but it is hard to discover factual information about current practices in the schools. In an article in the *Times Educational Supplement* (22 October 1971), Dr Brenda Preest wrote, 'The almost complete passing of the Nuffield Junior Science Project is very sad, but certainly not surprising.'

From our observations in over a hundred schools there is little evidence to suggest that a significant proportion of schools is being highly innovatory or experimental in their science teaching. While the team was fortunate in observing work of a demonstrably high standard being undertaken in a variety of settings, most of the schools visited, both at the junior and the secondary level, tended to follow a traditional rather than an experimental approach. Where changes had been made they were inclined to be of a tentative nature, most often involving only one or two teachers and their classes in any one junior school, and at the secondary level there was clearly concern and even anxiety that modifications to the syllabus should not result in falling standards, or adversely affect children's chances of success in external examinations.

We cannot claim to have visited schools where the discovery method had been adopted as the basic methodology in science teaching, although some of the schools included work of this nature in their courses, and the majority were doing far more than passing on to their pupils the end products of other people's discoveries. Our sample of secondary schools where the Nuffield materials were in use was far too small for any firm conclusions to be drawn, but it would seem that the use of Nuffield *texts* does not necessarily imply a full commitment to a completely Nuffield approach. The content of the various texts was highly praised by the teachers in all the schools we saw making use of them, but they also felt the need to modify, sometimes drastically, the amount of practical work which was suggested for the children. No teacher claimed to be cutting down on

156

this aspect of the work because it was felt to be lacking in value, but mention was made again and again about the shortage of time allowed to cover the course, and the time needed to allow children the opportunity to carry out their own explorations, especially if teachers recognized the importance of follow-up discussion, to ensure that the practical work was fully understood.

We have mentioned this aspect of our school-based observations because of much recent concern over what might be described as the swing towards discovery methods. This, it is felt, may be matched by a decline in teachers' concern over content and even standards of work. While we are not in a position to comment on the latter, it does seem important to point out that we saw little evidence in the schools to suggest a 'swing' in the direction of any particular methodology. Indeed, the institutions catering for middle-years children are so many and so varied that it seems extremely difficult to obtain anything like an accurate picture of current practices in the teaching of science throughout the middle years. Rather disturbingly, we have to report that we visited schools where very little science teaching of either a formal or informal nature was included in the curriculum. There are schools which seem to be lacking even the most elementary resources for science teaching and where extremely dated nature-study texts were all that was available. This is not to suggest that such schools are more representative of current practice than those following a closely planned syllabus or an open-ended discovery approach, but there are grounds for thinking that at present science teaching throughout the middle years of schooling displays extremely varied characteristics, not only between the different types of school institutions, but also between institutions of the same type.

There is much good material in the published guides and texts produced by the six science projects considered, but of course it will be some time before the effect of these on the education of children in the middle years of schooling can be assessed. Apart from Science 5–13, the projects have been concerned with developments either at primary or secondary level, and there is very little in their published guides which refer to the question of continuity throughout the middle years. Were it not for the work of the Science 5–13 Project this would amount to a dangerous neglect, emphasized by the sweeping generalization which opens an otherwise excellent introduction to the *Junior Science Source Book*: 'Scientific activity at the primary level is a very different affair from the more formal study in the secondary school. This, of course, is only to be expected since the children are at very different stages of intellectual, emotional, social, and physical development.'[5] While this almost complete encapsulation of science curriculum projects within the boundaries of particular types of school institutions can be rationalized, it presents something of a problem to those

157

concerned with the evolution of middle-years curricula. For most of these projects, the process of dissemination on a national scale is very recent and will undoubtedly be spread over a considerable period of time. This would seem to imply that for some years to come more and more teachers will be adopting, for the first time, a science course which makes little or no mention of this continuity of learning. What seems to be called for is an injection of the idea that the group of children at the top of the junior school and the bottom of the secondary school does indeed contain children 'at very different stages of intellectual, emotional, social, and physical development' but these children, at these different stages, are to be found in both junior and secondary schools, not segregated into one institution or the other.

Although the work of the major science curriculum projects is already familiar to many teachers, the dissemination of information is a protracted process. There would still seem to be a need to give a brief description of their work. The Nuffield Science Teaching Project was established early in 1962, and its first task was to produce courses leading to the GCE O-level examinations in physics, chemistry, and biology. Two years later, the work was extended to include junior schools (Nuffield Junior Science Project) and the sixth forms. Nuffield Combined Science was a later development (1965–1969) and its genesis has been described in the foreword to the *Teachers' Guides*:

> When the Nuffield O-level courses were first planned, early in 1962, it was not found possible to avoid the traditional division of school science into three subjects, Physics, Chemistry and Biology. But it was agreed that a combined science course was most desirable, especially in the first two years – for children between the ages of 11 and 13 . . . 'Combined Science' is therefore called upon not only to combine three science subjects, but also to be a preparation both for O-level work and for CSE or unexamined work later on.

The introduction to *Teachers' Guide I* states:

> [Combined Science] is an attempt to recapture the unity of outlook and consistency of method which belong to the whole of science and which enable us to make reasoned statements about the world we live in.[6]

The Nuffield Secondary Science Project, which began its work in 1965, is outside the scope of the middle years since it is concerned with the work of 'approximately three-quarters of the pupils in secondary schools aged between thirteen and sixteen . . . who are unlikely to take GCE in Science at Ordinary level though they may well take O-level papers in other subjects.'[7] However, it needs to be considered in any discussion on science in the middle years since it is likely

158

to be the follow-on course taken by many children who transfer from middle schools to secondary education at 13. Appendix 2 in the *Teachers' Guide* indicates the close relationship between Combined Science and Secondary Science, and it is claimed that in both the 'emphasis is put on discovery by the pupils through their own investigations', and again in both projects, 'it is assumed that the work for a class will be taken by one teacher.'[8]

Although the materials produced by the Chemistry Project are not likely to be used by more than a minority of middle-years children, the thinking behind the project seems to have wider relevance, especially for teachers working with older juniors, who may well be concerned about the approach to science likely to be offered to their more able pupils after transfer. The Nuffield Chemistry *Handbook for Teachers* begins with a quotation from H. E. Armstrong in 1891:

> The infant learns by experimenting – the vast majority of children naturally like such work; our system of education is mainly responsible for the decay of the taste with advancing years.[9]

The project proposes that:

> Pupils should gain an understanding that lasts throughout their lives of what it means to approach a problem scientifically. They should be taught to be aware of what scientists are doing and can do. This has little connection with the short-lived remembering of dictated information. Therefore science should be presented to pupils in a way in which *they* can conduct an inquiry into the nature of things, as well as a body of information built up by the studies of other people. Pupils must approach their studies through experiments designed to awaken the spirit of investigation. They must be given the opportunities to observe and explore so that they can develop disciplined imaginative thinking and are made fully conscious of the part that science plays in modern life.

They go on to add:

> Which ideas are discussed, how they are presented, what materials and techniques are used to develop them, depend on the level of development reached by the pupils and should be chosen accordingly. But what is taught must reflect up-to-date thought and technology.[10]

The project team recognize that the effect of these proposals on classroom techniques 'will, in many cases, be revolutionary' but they are clear about the importance of their proposals:

> They are based largely on what 'being scientific' means to a scientist – the application and the personal commitment involved; the importance of the

159

disciplined guess or 'hunch' as well as logical argument; the feeling of exploration; and the readiness to make apparently unwarranted jumps while knowing how to check their validity. This activity of science is nothing new and, in fact, is embryonic in much of the activity of younger children; but so far there has been little opportunity for it to take its place in the education of the age range with which we are concerned.[11]

There seems little doubt that the philosophy behind the chemistry, physics and biology projects is much closer to the thinking behind many contemporary developments at primary level than has been common in the past, and this may well help towards narrowing the gap which frequently exists between the primary and secondary institutions.

> One of the principal aims of the Nuffield Biology Course has been to foster a critical approach to the subject with an emphasis on experimentation and inquiry rather than on mere factual assimilation.[12]

And in physics:

> The emphasis is on teaching for understanding and not on collecting information or memorizing formal statements by rote or solving mechanical problems by formulae or carrying out routine measurements by following detailed instructions. We believe that the latter activities, however useful they may seem in training future scientists, fail to give the educated non-scientist an understanding of science, or even that liking for science which might make him preserve his knowledge.[13]

The work of the Science 5–13 Project is so central to the middle years of schooling that a brief synopsis of the project's work seems out of place. The introductory text, *With Objectives in Mind*,[14] is essential reading, and contains not only the philosophy behind the project, but information on how the project team set about preparing and evaluating their materials, and a thorough and detailed analysis of objectives. These have been developed from, and make meaningful, a series of aims which they have itemized in general terms under the heading, 'Developing an inquiring mind and a scientific approach to problems'. The aims are:

1  Developing interests, attitudes and aesthetic awareness
2  Observing, exploring and ordering observations
3  Developing basic concepts and logical thinking
4  Posing questions and devising experiments or investigations to answer them
5  Acquiring knowledge and learning skills
6  Communicating

160

**7**    Appreciating patterns and relationships

**8**    Interpreting findings critically.

From our study of these curriculum projects certain common elements emerge:

**1**    They all lay stress on the importance of maintaining children's interests in the work they are doing, and demonstrate that the nature of scientific inquiry is likely to appeal to the majority of children in the middle years. Science is generally seen as a 'popular' study for middle-years children.

**2**    They all emphasize that there should be a major element of practical work involving first-hand observations and personal experiment.

**3**    When considering content, they all mention the fact that there is a vast amount of material which is both relevant and worthy of inclusion in a school syllabus.

In 'Science in the middle years of schooling', an article included in *Science 5–13 Newsletter 2* (Spring 1971), the author comments: 'Recently, the sheer amount of science which could be learnt has become so great that the syllabus-making has become an exercise in deciding what can be left out.' But they urge that whatever content *is* selected it should be dealt with in a contemporary, scientific manner.

While there are many other common elements, these three seem to be of major importance and raise problems that may not easily be resolved. The emphasis placed on providing children with much direct observation and experimentation is to some extent in conflict with the practical situation which many secondary teachers claim to be facing. The enormous increase in relevant content has not always been matched by an increase in the amount of time allocated to the teaching of science. Many teachers, faced with an expanded syllabus, have to resolve the problem of fitting a quart of content into a pint pot of time. Often this is met partly by improved teaching techniques and by 'streamlining' or cutting down on time-consuming, experimental work carried out by children. Few teachers would regard the latter as desirable, but it frequently represents the only practical solution to the problem of covering an expanded syllabus.

For some teachers, the unresolved problem seems to be to know whether it is possible to include the amount of practical work seen as desirable, and maintain (or even improve) standards in examinations. Although external examinations are outside the age-range of the middle years, they are relevant in that they may have a backwash effect on the course of studies followed by middle-years children. 'Unless we start with the 11-year-olds, many of our children will fail to obtain the paper qualifications they are going to need' is by no means an uncommon statement. The implications of this are somewhat different from saying, 'A course of study which is based largely on inquiry, experiment and discovery will, if properly organized and professionally conducted, enable children to obtain paper qualifications which, in science, can be regarded as having genuine validity.'

Somehow a balance has to be struck, but in finding the right balance consideration has to be given to content, methodology, the children and the range of available resources. The weighting given to each of these factors will depend a great deal on the beliefs and attitudes of the teachers involved, for teachers remain the key consideration in curriculum development.

At the junior level, and to some extent the middle-school level, the problems are somewhat different. If the resource material provided for the non-specialist teacher has too strong an emphasis on content, there is a danger that this might be presented in a manner incompatible with the spirit of scientific inquiry. Conversely, an over-emphasis on scientific methodology may leave some teachers insecure when it comes to making decisions about content priorities. The various curriculum projects have sought to find ways of avoiding those polarities and generally offer a wide range of possible content together with varying degrees of guidance over methodology. Much recent writing about science in the middle years has also been concerned with effecting a satisfactory mix of these two important elements (sometimes referred to as the *how* and *what*). The question as to whether a greater emphasis should be placed on content or on methodology presupposes much knowledge about what schools are doing at present. Some would appear to be in need of encouragement or even persuasion to include more science in the curriculum; others need help in broadening the scope of a somewhat narrow emphasis on nature study. Many have already developed extremely valuable courses and would welcome expert guidance on ways of making further progress. Perhaps the least helpful writing is that which polarizes thinking, and stresses one aspect of science teaching as opposed to another. The danger with this approach is that its chief effect is likely to be to provide support for extremists in their entrenched positions, rather than to bring about fresh and unprejudiced thinking about what is right for the children.

An article by N. Booth published in the October 1971 issue of *Trends in Education* stated that: 'No one has yet produced a nationally acceptable core of material suitable for young children, capable of being soundly taught by class teachers without specialist qualifications in science, and acceptable as a foundation for what comes later.' The writer argues the case for the provision of such a common core and suggests that middle schools 'should accept as a required

162

component of its curriculum a core, preferably the same for all schools, of low-level but fundamental notions in science which will be taught to all children, the teacher selecting whichever method of approach he believes right for his children.' This common core is seen as occupying between 50 per cent and 75 per cent of the time devoted to science activities. The remainder of the time would be devoted to activities which should 'arise from the spontaneous, probably prompted but unforced, interests of the children.'[15] Although specific mention is made of middle schools, it would be difficult to justify a limitation of such proposals to these particular institutions. Children are the same people, whether they are living within an area that has adopted middle schools or one which continues to operate junior and secondary schools. Certainly the idea of a core curriculum has been canvassed elsewhere. It forms the basis of the text produced by the Oxford Primary Science Project[16] in which four major groups of ideas covered by the themes of energy, structure, chance and life were explored. It is also postulated by the Schools Council Science Committee in a paper, 'The place of science in the middle years of schooling', where it is stated that 'it seems necessary to redress the balance [referring to the current swing from traditional factual learning] by suggesting certain key areas in science which could (and should) be profitably explored by children'. The Association for Science Education publication, *Science for the Under Thirteens*, also supports the idea.[17]

Many suggestions regarding syllabus content have been made: by the Schools Council Science Committee, in the article in *Trends in Education*, and by the Oxford Primary Science Project and the Science 5–13 Project. Before looking at these suggestions, it seems important to point out that the author of the article in *Trends in Education* leaves methodology alone – 'the teacher selecting whichever method of approach he believes right for his children'. A similar stand is taken by the Oxford project – 'if the teachers themselves have an understanding of the physical universe in terms of energy, structure, chance and life, and feel confident about these concepts, then their teaching and the children's experience will be true to the nature of the world around them. It follows that no specific method of learning or teaching is either recommended or deprecated in this approach to science.'[18] To some extent the Schools Council Science Committee paper, and to a greater extent the Science 5–13 Project, are concerned with methodology as well as content.

The Schools Council paper suggests that 'children should gain experience in certain areas of knowledge.' These are set out below but they do not constitute a syllabus, nor is any teaching order implied:

1 Interdependence of living things and the related aspects of conservation and exploitation

**2** The main processes which enable organisms to exist

**3** The differences between, and similarities of, organisms and the conditions which give rise to these

**4** The differences between, and similarities of, materials, changes in materials and how these changes can be effected and controlled

**5** Stability and change in systems and materials and the component ideas of equilibrium, force and motion

**6** Energy changes which accompany material changes; the manifestations and transformation of energy

**7** The social implications of man's changing use of materials and energy

**8** Conditions of the environment – on earth and in space.

The article in *Trends in Education* puts forward three main themes as the basis for a 'core' – matter, energy and life. These are briefly expanded as follows:

1. *Matter.* Experiments which show that weight is not conserved. It depends where we measure it. Something (mass) is. Experiments on forces leading to the general notion of how we recognize a force when we meet it, how we can measure it and some of the ways in which a force can be set up. The notion of buoyancy.

2. *Energy.* Experiments which show that rearrangement of matter (mass still being conserved and hence, if measured at the same place under the same conditions, weight also) involves a phenomenon we call energy. This can be what we call a physical rearrangement or a chemical rearrangement.

3. *Life.* Experiments and observations which show that living things have the capacity to reproduce themselves: that one of the methods for doing so requires the presence of maleness and femaleness and a certain stage of maturity. That offspring are similar to, but not identical with, their parents.[19]

The Oxford project's proposals for an examination of energy, structure, chance and life are examined and described in detail in *An Approach to Primary Science.* This looks at these major topics at an adult level, and provides a basis of factual scientific information as a guide to the non-specialist teacher. There are also supporting chapters for each topic which indicate many of the ways in which the work might be introduced and developed at the children's level.

In 'Science in the middle years of schooling', the Science 5–13 Project suggests possible content under seven main headings:

164

1. *The environment*
   Conditions on earth and in space
   Simple geology and oceanography
   The environment as a source of materials
   Weather and climate
   Simple astronomy.
2. *The wealth and nature of plant and animal life*
   The main differences in environments
   Life histories of selected animals and plants (arising from the study
   of the environment rather than selection based on the traditional
   evolutionary sequence); adaptation.
3. *Man and his place in the order of things*
   Man as a social and intelligent animal
   Conservation and exploitation
   Pests and their control
   Pollution
   Food: health.
4. *Differences, similarities and patterns*
   Grouping materials according to properties
   Grouping plants and animals according to their observable charac-
   teristics and behaviour
   Classification as an aid to scientific thinking.
5. *Interaction and change*
   Effecting changes and controlling changes
   The main processes which enable organisms to exist
   The idea that evolution took place and is continuing
   Stability and instability in systems
   Equilibrium, force and motion
   Material changes: some effects of heat and electricity; chemical
   interaction, change of state
   Rates of change.
6. *Energy changes which accompany material changes*
   Forms of energy: energy and work
   Sources of energy
   Energy conversions (including those in living things)
   Energy chains: energy storage
   The electro-magnetic energy spectrum.
7. *The organization of matter*
   The way larger organisms and objects are made from smaller parts
   The particulate nature of things

165

Structure: organisms, mechanical structures, matter
Levels of organization
Pattern: structures made from repeating units
Shape related to purpose
Conditions controlling size: size and volume, size and weight, size and surface area, size and strength
Measurements: degrees of accuracy.

It is important that the above statement of main areas of study should not be looked at as an 'Eleven to Thirteen Course'. It is an overall picture of the science which we would like all children to have sampled widely by the age of thirteen. The stage of mental development they have reached will usually be the main thing which determines how much they can cover and to what depth. The Science 5–13 units will give some indication of what might be expected at the different levels (Stages 1, 2 and 3) in a few selected areas.

Although there are overlaps within the areas of study suggested by these four sources, they give some indication of the amount of relevant material which might be considered as a suitable content for the middle-years curriculum. The brief headline notes provided in this synopsis do less than justice to the writers concerned, nor have we included any analysis of the content suggestions which are contained in the various guides and texts.

Science is clearly an area of the curriculum where a wealth of resource material is available to teachers in the middle years. To some extent this may face the non-specialist teacher who has responsibilities for many other aspects of the curriculum with the problem of evaluating the material and selecting from it the best for his own particular situation. It is to be hoped that every local authority will establish centres, readily accessible to teachers, where collections of teaching materials can be studied. Perhaps one of the most useful steps forward might be for teachers working in any given area to discuss the various alternatives, and ideally to reach agreement to invest in one of them; this would then be common to all schools in the area. This is a long way from adopting a 'common core', for within each of the individual projects there is considerable scope for choice over both content and approach.

A useful summing up of the present position comes from the article in *Trends in Education*: 'It remains for the teacher to select and to prompt, and whether or not he is consciously trying to lay the foundations for what comes later, the foundations will be laid and they ought to be sound ones. It comes back in the end to the need for good teachers who know what are the productive lines of development.'[20]

166

## References and notes

1. The Nuffield Biology, Chemistry and Physics Projects (1962–65) covered the age range 11–16 (O-level courses published by Longman/Penguin Books, 1966–68); Nuffield Junior Science Project (1964–66), age range 5–13 (materials published by Collins in 1967); Nuffield Combined Science 11–13 Project (1965–69), was based at City of Birmingham College of Education and directed by M. J. Elwell (publisher: Longman); Nuffield Secondary Science 13–16 Project (1965–70), was based at Centre for Science Education, Chelsea College of Science and Technology, and directed by Hilda Misselbrook (publisher: Longman); Oxford Junior Science 5–13 Project (1964–67) on the formation of scientific concepts in children was based at the Oxford Institute of Education; the Science 5–13 Project (1967–74) was established to consolidate and extend the work initiated by the Nuffield Junior Science Project – it was based at the School of Education, University of Bristol, and directed by L. F. Ennever (publisher: Macdonald Educational).
2. Central Advisory Council for Education (England), *Half Our Future* (HMSO, 1967), p. 142.
3. Central Advisory Council for Education (England), *Children and their Primary Schools* (HMSO, 1967), Vol. 1, para. 669, but see also paras 663–76.
4. Foreword to Teachers' Guides, Nuffield Biology, Chemistry and Physics Projects.
5. J. W. BAINBRIDGE, R. W. STOCKDALE and E. R. WASTNEDGE, *Junior Science Source Book* (Collins, 1970), p. iv.
6. Nuffield Combined Science, *Teachers' Guide I* (Longman/Penguin Books, 1970), Introduction, p. xi.
7. Nuffield Secondary Science, *Teachers' Guide* (Longman, 1971), p. ix.
8. Ibid., p. 102.
9. Nuffield Chemistry, *Handbook for Teachers* (Longman/Penguin Books, 1967), p. 1.
10. Nuffield Chemistry, *Introduction and Guide* (Longman/Penguin Books, 1966), pp. 1–2.
11. Ibid., p. 3.
12. Nuffield Biology, *Teachers' Guide 1: Introducing Living Things* (Longman/Penguin Books, 1966), p. xii.
13. Nuffield Physics, *Teachers' Guide 1* (Longman/Penguin Books, 1966), pp. 1–2.
14. Science 5–13, *With Objectives in Mind* (Macdonald Educational, 1972).

15. N. BOOTH, 'Middle school science', *Trends in Education*, No. 24 (October 1971), 14, 15.
16. S. REDMAN, A. BRERETON and P. BOYERS, *An Approach to Primary Science* (Macmillan Education, 1969).
17. Association for Science Education, *Science for the Under Thirteens* (ASE, 1971), pp. 16–17.
18. *An Approach to Primary Science* , p. 132.
19. N. BOOTH, 'Middle school science', *Trends in Education*, No. 24 (October 1971), 14.
20. Ibid., 13–14.

# X. Social and environmental studies

This chapter describes some different approaches to social and environmental studies in the middle years of schooling, particularly as expressed in the work of Schools Council projects. It is partly analytical and partly descriptive and does not attempt to supplement the work of the major development projects in this field by offering original and creative material.

A visitor to this country might be forgiven if, after seeing the words 'social studies' and 'environmental studies' on two timetables, he inferred that 'social studies' implied a study concerned with man and man's society, while 'environmental studies' implied a study concerned with man and man's physical world. In common language his distinction would be understandable and in principle it would appear to be sound. In practice, however, if only for the reasons which follow, it would be an over-simplification of the educational reality.

In primary, middle, and secondary schools throughout England and Wales there is no shared, definitive concept of social or environmental studies. The terms may not be taken to mean in one curriculum what they mean in another. In themselves they tell the visitor nothing about course objectives or course content, and nothing about the type of disciplinary sources or the nature of the theory which underpins them. When, therefore, the Schools Council Social Studies 8–13 Project asked schools to provide information about their social studies work, they were careful to point out that 'our definition of social studies to these schools was deliberately broad, to include any kind of learning which fosters the development of social concepts, general social awareness, and the understanding of modern industrial society.'[1]

Since there is no generally accepted definition of social or environmental studies in the middle years, it follows that in practice there is a degree of overlap between them. For example, when the director of the Schools Council Environmental Studies 5–13 Project was asked how social, economic and political concepts were developed by his project he replied, 'We don't ignore these – we get at them through their physical expressions. For example, shops are studied and the pattern of production and retail trade may develop out of them. We might visit a particular industrial site and then study associated documents to develop ideas of industrial control and change and so on. There may be other ways of doing this – but I'm talking about how it can be done through Environmental Studies.'[2] This project involved nearly 240 schools in its work, taking as a working rule that 'the schools were not presented with a model of how environmental studies "ought" to be conducted, but were asked to continue with their usual work.'[3] This traditional autonomy of schools, in which each one is responsible for its own area of curriculum innovation and development, seems to suggest two consequences for conceptions of social or environmental studies. Firstly, an antipathy to any nationally uniform conception; secondly, a continuing flexibility and mutability in the concepts as they are applied in middle-years schools. One primary-school head could therefore feel quite comfortable in writing, 'We do not at the moment have a scheme for urban studies as such, but we are building up a framework of ideas under a general heading of environmental studies which of course will include geography, history, science, mathematics, English, art, etc.'[4]

At this point it might be useful to mention some of the ways in which social or environmental studies may be observed to vary. In terms of curriculum time, they may be allowed set periods each week or form part of a largely unstructured timetable. Aspects of the work may be extended, especially at the primary- or middle-school level, to occupy a whole day or several days of almost continuous study, especially when undertaken in the form of a project. Alternatively a theme may be developed at different times throughout a whole term or even over a longer span of time. Geographically they may be confined to the immediate environment of the school, or they may take in a town or country or even other countries. The number of children and staff involved in these ventures is highly indeterminate, ranging from a small group undertaking a special study within one class to more than a whole year group. Ventures may be run by a teacher, a teaching team, a school staff, a local education authority, or by voluntary groups of parents, teachers, or advisers. Expenses involved and resources engaged may be nominal, as in the case of a teacher taking a class on a visit to the local fire station; or they may be considerable, as in the case of excursions undertaken to Greece and the Adriatic, using luxury liners as floating schools. Another important variable is the degree to which children physically move beyond the bounds of a school during such studies. There are some schools where virtually all that is done within the field of social studies takes place within a given room. While this is seldom true of environmental studies, there is nevertheless considerable variation in the degree to which children make physical use of the environment in such studies. In some cases teachers go to considerable trouble to bring into the classroom materials and visiting speakers to highlight aspects of the environment; in other cases much direct field study is involved, with children themselves being engaged in the collection of materials, data and other forms of information.

170

Ostensibly each school is free to chart and direct the course of its curriculum. This does not mean that a discussion of the relative merits of different forms of social or environmental studies is redundant. However, it makes for difficulties and tends to force the discussion away from the realities of school life and towards a more theoretical discussion, in which the question changes from, 'What is happening in social and environmental studies?', to 'What should be done in social or environmental studies, and why?' Questions of the 'What should be done?' variety are notoriously involved and difficult. That is why this chapter has recourse to the thoughtful, systematic, and sophisticated work of the Schools Council projects, in which project teams have sought to justify and make explicit to a wide circle of critical opinion what they are trying to achieve and why.

Two basic problems which condition the whole argument about the nature of social and environmental studies should be kept in mind. The first is that social or environmental studies for the primary years assumes the existence of primary institutions. A similar assumption is made regarding the secondary years. Social or environmental studies for the age-range 8 to 13 (or thereabouts) assumes either the existence of middle schools, and a range of sympathetic institutions, or some attempt at curriculum continuity across primary and secondary institutions.

The second problem is even more pertinent and is concerned with whether either social or environmental studies have a rightful place in the middle-years curriculum. What do such studies offer that cannot be more conveniently and effectively taught in other ways? This problem, which broaches the whole question of defining and justifying social or environmental studies for the middle-years curriculum, cannot easily be resolved. It is as yet an open question whether the advocates of various approaches can be brought to agree on the grounds for an adequate resolution. In these circumstances it seems more realistic to allow the problem to gain definition as the chapter progresses, through an exposition of the assumptions, beliefs, and practical suggestions of different workers in these areas, rather than attempt a direct, lengthy and rather abstract analysis of the problem in terms of uni-, multi- or inter-disciplinary approaches.

In secondary schools, social studies has its modern roots in the period just after the Second World War. At that time it appeared often as a liaison of geography, history and civics – partly as an attack on the 'tyranny of examinations', partly as a new attempt at the American concept of 'education for democracy', and partly as a way of stimulating and involving less able or committed pupils.[5] By the mid-1950s, however, it had almost disappeared. Graves accounts briefly for its decline in the following words.[6]

The increased output of history and geography graduates from the universities and the development of geography in the Colleges of Education led to a teaching force which had, to some extent, invested its intellectual capital in one or other of the subjects and naturally preferred to teach either history or geography. Further, the subject associations were generally hostile to such developments and continued to foster the development of their individual subjects in the schools.

Significantly:

Only in the primary school, where systematic study of the individual humanities subjects had never been felt to be desirable, did the study of the environment, especially the local environment, develop on a 'centre of interest' basis regardless of the subjects involved.[7]

Much of the work which now tends to be categorized as environmental studies has long had a place in some of our primary schools, but the phrase itself is of more recent origin. It appears in the Plowden Report[8] under the heading 'Use of the environment', and the report states that 'another effective way of integrating the curriculum is to relate it through the use of the environment to the boundless curiosity which children have of the world about them.' However, the report does not describe how such curriculum integration should be conceived, in terms of the major concepts which might be employed from, say, history, geography or science.

Contemporary support for social and environmental studies in official educational circles is indisputable. The Schools Council has financed several projects in the 8 to 13 range[9] including one major development project. Between 1968 and 1971 the number of colleges of education offering environmental studies as main courses almost doubled.[10] In a recent publication on middle schools, the Department of Education and Science[11] suggests that two groupings of subjects (among others) could be used to advantage in these studies. The first, which emphasizes first-hand observation, would encompass science, some geography and some history, and would make use of mathematics, art and language as tools. The second suggests that history, geography and such related fields as anthropology could be 'blocked' as social studies.

Nevertheless the contemporary strength of social or environmental studies in the schools is difficult to assess. *Social Studies 8–13* confirmed the view 'that social studies is a sadly neglected part of the curriculum in the vast majority of schools.'[12] It is difficult to assess how quickly favoured ideas spread throughout the educational system. What is actually happening in schools may be hidden by,

172

or take place under, a profusion of headings.[13] Activities which could fairly be described as having social or environmental knowledge, skills, and attitudes as objectives may therefore be taking place under history, geography, science, social science, inter-disciplinary inquiry, humanities, etc. Similarly, it is not easy to be clear whether research or development projects are a cause of change or an effect of change in the educational system, or whether they are both.

Further speculation as to why contemporary social and environmental studies have received a degree of official support may be examined under the by now familiar headings of educational aims and objectives. In this context aims are affected by broad social pressures for curriculum change, as these are mirrored in the communications media, as well as by the individual assumptions and beliefs of educationists about child development and about the structure of educational activities. Objectives take in the way in which aims are substantiated, e.g. in the assumptions, design, and strategy, of development projects, and in the work of schools.

Although the impact of social pressure on the nature of schooling is indeterminate, and the processes by which social trends and opinions affect, influence, or change what goes on in schools are not easily measured, it seems likely that at least one form of pressure is making itself felt. In recent years concern with the environment has been gathering momentum. Problems associated with the population explosion, pollution, wild-life conservation, and starvation vie for coverage in the mass media with problems of urban sprawl and decay, racial conflict, and the economic and social consequences of rapid industrial and technical change. Physical and social problems which seem to be inextricably interrelated have become the province and concern of numerous conservation and preservation societies. The ecological approach to these problems is implied by that telling American phrase, 'spaceship earth'. Significantly, Project Environment 8–18 (1970–73), which was established following recommendations made in Schools Council Working Paper 24, *Rural Studies in Secondary Schools*, took as one of its aims a closer examination of the part which the subject might play in educating children through the environment and encouraging an enlightened interest in the quality of the environment and a concern for its intelligent management.

It might be useful, at this point, to try to indicate some common beliefs and assumptions about what could be called a social and environmental approach to learning. Firstly, such approaches draw heavily on the researches of Piaget and Bruner in making certain assumptions about concept development, the ways in which children learn and, by implication, the ways in which they should be taught. Secondly, in line with these assumptions, the social and environmental

173

approach tends to support the view that the Gradgrind image of schooling, with its emphasis on children learning streams of inconsequential facts, is educationally wrong. Thirdly, it suggests that the classroom, or even the school, is at its best too impoverished an environment in which to stimulate effective learning. Fourthly, there is a belief that children should be physically as well as intellectually active and that, consistent with age and responsibility, they should be allowed some independence and freedom of movement outside the school. Fifthly, there is a stress on effective motivation as a key to effective learning, and in this context a belief that while it is the task of the teacher to interest the child in what is to be learned, this is often best accomplished by giving the child some opportunity to develop and follow up his own interests. It should be added that these are intended as common rather than definitive characteristics for the projects mentioned.

The Environmental Studies 5–13 Project illustrates very well a number of these characteristics. Here the child is assumed to be both active and curious about his surroundings. This is fundamental in the project's emphasis on the significance of direct experience for learning. The use of secondary sources is by no means ruled out; pictures, books, radio, television, slide projectors and tape-recorders may all have a part to play, and their exclusion in the context of much contemporary school work would obviously be quite unrealistic. But this is 'not the core of the approach' in the project.[14] The project holds that direct experience, in which the child goes out from his school and under his teacher's guidance explores first his own locality, and then perhaps the wider horizons of his world – visiting farms, shopping centres, touching, talking about, observing and recording his impressions – is the key to the development of a wide range of what are called 'study and communication skills'.[15] The environment is therefore conceived to be a 'resource', through which children develop both language and number skills. These are constantly and progressively developed under the guidance of the teacher. The approach deliberately encourages children to classify, to record accurately, and to attempt to measure environmental phenomena. In this sense it could be called a scientific approach; though since it utilizes the observation, recording, and mapping techniques of the geographer it could also be regarded as a geographical approach. The following extract from a teacher's report about a visit to a marsh may help illustrate the kind of work suggested by the project:

> During the summer holidays I paid a visit to the marsh and took some slides of the river, the bridges, the dykes which kept the water flowing over the marsh, and the sluice gates which allowed the river to run out into the sea when the tide had ebbed. During the first week of term, these slides

were shown to the children, and we discussed what we would need to take with us on our first visit. The children were also introduced to two folk songs which were concerned with the marsh.

On our first expedition, we visited the sea end of the marsh and had a good look at the dyke. Two of the boys measured the angle between the ground and the top of a large viaduct which crosses the marsh. Others measured the length of one of the arches, and from this worked out the length of the viaduct. We looked closely at three bridges crossing the river, made a note of the trains, and gathered rushes and wild fruits. While we were there, I took many slides of the marsh and of the children at work.

The following week, one of the boys brought a steam engine to school, and a group became very interested in how it worked and in the history of trains. They started experimenting with steam, and during the following weeks discovered how a steam engine works, and how to get clean water from dirty water, and they wrote a book about their experiments. Three of the boys were very interested in bridges and, after finding the height of the viaduct with a scale drawing in school, they made models of four different types of bridge. They tested these to find which could support the greatest weight. Their experiments showed that an arch gives strength to a bridge. They experimented with other shapes, and found that a triangular construction gives strength to an even greater degree. From here they went on to curve-stitching, and wrote a book about this work.[16]

It is no coincidence that a project called Environmental Studies should use scientific and geographical skills and techniques. For a number of years now pioneering work in school science and geography has used approaches complementary to those of the Environmental Studies Project. Both the Nuffield Junior Science Project, with its emphasis on case-studies, and the Science 5–13 Project (1967–74) (which followed on from and extended the Nuffield work), emphasize direct experience in experimental situations in which the child is given the opportunity to handle materials and equipment, and is faced with problems which he needs scientific skills and techniques to resolve. Science 5–13 also pays careful attention to the work of Piaget and uses his notion of conceptual stages in the project's design and strategy. Similarly, geographers in schools have been developing techniques to use first-hand material in rural and urban settings – taking children out of the schools to use maps in a more or less sophisticated fashion, and with undoubted success, even in the infant school,[17] and to undertake compass surveys and orienteering with juniors.[18] It is significant from a social or environmental perspective that both Science 5–13 and the Geographical Association in *Geography in Primary Schools* link interdisciplinary aims, such as

175

the development of scientific or geographical knowledge, skills or attitudes,[19] with educational aims which transcend both science and geography. Science 5–13, for instance, takes as a broad aim the development through science of 'interests, attitudes, and aesthetic awareness'; the Geographical Association stresses that it should be one aim of geography to encourage children to 'establish tolerant attitudes that will eventually lead to sympathy and understanding of those whose lives are different from our own'.[20]

There are also instances of innovation in history teaching. Fenton[21] has argued that if history is created by historians then it is the modes of inquiry or the methods of historians which give it its structure, and we ought to concentrate on the process rather than the product. Combining this idea with a judicious use of Bruner's discovery methods, Fenton devised secondary-school courses which aim to promote the pupils' thinking skills mainly, though not exclusively, using primary source materials. As Fenton himself succinctly puts it, instead of giving the pupils explanations of data, he gives them data to explain. The Schools Council History, Geography and Social Science Project (in an unpublished paper) stated: 'this is one point at which the Piagetian "model" of thinking and the Brunerian "model" of instruction seem to complement each other, and we would regard the development of critical thinking, using a variety of primary and secondary sources, as an important general objective, the core of the historian's contribution.'

Such enterprise within subject areas seems to force a reconsideration of that difficult question which was deliberately shelved earlier. It could be argued that if separate subjects in the middle years can be so structured from the points of view of objectives and content, and so designed that they encompass social or environmental aims, why should social studies or environmental studies be necessary in the curriculum at all? There are obviously different views about this, and not all the projects or writers considering the place of such studies in the middle-years curriculum adopt the same modes of expression. Furthermore, it is obvious that some of the statements which *are* made seem equally applicable to the notion of teaching separate subjects, or may even be expressed in terms of such subjects.

The writers of *Social Studies 8–13* look at history and claim, 'It is not our view that history should be abolished from the curriculum, but that history alone is not enough.' They think that children need not only to know something about societies of the past, but also to have a greater understanding of contemporary societies. While they feel that geography is the 'interdisciplinary subject par excellence', they add 'but once again it does not set out to achieve all that we think should be included in the curriculum.'[22]

They make a case for social studies on the grounds that:

176

1    'Any item of a syllabus or area of a curriculum can be justified in terms of a theory of knowledge, and in terms of social or individual relevance. It is possible to justify social studies on all these counts. Knowledge of society is something which exists, is regarded as important, and is or can be interesting to young people.'

2    The various official reports have suggested that young people should be helped 'to find their way about the modern world, or to find some basis for their values, or that schools should prepare pupils for the future and make the world a slightly less confusing place. These kinds of statements are important . . . but they sometimes appear to be slightly ambiguous in as much as they could be seen to suggest social integration rather than social awareness – conformity rather than real understanding.'

3    While it is important that young children should know more about the welfare state and the social services, 'it is not only knowledge that is needed, but the ability to find out, and an attitude towards finding out.'

4    'The social sciences now represent an important form of knowledge in our society and it is no longer possible to regard anyone who is totally ignorant of them as a completely educated person.'[23]

Secondly, there is the view of Melville Harris, Director of the Environmental Studies 5–13 Project. He has justified such studies in the following terms:

1    'The culture of the community in which a child grows is his heritage, and it is felt by many teachers that it is part of the function of schools to enable the child to experience this as something to be preserved, enriched and transmitted.'

2    'This growth of awareness in a child, of the society in which he lives, his appreciation of his existence as part of a stream of humanity reaching back into the past and extending into the future is one of the major objectives of this approach.'

3    'At a time when the problems of conservation and pollution are concerning governments and planners, teachers want children to develop a respect and concern for the quality of their surroundings. Such respect and concern may best be served by direct active involvement with the environment itself, over a long period and as a normal part of school activities.'

4    'While such involvement can provide ways of developing analytical modes of study and expression, it can also intensify children's visual perception.'

5    Environmental studies are 'intended as a means of helping children develop a wide range of skills for observing, recording and interpreting their world. Many of these skills will be those used by scientists, geographers, historians

and sociologists, though these separate specializations are not relevant at this stage of children's development.'

6 'The activities in which the children are involved also provide experiences which will enable them to develop the varied concepts of space, structure and time through which they can relate to the physical and social worlds about them.'

7 Such studies will give experience in the 'techniques of collecting, grouping and classifying material objects, such as plants, stones, snails and cars, as well as non-material items such as pupils' ages, door colours or the functions of different buildings.'

8 They provide 'opportunities of experiencing stages of question-posing and record-keeping under control conditions . . . and in the drawing of conclusions.'

9 'Plans and maps have to be drawn and interpreted, thereby aiding the growth of concepts of scale, direction and so on . . . the use of simple statistical methods developed in mathematics.'

10 There is also the 'use of books and documents . . . part of the essential development of language skills . . . precise and accurate description and recording . . . pictorial representation (e.g. forms such as diagrams, sketches, and photographs) . . . Language, together with mathematics and visual art forms, will be constantly used and developed by such studies.'

11 'It may well be the ultimate aim of some teachers to base the school curriculum upon the study of the environment – widely defined.'[24]

The History, Geography and Social Science 8–13 Project (1971–75) approaches the problem through the *interrelation* of history, geography and social science, rather than through *integration*. In this way the academic integrity of the separate disciplines is acknowledged, each being considered to have a useful role to play on its own account. At the same time, the door is left open for the three disciplines to co-operate in achieving those objectives which may be best achieved through their interrelation.

While these various projects have certain elements in common, such as their concern that children should be encouraged to think critically, to assess evidence with care, to be wary of emotionally-based arguments and to avoid premature commitment to unsatisfactory explanations, there are other marked differences. These differences are so considerable that they raise the question as to why this chapter has linked together social studies and environmental studies. The answer is chiefly to be found in the work of schools at the present time. By no means all of the institutions catering for middle-years children have included either social or environmental studies in the curriculum, and of those that have few at present make a clear distinction between the two. By considering them both together, it seemed that schools would be in a better position to assess their joint claims for inclusion in the middle-years curriculum.

The claim for social studies is framed in terms of adding another subject to the curriculum, not a substitute subject designed to replace, say, history or geography. Admittedly this will be a subject which can be, and perhaps ought to be, approached through investigations carried out in the real world beyond the classroom. However, this is somewhat different from the environmentalist approach which sees the environment as a major resource area which can be used by children in a variety of ways prior to, and in part as a preparation for, a move towards a more formal, subject-based curriculum. Thus social studies can be seen to have certain methodological elements in common with, say, history, geography and science in the middle years, namely that children undertaking these studies should spend some time on practical field investigations and not follow the entire course within the confines of a classroom. From this it seems clear that the relationship between social studies and environmental studies is no greater than the relationship that exists between history and environmental studies, or geography and environmental studies.

At first sight this seems to offer teachers in the middle years a reasonably simple choice and the approach which they decide upon will depend a great deal on their view of what the curriculum in the middle years ought to be.

1   They may decide to structure the curriculum in the form of subjects to be studied, and at appropriate times and for specific purposes arrange for fieldwork to be carried out as the most effective way of helping children to learn. For example, children might use the environment when carrying out a survey of types of work common to their local community. This investigation might form part of a larger study of man at work in different communities and perhaps at different times, and this larger study would itself be part of a course covering other aspects of social studies.

2   The environmentalist approach would have at least part of the curriculum unclassified in terms of traditional subjects. The teacher would consider the learning possibilities offered by some aspect of the local environment such as a river, a wood, the high street, or a ruined church. He would probably prepare for his own guidance a flow diagram of some possible lines of development and undertake the preparation of resource material to be available for use both on field studies and within the classroom afterwards for the follow-up and development of the study. At this stage, the teacher is unlikely to know in detail the ways in which the investigation will develop, or the different emphases that will be given to the study by

179

different groups or individuals within the class. If the visit is a success, children would be motivated in a variety of different ways, and work would develop that could be classified under a range of different subject headings. It would not be unexpected, for example, that after a visit to a ruined church some art, written English, history, biology, religious studies, etc. would emerge. The depth to which individuals or groups might take their studies would depend not only on their personal abilities, but also on the teacher's ability to guide and stimulate inquiry and to provide adequate resources.

The first approach is obviously more structured and offers the teacher a greater security in knowing 'what to do next'. It is possible to be reasonably sure about what is likely to be 'covered' by the course. The alternative is, by its very nature, less clearly defined; however, it would be quite wrong to assume that this implies it is random or haphazard. While argument is likely to continue about which approach is the better, there is sufficient evidence now available to show that both approaches can result in work of high quality produced by children who are keenly interested and highly motivated. Unfortunately, however, it is also possible for results from either approach to be less happy and successful. Although it was said earlier that the alternative chosen depended to a considerable extent on the teacher's view of the middle-years curriculum, there is perhaps another strong deciding factor and this is the personality of the teacher. Some teachers may best be able to teach within the framework of the classroom, following a reasonably clearly defined course. Other teachers find this a less happy and satisfying way of working. The former might well feel threatened and insecure when faced with the prospect of taking a large group of children beyond the confines of the classroom for a variety of activities. The latter may find the challenge stimulating and the teaching experience much more rewarding.

If it is agreed that some form of social or environmental studies is desirable in the middle years, further questions now arise. Firstly, what is to be the scale of activities in either study in relation to other curriculum activities? How much time, and physical and material resources should be allocated to the social or environmental part of the curriculum? The environmentalist answer is likely to be different from that given by the advocate of social studies. To start with, it is almost impossible to make any precise statements about where environmental studies might end and other aspects of the curriculum begin. Is the girl producing a painting of the high street engaged in environmental studies or has she moved over to art? While some schools make little use of the environment as a teaching resource, in others it is used as the genesis for studies in many aspects

180

of the curriculum. Indeed, Melville Harris has gone so far as to claim that, 'it may well be the ultimate aim of some teachers to base the school curriculum upon the study of the environment – widely defined.'[25] However, most teachers are likely to view environmental studies in relation to their view of the whole curriculum and the other priorities they have established.

One school visited by the project team had planned much of the curriculum around the environment, but it was fairly clear that the children had been able to visit so many places and meet so many officials to discuss their work mainly because few other schools in the area were undertaking similar exercises. During one fourteen-day survey of the River Thames from London Bridge to Westminster, the children met more people connected with the river and visited more riverbank buildings and institutions than most Londoners would achieve in a lifetime. The extent of the co-operation offered by the river police in putting boats at their disposal, by the Customs and Excise authorities, by the Port of London Authority, the various docks and warehouse officials and by a number of the Livery Companies simply could not be repeated for schools generally, or even for a reasonable minority of schools. On another occasion, several classes were able to spend an entire week working full-time in a museum, and the curator and his assistants were able to offer access to reserve stock for the children to handle in a manner that would have been impossible had more schools wished to exploit such a resource.

It might be expected that a more precise answer about curriculum weighting could be obtained from those advocating social studies, for here, although there is obviously an enormous possible content, it is conceived as taking a place in the curriculum alongside other defined subjects. Denis Lawton's claim is reasonably succinct: 'Briefly, we are not suggesting social studies as the core of the whole curriculum for the middle years, but rather as *one* very important area of learning which often overlaps other *subject areas*. In the earlier years, the overlap with many other subjects should be encouraged. As the pupils approach the end of the middle years, it will be more appropriate for children to focus on the materials and methods of the social sciences and begin to realize the nature of the evidence they are using.'[26] Nevertheless, the Social Studies 8–13 Project did produce a framework for social studies in the middle years which was based on the assumption that 'not less than 20 per cent of the school time is given to social studies.'[27]

From what has been said, it is clear that although there are some similarities, there are also some differences of opinion regarding the role, function, and scale of operations both of social and environmental studies. The concept of balance in the curriculum is not an easy one to define or put into operation, but in its broadest interpretation it does seem to cast some doubt on the viability of having

181

both a social studies course of the nature envisaged by the Social Studies 8–13 Project, and also a programme of work based on the environment as envisaged by the Environmental Studies 5–13 Project. However, it does not rule out the viability of having, say, an environmental studies course for part of the middle years, followed by a social studies course at a later stage. Or as another alternative, having social studies subsumed under the more general activities carried out in environmental studies. There is an obvious appeal in these two suggestions, for they appear to offer the best of both possible worlds. However, the conditions under which they might operate would need careful examination to ensure that the best and not the worst of both worlds was being obtained.

A noticeably broader stance on the relationship between environmental studies and the whole curriculum is taken by Project Environment 8–18. As the project's director, R. W. Colton, explained to us, their approach is based on developing an understanding of the basic ecology of human existence which involves the working of the great natural systems of the earth both physical and biological, the place of living organisms including man in the working of these systems, and the extent and consequences of human interference in these systems. They argue that there is too much teaching *about* the environment, much of which is detached and lacking in commitment. What is needed is more teaching *from* the environment, using the real world as a basis for study, as well as teaching *for* the environment, that is, teaching designed to develop a sense of concern for, and responsibility towards, the environment. Their conception of environmental studies is not simply as a subject, or as an integrated approach to the teaching of skills and techniques, or even as the linking or interrelation of disciplines. Rather they are making a plea for a new conception of educational priorities. At the secondary level they see little purpose in tacking on 'a bit of conservation to the end of the biology syllabus'. Similarly, they see no point in 'squeezing one more subject into an overcrowded curriculum'. What they would wish to see is the adoption of a new set of values 'for the impregnation of the whole of our education by the subject matter, principles, methods and spirit of environmental education.'

Here then are several differing judgements about this aspect of the middle-years curriculum. The debate is not ended, however. Several projects have yet to complete their work. Even when this has happened, it is the teachers in the schools for middle-years children who will decide the extent of the experiment and innovation which will follow. Critics of environmental studies have not been slow to point out that the child who does little more than colour the butcher's shop red or the grocer's green on his duplicated map of the locality, or who sits by the kerbside making a count of the number of cars and lorries rolling past, is not likely to be better educated than the child who copies material from his

182

history and geography textbooks into the appropriate notebooks.[28] That point is well made; the answer can be given by Melville Harris in writing of his own concept of environmental studies. '[It] is not made up of unorganized "happenings". It has structure and purpose, though much of the structure lies in the organization undertaken by the teacher prior to the involvement of the children.'[29]

## Home economics

We end this chapter with a section on home economics since this subject, as developed now in many schools, is clearly capable of providing many of the learning experiences mentioned above. The subject has the great advantage of being 'home-centred' and uses the home as a resource to be exploited in an approach to understanding the wider environment. Home economics is now seen as dealing principally with the following overlapping areas of interest:

> People and their environment
> Home
> Food
> Fabrics
> Consumer education.

An analysis of the first topic carried out by the Schools Council Home Economics Subject Committee produced the following themes:

> Personal relationships
> Child care and development
> Housing and the community
> Patterns of family living.

Developed in this way, the subject clearly provides an alternative though distinctive approach to problems which can be pursued as social studies. Similar overlaps occur in the other topics.

The Schools Council Home Economics Subject Committee describes the subject as a vital component of the middle years of schooling, and develops the case pointing out that there are particularly valuable contributions in the mathematical, psycho-motor and aesthetic as well as in the empirical area. It is apparent that no balanced curriculum could possibly simultaneously provide full programmes in geography, history, science, social studies, environmental studies and home economics. How the school approaches this area of study will depend to some extent on local factors – strength of the staff, special facilities and opportunities, likelihood of outside support, and so on. In reaching decisions

183

some schools will wish to consider home economics alongside the other subjects if only because many schools (including former secondary-school middle schools) have equipment and staff for the subject. Provided it is realized that the subject is being developed across the middle years for learning outcomes much broader than those relevant to the subject itself in its narrow concept, there is every reason for seeing home economics developed, for boys and girls, as a principal way into the empirical area. The paper prepared by the Schools Council Home Economics Subject Committee suggests adapting the traditional purpose-built home-economics room (composed of 'unit kitchens') to provide spaces for individual and group study plus areas for library and media, food preparation and eating, mathematical and language activities. It is apparent that there are special in-service requirements here. Non-specialist primary-school teachers need training in the home economics approach and home economics specialists need to be trained in methods appropriate to the children of upper primary-school age. An important corollary to moving the subject into the mainstream of the middle-years curriculum is that 'finding out' replaces demonstration-followed-by-practice as the principal teaching method – this will lead, if not to the waste, at any rate to a greater consumption, of materials than has been customary in home economics teaching. Another corollary is that the subject – since it will to some extent supplant others that might have been taught – must consciously enlarge its coverage, seeking to 'pick up' some of the subject matter not being studied directly because of the decision to use home economics as a principal way into the empirical area of the curriculum.

## References and notes

1. See the project's report, published as Schools Council Working Paper 39, *Social Studies 8–13*, by DENIS LAWTON, JAMES CAMPBELL and VALERIE BURKITT (Evans/Methuen Educational, 1971), p. 13.
2. 'The environmental studies approach', *Dialogue*, Schools Council Newsletter No. 6 (Autumn 1970), 8.
3. Schools Council Project Profile on Environmental Studies 5–13 Project.
4. Quoted in *Geography in Primary Schools* (Geographical Association, 1970), p. 16.
5. D. LAWTON, 'Social studies and the social sciences', *Ideas*, No. 4 (September 1967). Journal of the Curriculum Laboratory, Goldsmiths' College, University of London.
6. N. O. GRAVES, 'Geography, social science and interdisciplinary enquiry', *Geographical Journal*, **134** (1968), 391.
7. Ibid.

8. Central Advisory Council for Education (England), *Children and their Primary Schools* (HMSO, 1967), Vol. I, paras 543–8.

9. Social Studies 8–13 (1968–70), based at the University of London Institute of Education; Project Environment 8–18 (1970–73), based at the Department of Education, The University, Newcastle upon Tyne; Environmental Studies 5–13 (1967–71), based at Cartrefle College of Education, Wrexham, Denbighshire; History, Geography and Social Science 8–13 (1971–75), based at the School of Education, University of Liverpool.

10. W. E. MARSDEN, 'Environmental studies courses in colleges of education', *Journal of Curriculum Studies*, III (November 1971), 162.

11. Department of Education and Science, *Towards the Middle School*, Education Pamphlet No. 57 (HMSO, 1970), pp. 15–17.

12. Schools Council Working Paper 39, *Social Studies 8–13* by DENIS LAWTON, JAMES CAMPBELL and VALERIE BURKITT (Evans/Methuen Educational, 1971), p. 7.

13. See Schools Council Working Paper 42, *Education in the Middle Years* (Evans/Methuen Educational, 1972), chapter IV.

14. 'The environmental studies approach', *Dialogue*, Schools Council Newsletter No. 6 (Autumn 1970), p. 7.

15. Ibid.

16. MELVILLE HARRIS, *Environmental Studies*, British Primary Schools Today Series (Macmillan Education, 1971), p. 8.

17. O. GARNETT, *Fundamentals in School Geography* (Harrap, 1965).

18. Geographical Association, *Geography in Primary Schools* (Geographical Association, 1970).

19. Science 5–13, *With Objectives in Mind* (Macdonald Educational, 1972), and *Geography in Primary Schools*, chapter I.

20. *Geography in Primary Schools*, p. 5.

21. E. FENTON, *Teaching the New Social Studies in Secondary Schools: an Inductive Approach* (Holt, Rinehart & Winson, 1966).

22. Schools Council Working Paper 39, *Social Studies 8–13* by DENIS LAWTON, JAMES CAMPBELL and VALERIE BURKITT (Evans/Methuen Educational, 1971), p. 16.

23. Ibid., pp. 9–10.

24. MELVILLE HARRIS, *Environmental Studies* (Macmillan Education, 1971), pp. 17–23.

25. Ibid., p. 23.

26. Schools Council Working Paper 39, *Social Studies 8–13* by DENIS LAWTON, JAMES CAMPBELL and VALERIE BURKITT (Evans/Methuen Educational, 1971), p. 18.

27. Ibid., p. 153.
28. See MICHAEL STORM, 'Environmental studies', *Teacher's World* (4, 11, 18 September 1970), and FLORENCE SMALLWOOD, 'Environmental studies', *Teacher's World* (31 July 1970), 12.
29. MELVILLE HARRIS, *Environmental Studies*, British Primary Schools Today Series (Macmillan Education, 1971), p. 29.

# XI. Moral and religious education

Readers of this report will not need to be reminded of the difficulties attaching to moral and religious education in all schools, including voluntary schools; nor will they wish to have pointed out to them the implications of the fact that schools are required by law to include religious instruction and worship in the curriculum. The difficulties are such that some teachers (including some 'believers') prefer not to take part in teaching this part of the curriculum, and others fulfil the statutory requirement in a way which would surprise – if not shock – some of the legislators of the 1944 Education Act. There are teachers who enthusiastically support religious education but who would welcome its removal from the unique if not anomalous position of being the only 'required' subject in the curriculum. Such teachers claim that the subject is well capable of justifying its place in the curriculum of all schools – schools catering for those of whom many are the children of 'second-generation non-Church-goers' as well as church schools seen to be part of a thriving parish. They claim too that it has a place in the curriculum for schools serving racially mixed areas which have pupils of many religions other than Christian, or of no religion at all.

The model of the curriculum put forward in Chapter I included a content area called morality which provides for the accumulation of experiences concerned with ethics and value systems. It is certainly true that this area can be explored from starting points in the empirical area (social studies, for example) and from other directions (physical education, English, science), but moral and religious education offer the most direct approach. A curriculum which does not provide for experience in this category cannot be regarded as 'whole'. The problems surrounding moral and religious education are considerable but they must, nevertheless, be faced.

Development in this field has been impeded to some extent by the statutory obligation already mentioned. It has, of course, been pointed out that although the Education Act of 1944 calls for a corporate act of worship it does not state worship of what or whom; the appendices to the act make the position quite clear. The legislators of 1944 undoubtedly saw the clauses concerned with religious education as being concerned with the promulgation of a moral code. Many schools and teachers accept that position today. Many do not. Many publications sponsored by religious bodies do not. Religious education can be shown to be capable of making a significant contribution in its own right to an understanding of the world. It is the justifiable claim of some of those who devise materials for use in teaching religion that they can be used by believer and non-believer alike. There is less emphasis upon the use of materials to lead children towards a particular view of morals, though this outcome is equally possible. There are teachers who are anxious to encourage the acceptance of a particular moral code but who do not wish to take the religious position as the starting point. The development of moral education quite separate from religious education has been the result. This chapter deals with both approaches and begins with religious education.

In recent years there has been no dearth of advice from public bodies. In 1969 the Department of Education and Science issued a leaflet, *Religious Education, Present and Future* (Reports on Education No. 58); in 1970, the Social Morality Council issued *Moral and Religious Education in County Schools*; and, also in 1970, the Commission of Religious Education in Schools, appointed in 1967 under the chairmanship of the Bishop of Durham, published their report, *The Fourth R*.[1] Many local education authorities have revised the versions of the agreed syllabus which they are using. The Schools Council has not been inactive either. In 1969 *An Approach through Religious Education* was published as part of the Schools Council Humanities for the Young School Leaver programme.[2] This was followed in 1971 and 1972 by Schools Council Working Papers 36 and 44, *Religious Education in Secondary Schools* and *Religious Education in Primary Schools*.[3] Following the recommendations made in Working Paper 44, in 1973 the Schools Council set up a three-year development project on religious education in primary schools, based at the University of Lancaster and directed by Professor Ninian Smart and Donald Horder.

The considerable amount of advice contained in the publications mentioned above provides a suitable background for the decisions teachers are required to take about religious education in the middle years of schooling. In writing this chapter we also had available a paper written by the Schools Council Religious Education Subject Committee, and the views of teachers in the discussion groups which assisted the project. One such group reported:

> Primary teachers felt that, while assemblies should be retained, formal religious education might well be removed or reduced on the grounds that moral/religious education should form part of the whole range of 'humane studies' as well as of school life . . . Secondary teachers were in substantial agreement with their primary colleagues to reduce the formal religious education allocation.

The implication in this quotation that whatever it is that religious education is capable of doing for the child it may also be done in other subjects, or through school life in general, is to be noted – though it does not necessarily follow that it can be done as well or better. But the aims implicit in such an approach clearly go far wider than giving children a knowledge of the Bible. The case for religious education can certainly be related to the broad intention to give children the means of understanding the world as it was, as it is and as it might become. It can further be related to giving the child important experiences in terms of facilitating self-development and self-fulfilment and, because of this, important in preparing him for his future life as an adult. There is no reason why such a programme of experiences should in any way conflict with an additional scheme of religious education provided at home, in chapel or church, which goes on to consider propositions about a 'future' life of another kind.

Religious educationists are well aware of the dangers (indeed the immorality) of indoctrination, oppression and authoritarianism, and have therefore embraced the 'open' approach. *Religious Education in Secondary Schools*,[4] for example, calls for 'procedural neutrality' when discussing value questions. The case of younger children may not, however, be the same. The concepts used in religious education appear to develop more slowly than in some other subjects and it may not be possible to parody in the middle years the modes of thought distinctive of the mature student of the subject. In some sense the child of 13 can tackle a mathematical problem using strategies and concepts which are recognizably mathematical. It is more difficult to say that this can be done in religious education if one is thinking of the concepts used by adults, much less by theologians and students of religion. This does not imply that religious education has no place in the middle years. Without an appropriate experience at this stage the concepts will emerge less easily at the appropriate time.

Some teachers, especially in the lower forms of secondary schools, believe that these problems can to some extent be overcome if the subject is integrated with environmental studies, history, geography, social studies, and perhaps English. Using the empirical method – 'let us see what we can find out' – children are encouraged to use religious as well as other concepts as a way of making sense of the world and human behaviour, as it can be observed by children. To add a further dimension to the mode of inquiry is itself desirable but, properly guided, such studies are capable of producing a deeper understanding, and this, because of its emotional and attitudinal content, may in some cases have a lasting effect upon the development of the individual. We can perhaps see more clearly the contribution of religious education generally if we ask what it is that religious education provides in an integrated studies programme that cannot equally well be provided through the medium of history, geography, social studies, English, physical education and other subjects. This additional element is to be found in experiences – structured if need be – designed to help a child to develop a dimension of awareness of a range of problems, understanding of which is

189

needed to achieve a fuller understanding of himself, of his relationships with others and of the questions related to arriving at an idea of the purpose of life. This is something which has as much to offer to the child who rejects the existence of God as it does to the child who accepts it as an unchallengeable presupposition. It can lead to the development of a series of attitudes which together form a value system. Just as in other contexts teachers of middle-years children are asked to ensure that by the time the child is 13, his experiences have been such as to develop a 'favourable' set of attitudes (for example, towards going on with the study of mathematics), the aim would be to encourage 'favourable' attitudes towards the idea of being prepared to discuss fundamental questions. It is at this point that problems emerge, for sets of attitudes produce value systems and many teachers do not wish to be over-positive in this respect. This is a problem which cannot be avoided. A decision to be strictly non-controversial or to ignore the area entirely is, in effect, a powerful statement of opinion which the children will quickly perceive and interpret. Besides, there is the hidden curriculum of the school which expresses at every point what people are, how they treat each other and what the purposes of life are thought to be. Deliberately to develop a set of experiences designed to give children the opportunity of recognizing that judgements can be (and are) made, and that many judgements are made in the light of standards of value which vary, can thus be an important contribution made by the religious and moral education programme. The 'open' approach will certainly take teachers and children to this point of tolerance. To consider whether or not there are bounds to this tolerance is an important question and we shall return to this. A further question – and one of equal importance – is whether or not it is legitimate to promulgate certain value systems as being better than others. *Religious Education in Primary Schools* is quite clear that if this means instilling Christian beliefs, teachers should not do so. 'They were appointed as teachers, and it is important that they should be faithful to their appointment and accept their role as educationists.'[5] The problem is, alas, less simple than this statement indicates, especially when we move into the area of precepts which can be regarded as moral rather than religious. We shall return to this point later also.

The paper by the Schools Council Religious Education Subject Committee recommends for middle-years children the topic-centred approach involving integration with other subjects, but sees also the need for some independently structured 'informational' courses on religious ideas and institutions. It is not surprising that the claim is also made for teachers of middle-years children to have available to them within the school a consultant specialist who would help them to develop programmes designed to lay down the foundations for the development of religious ideas and attitudes. The paper claims:

190

There are certain areas of work where the religious education specialist can, and should, make a quite specific contribution to the overall educational process. His particular, direct concern with 'ultimate questions'; his particular knowledge of the roots and development of religious belief and expression, his expertise in the skills of the religious 'language game', and in the analysis of religious literature; his concern with the development of religious tolerance, and his general concern with moral issues – all these would seem to demand quite specific time and opportunity for expression and application in the classroom.

We turn next to moral education, and it should be made clear at once that such a title may never appear on any timetable and yet still embrace a significant part of the school's aims. The religious educationist will often find himself dealing with moral questions but not all moral questions arise in a religious context. Furthermore there are teachers who would prefer to explore the ethics area from a non-religious starting point. The case for exploring it, especially in the middle years, overlaps to some extent the propositions put forward on behalf of religious education. To understand and to tolerate differences between peoples, children require learning experiences which give the opportunity of savouring what it is like to make a judgement and of learning that such judgements relate to systems of value which can differ from person to person and group to group.

As with religious education there is an increasing amount of advice available. In 1968 there was the first publication from the Farmington Trust Research Unit at Oxford (set up in 1965), *Introduction to Moral Education* by J. Wilson, director of the unit, N. Williams and B. Sugarman.[6] In 1969, a guide for teachers, *Moral Education and the Curriculum*, by J. Wilson, was published.[7] The Schools Council Moral Education 13–16 Project was started in 1967 and publications from this include a teachers' book, *Moral Education in the Secondary School* by Peter McPhail, the project director, J. R. Ungoed-Thomas and Hilary Chapman, and teaching materials published under the title *Lifeline*.[8] Peter McPhail is now directing a four-year Schools Council project, Moral Education 8–13 (1972–76), to develop a programme of moral education for middle-years children.[9]

It should be made clear that, though some may see moral education as the means of supplanting religious education in schools other than voluntary schools, many of the teachers and researchers engaged in developing moral education see it as an addition to the curriculum existing in its own right, not as a new subject on the syllabus, and not as a replacement for, or an equivalent to, religious education. The Farmington Trust Unit has analysed moral behaviour into various components such as attitudes (of mind – especially towards others),

191

abilities (particularly those which make it possible to know what other people are feeling), knowledge, know-how, and the ability to plan and execute an action which follows from a moral judgement. McPhail approaches the problem through experiences designed to sensitize the child and then, by discussion, to enable him to develop an understanding of what is implied by a moral judgement and its possible consequences. It will be seen at once that the range of feelings and abilities called upon are those which are developed and are, for many children, transformed across the middle years. There can be no doubt that the schools responsible for middle-years children have therefore a responsibility to provide an appropriate range of experience designed to apprise the child of the nature of an ethical judgement. Schools have traditionally allowed religious education to be a principal means of communicating this awareness of moral questions. As religion has lost some of its force in society, in schools and in the teaching profession, the schools seem to have approached the question of positive moral teaching with increasing uncertainty. The fact that value systems have been changing rapidly, and that our society is increasingly pluralistic, has strengthened the case against positive moral teaching. It would be difficult, however, to defend the position that we should give no guidance at all. What is needed now is an agreement among those most nearly concerned – the parents, the teachers, the governing/managing bodies and the providing authorities – as to the positive steps that can legitimately be taken. It is clear that a curriculum which leaves unexplored the area of ethical and moral values, and which gives no opportunity for experiences likely to arouse the awareness needed when moral and ethical decisions have to be taken, cannot be 'whole'. It is clear also that the solution must be one as satisfying to believers (of whatever kind) as to non-believers (of whatever kind) whether they be teachers, parents or pupils. In particular it is important to make the point that the basis for establishing a code of moral behaviour has not necessarily been removed if organized religion is rejected. Considerations such as these have led to the great interest in moral education developed in recent years and there can be no doubt that, in considering the place of the ethics sector in the curriculum, moral education must be considered alongside religious education. Both moral and religious education can make a contribution to the empirical sector – that is, they can be used as a way of helping the child to discover more about the world around him. But to stop there is, in the opinion of many, not enough. What distinguishes moral and religious education from other subjects in the curriculum is their facility for taking the child directly into the area of ethics and morality. This is not to say that the programme should be designed to produce theologians or philosophers, though it is legitimate to draw the parallel with other subject areas and to ask what kind of learning experiences are appropriate in view of the fact that a few

192

*will* become theologians or philosophers. But just as a science programme must consider all 13-year-olds and not only those who eventually become physicists and engineers, so must the ME/RE programmes keep in mind the objectives appropriate to a broad range of middle-years children. What is being sought here is experiences, graded according to age, ability and maturity, designed to help a child to develop that awareness from which will grow congeries of attitudes which will give rise to a code of behaviour, a set of values and, in many if not all cases, something which might fittingly be described as a purpose in life.

In this area children's behaviour is influenced as much by 'signals' quickly observed and interpreted as by formal teaching. The total atmosphere of the school may speak more powerfully than the voice of the teacher. It is perhaps one of the more daunting of the responsibilities which go with being a teacher that the unconscious teaching of his own example may communicate to middle-years children those all-important 'learnings' from which moral positions are derived. When the 'signals' conflict, between home and school, between teacher and teacher, the younger child may be left in a state of confusion, especially when the concepts implied are at the periphery of his understanding.

It is at this point that we return to the two difficult questions raised earlier, and it will be seen that they are related. Firstly there is the concept of tolerance. The open approach demanded in a pluralistic society makes it incumbent on us to develop in the young a measure of tolerance of different styles of life, patterns of behaviour, modes of worship and codes of values.

In seeking to allow our children to develop themselves in the best way possible and to help produce a society in the future more just than that which exists today, the thinking teacher and the observant child cannot but be aware of the harm wrought by attitudes created by the dividing characteristics in our society – race, accent, region, intelligence, class, wealth, sex, to say nothing of smaller groupings such as gangs and supporters of teams. Fostering understanding of the differences between peoples, helping children to recognize and accept that others may make different but equally valid judgements, are examples of learning out-comes capable of helping the child to develop himself as a person and of pro-ducing a more just society. The question of how far this tolerance is to stretch has now to be put and it cannot be answered without making statements which are as much political as educational. The point is expressed well by a 'semi-anonymous' reviewer:

> To impose any particular system of values upon the young – to force or wheedle them into uncritical conformity – is itself immoral since the aim should be to stimulate and encourage our pupils to personal independence

193

of mind. It is equally true, however, that a democratic society, indeed any society, maintains itself by the veneration and transmission of those values which define its nature and relationships . . . What we need is a mode of moral education that combines the two – encouraging critical thinking and eschewing rigidity, while offering experiences that bring home the importance of civilized values.[10]

The case of the middle-years child poses a particular problem. In one sense he is 'ready' to discuss important ethical problems, but for only a few will the ability to think critically about fundamental questions be present even at 13 years of age. Given that the child is at the stage of being influenced significantly by the actions and opinions of 'significant others', such as parents, teachers, peers and public figures, it would seem reasonable for the school to bring at least one point of consistency into the situation. It is here that our second problem occurs. Can it be agreed that there is, for any one society, a cluster of values judged to be 'better' and which will be reinforced at every suitable opportunity? The agreed syllabuses of religious instruction established, for a generation, an agreed 'core' of religious teaching. Would it be possible for schools to work out, as part of the curriculum, a statement of principles accepted by the staff and known to the parents which would to some extent set a standard for the school? Such a list could not be extensive for it would soon enter areas obviously of political debate, but propositions about respect for the integrity of the human person regardless of all distinguishing characteristics, recognition of the legitimate rights of others, adherence to the highest standards of honesty, truthfulness, kindliness and co-operation, would not be questioned, and could be encouraged with positive reinforcement wherever possible. There is much in the educational system of the USSR which would be quite unacceptable in Britain, for educational systems, like constitutions, do not travel well. Nevertheless, the study of Russian education by Bronfenbrenner[11] is not without significance for those who accept that there is a connexion between public standards of morality and life in the nation's schools.


### References and notes

1. *The Fourth R*: the Report of the Commission on Religious Education in Schools appointed in 1967 under the chairmanship of the Bishop of Durham (National Society and SPCK, 1970).
2. Schools Council, *Humanities for the Young School Leaver: an Approach through Religious Education* (Evans/Methuen Educational, 1969).

194

3. Working Paper 36, *Religious Education in Secondary Schools* (Evans/Methuen Educational, 1971) is from the Schools Council Religious Education in Secondary Schools Project (1969–73), based at Cartmel College, University of Lancaster, and directed by Professor Ninian Smart and Donald Horder. (Teaching materials from this project to be published by Hart-Davis Educational from 1976.) Working Paper 44, *Religious Education in Primary Schools* (Evans/Methuen Educational, 1972) is the report of the Schools Council Religious Education in the Primary School research project (1969–71), based at the Institute of Education, University of Leeds, and directed by C. M. Jones. The development project, Religious Education in Primary Schools (1973–76), is based at University of Lancaster, and directed by Professor Ninian Smart and Donald Horder.

4. Schools Council Working Paper 36, *Religious Education in Secondary Schools* (Evans/Methuen Educational, 1971), chapter XII.

5. Schools Council Working Paper 44, *Religious Education in Primary Schools* (Evans/Methuen Educational, 1972), p. 59.

6. J. WILSON, N. WILLIAMS and B. SUGARMAN, *Introduction to Moral Education* (Penguin Books, 1968).

7. J. WILSON, *Moral Education and the Curriculum* (Pergamon, 1969).

8. The Schools Council Moral Education 13–16 Project (1967–72) was based at the Department of Educational Studies, University of Oxford and directed by Peter McPhail. *Moral Education in the Secondary School* by PETER MCPHAIL, J. R. UNGOED-THOMAS and HILARY CHAPMAN was published by Longman in 1972. The teaching materials, *Lifeline*, are published by Longman.

9. The Moral Education 8–13 Project is based at Hughes Hall, University of Cambridge.

10. J. H., book review, *Trends in Education*, No. 26 (April 1972), 54.

11. U. BRONFENBRENNER, *Two Worlds of Childhood* (Allen & Unwin, 1972).

# XII. Other languages and cultures

In this chapter we deal with modern languages other than English and with classics. They are dealt with here under two headings for convenience, but it will be recognized that both share the broad aim of opening the child's mind to cultures other than his own. The basis for comparison thus introduced makes possible the development of greater understanding of the first or native culture, and at the same time leads to the possibility of developing an important range of values including that of tolerance for cultural differences. Seen in this way, these studies are obviously much more than linguistic. Indeed those who support the cause of classical studies claim that the subject has much to contribute to middle-years education even without any start being made on the learning of Latin or Greek. In the case of modern languages other than English, learning to understand, speak, read and perhaps write the language has been given a high priority. Seen as the development of a linguistic skill, the subject clearly finds its starting point in the basic skills area, but if the broader aims mentioned above are to be fulfilled it clearly has an important part to play in the empirical area and has contributions to make in the aesthetic and moral areas also. As in so many other cases, there is no reason why the subject, properly developed, should not make a significant contribution in almost any quarter of the curriculum. Our concern here is to examine the point at which the subjects make their principal contribution, while recognizing that this by no means covers all that they provide. The extent to which they permeate the rest of the curriculum depends on teaching skills, the pattern of organization and the environmental circumstance of each school. While a good deal of language teaching other than English, especially in the upper-primary sector of the middle years, is to be judged by the criteria relevant to the communication of basic (in this case linguistic) skills, it would be improper not to recognize that modern languages as they are studied across the middle years begin to develop dimensions which need to be measured by the criteria used for literary studies, especially those calling for sensitivity to what is implied in the making of judgements. The study of modern languages can be seen as encompassing learning the language *as* language for practical and literary use, studying the literature either in translation or in the original *as* literature, and finally studying the society from which language and literature sprang. This analysis, with appropriate adjustments, can be applied to classics also. Professor P. Strevens predicted:

Foreign languages will increasingly be taught for practical use and for insight into other societies rather than for literary studies, perhaps they will even be taught *through* other subjects; above all the language teaching profession will regard itself as dynamic and changing rather than static and unchanging.[1]

It is against a background of changing ideas that the teacher of middle-years children has to judge what part of the school's resources shall be applied to foreign languages and to classical studies.

## Modern languages other than English

This heading is intended to draw attention to the point that the teaching of English already encompasses much language teaching. The distance which in some cases seems to exist between those teaching English language and those teaching foreign languages may be expected to decrease as a new generation of teachers, armed with tools forged in the rapidly developing study of linguistics, begin to apply their skills to the task of communicating language skills. In this connexion the development of 'linking studies' in some institute of education BEd courses is interesting. Their aim is to help teachers of foreign languages to link their teaching with teaching the mother tongue and break down existing barriers between these two areas of the curriculum. The heading also gives 'languages' in the plural. This is intended to draw attention to the fact that the teacher of middle-years children should consider languages other than French, and also the possibility of offering a start in more than one foreign language. The rapid spread of French in primary schools during the 1960s has often been said to be a cause for concern in so far as it is likely to inhibit the development of other languages. It is almost inevitable that such languages will be second foreign languages and the figures given in *Development of Modern Language Teaching in Secondary Schools* (Schools Council Working Paper No. 19) showed then that even in grammar schools only about one-quarter of the pupils were taking a second foreign language by 13.[2] Nevertheless, O-level entries in German and Italian rose significantly between 1961 and 1971.[3] Clearly European languages deserve special consideration but if the broader aims are to be achieved there is a case for developing the study of the cultures (even something of the language in some cases) of peoples who speak Russian, Chinese and Arabic, since these languages are, in world terms, so important. Just as modern European languages can be developed into an area study such as European Studies so can these other languages point the way to area studies of other significant parts of the world. This suggestion may not be too outlandish if there

197

is a move towards reorganizing the curriculum in such a way as to make it possible for children to be kept for periods of time in environments in which they hear and speak only the language of one culture.

The most significant development in modern language teaching has been the major effort which has resulted in 35 per cent of primary-school children having some French tuition.[4] The aims of such teaching are clearly different from those which informed the teaching of French in selective secondary schools. Even though by the mid-fifties much more attention was being paid in such schools to practical competence in the language, the then Ministry of Education was clear about priorities: 'Whatever the claims of modern languages to an important place in the curriculum, it must be said at the outset that they cannot be justified unless the course contains intellectual discipline.'[5] Perhaps it should be noted that there is no necessary incompatibility between achieving academic goals of the traditional kind and gaining a practical command of the language. The teacher of middle-years children will seek out a programme of work which emphasizes practical competence in the language; but he will also have children who, by the age of 13, have seized on the learning of foreign languages as the way by which they may develop themselves both as scholars and as individuals. The middle-years teacher has to encapsulate in five years (8 to 13) the thirteen years of experience in the child's first language. Inevitably work in the earlier middle years mimics (but not exactly, for the organism is more mature) the processes which helped the child to acquire that first language. The later years of the age-span provide, in the new language, experiences which complement, and to some extent replicate, the learning being simultaneously developed in other subject areas. The aims at the earlier stage have been summarized in *French in the Primary School: the Joint Schools Council/Nuffield Foundation Pilot Scheme* (Schools Council Working Paper No. 8) as follows:

**a**   To understand the foreign language when spoken by a native speaker at the normal speed of conversation
**b**   To speak the language fully intelligibly to the native speaker
**c**   To read the language with ease
**d**   To write the language correctly in expressing his own thoughts
**e**   To be well informed about the way of life (i.e. customs, culture, history, etc.) of the people who speak the language as their mother tongue.[6]

Applying these aims to the first three years of language learning, the following outcomes are sought:

**a**   An oral competence developed from accurate listening and understanding
**b**   A lack of inhibition and a readiness to talk in simple situations

198

c    A limited recognition of the printed word and a power of reading the familiar, the beginnings of skill in the handling of books

d    A more rational attitude to language in general

e    Some knowledge of a foreign country and its way of life

f    A readiness, certainly on the part of the more able, to begin a second foreign language.

The possible effects of teaching which is geared to these objectives may be judged by reference to the reports published by the National Foundation for Educational Research, describing the evaluation of the pilot scheme for teaching French in primary schools.[7] Some 12 000 children were followed through from their primary schools into the secondary stage. As was to be expected, their fluency was greater, especially where they had been taught by fluent and enthusiastic teachers in schools whose headteachers were enthusiastic about the teaching of French. Children in small rural schools did better on the whole than children in large urban schools. Girls did better than boys and children with 'good' home backgrounds also did better than average. The fluency was, of course, almost entirely verbal and by 13 the 'pilot' children could speak French better than children who had learned in a more traditional way from 11 onwards. Grammar-school teachers found the written work of the pilot group below standard. A Department of Education and Science summary of the conclusions to be drawn from these findings is admirably succinct:

> Experience now shows that clear conditions must be fulfilled if primary-school French is to succeed. Some local education authorities wisely insist on continuity between primary- and secondary-school French; on adequately qualified staff; on a reasonable time allocation; and on the use of appropriate materials. Without these minimum conditions it seems better to leave the subject alone.[8]

It would be more difficult to decide to leave the subject alone for the whole of the middle years; but before turning to those years it is appropriate to refer to the substantial investment made by the Nuffield Foundation and the Schools Council and others in the teaching of modern languages at the secondary stage. Outstanding is the Modern Languages Project (1963–75) based at the University of York.[9] The materials produced have relevance to the later part of the middle years but the task in modern language teaching of marrying the upper primary to the lower secondary has still to be worked out in detail. The middle-years project was greatly assisted by a paper from the Schools Council Modern Languages Subject Committee which offered valuable suggestions. The paper sees the mid-1970s as a time for stock-taking since by then the many projects under way will have come to fruition and pupils who have followed experimental courses will have proceeded to the point at which some form of long-term evaluation will be possible. The paper suggests that if the picture which then emerges is favourable, a further period of rapid expansion in foreign language teaching for the 8 to 13 age-group will have been justified. If it is not favourable, expansion will probably be limited to children over 11 years old, and to the upper half of the ability range. The linguistic justification for adding languages to the pre-secondary curriculum is given as follows:

> An early start to the learning of the first foreign language may make it possible:
> a    to exploit the child's imitative ability, his comparative freedom from inhibitions and his desire to learn;
> b    to lay a firm foundation for the later development of linguistic performance;
> c    to achieve higher standards by age 16;
> d    to begin learning a second foreign language earlier;
> e    to provide more time for exposure to the language and practice in using it.

These arguments obviously proceed from the question, 'What can the child do with the subject?', but the paper deals also with the reverse – 'What can the subject do for the child?' Not all the reasons given will commend themselves to all teachers but many will and they are therefore given here in their entirety:

> There are cogent reasons which support the claim that foreign language teaching can play a useful and important role in the education of children in the junior school . . . Learning a foreign language at this age is:
> a    *Appropriate to the children's abilities and interests*
> It appeals to the child's curiosity about the wider world outside the classroom.
> The thematic and linguistic content of the teaching programme can be geared to the pupils' interests.
> A satisfying degree of achievement is possible for most children, particularly at the oral stage.
> b    *Educationally productive*
> The introductory stages of the language learning process help to develop educationally useful skills, e.g. listening carefully, repeating accurately, oral memorization and recall, oral expression, reading (for pleasure and for information), and writing (copywriting, letter-writing, etc.).

Language awareness and the basic language skills which will be needed for foreign language learning in the secondary school are also developed at this stage.

The children are involved in acquiring reasoned attitudes and forming valid judgements about a foreign people and their way of life.

c *Consistent with the aims, methods and ethos of junior schools*
Learning a language involves active participation by the pupil.

The child's personality is developed through conversation, role-playing and general oral performance.

The content of the teaching can be linked to other areas of the curriculum, e.g. art, music and home economics, in the early stages, and history and geography later.

The language can be presented in situational contexts which are meaningful to the child and which are bright, colourful and stimulating.

The teaching methods involve not only classwork but group and individual teaching, especially after the initial introduction.

A foreign language can be successfully taught at this level by junior-school teachers after a suitable period of training.

d *Relevant to the needs and possibilities of Britain in the 1970s*
The inclusion of foreign language teaching provides one positive means of achieving an outward-looking curriculum.

It is consistent with entry into the EEC and with the growing demand for foreign languages for leisure as well as business.

A variety of suitable teaching materials and teaching aids are now available.

The training of adequate numbers of teachers capable of teaching the foreign language to pupils up to the age of 13 does not present any insuperable problems either to colleges of education or to the organizers of in-service courses.

A considerable amount of in-service backing for teachers of foreign languages is now provided at both the national and local levels.

The paper recommends that the teaching in the 11 to 13 period should be consistent with the above. 'This does not mean, of course, the wholesale transfer of junior-school methods into the secondary school, but rather the continuation of an attitude to foreign language teaching as a means of communication and the consolidation of an established set of basic skills.' The following is then given as a starting point for a list of such skills:

Aural comprehension
Aural discrimination
Oral repetition
Oral production of responses to oral stimuli
Production of utterances in response to visual clues
Role playing
Production of utterances with help of oral prompts
Reading orally familiar material (with and without visual and oral props)
Reading orally familiar material in new re-combinations
Copy writing
Memory writing
Reading (extensive and intensive) material containing a controlled amount of new lexis
Guided oral composition (descriptions and dialogues)
Writing to dictation of material which is familiar orally and as reading material
Guided written composition (letters and dialogues)
Assisted reading of selected material containing unfamiliar grammar and lexis
Assisted free composition (letters and dialogues).

In dealing with the content of language teaching in the 8 to 13 period, the paper mentions the usual criteria (interest, utility and relevance both in relation to the child's experience and to the understanding of the foreign country). Vocabulary will need to be restricted to those elements justified by frequency of occurrence and 'teachability'. The paper's comment on the much debated question of overt phonetic drilling is to avoid this until found to be necessary – that is, for certain pupils and for certain phonetic features only, and then in small doses. Nevertheless, the teacher must 'from the start . . . encourage and provide ample opportunity for careful listening and accurate repetition.'

No part of the middle-years curriculum is without problems and the modern languages part is no exception; indeed it has more problems than most other parts of the curriculum. The paper provided by the Schools Council Modern Languages Subject Committee refers to 'unsolved problems and unanswered questions'. One of these is the balance between class and group work, especially in unstreamed schools or schools working to an 'integrated timetable'. The paper states bluntly that successful teaching of foreign languages absolutely demands smaller groups and individual work for *some aspects* of the process. It may well be thought that the ritual gestures towards new methods and more flexible systems of school organization are not a sufficient reply to the teacher who asks how this problem is to be tackled. Professor H. Rée of the University of York spoke of this problem in 1972 when he expressed concern at the inefficiency of what he called the 'driblet approach',[10] that is, small amounts each day interspersed between experiences of a very different kind. His solution is for concentrated periods of skill learning outside the school (perhaps taken after the person has left school) and residence abroad. These suggestions apply only to the language-speaking aspect. French – or perhaps it should be called French studies – encompasses (like classics) more than the linguistic component. Nevertheless, the objectives of middle-years language teaching must, as things stand at present, include practice in speaking the language. It is clear that the able, enthusiastic teacher can succeed with the well-motivated child. When an innovation is generalized it faces judgement on what can be achieved with the less exceptional teacher and child. It may be that here, as in other parts of the curriculum, there is a case for periodic saturation during which additional resources and staff become temporarily available and other activities are left on one side. Such arrangements would be the result of local authority, rather than school, organization and would be part of that larger primary/middle/secondary co-ordinating task which must be undertaken if the pattern of language teaching in an area is to make sense. Such co-ordination should have particular concern with the teaching of foreign languages other than French, and with the introduction of second foreign languages. The resources of the whole area, not just those of a single school, should be available to solve particular problems. If this means establishing Saturday morning clubs for those interested in developing skill in languages other than those taught in the schools on week-days, then so be it, once the necessary financial and professional arrangements have been made. If it means periods of exchange with children in other countries, this can be done too.

The Department of Education and Science publication, 'Modern language teaching today', issued on the eve of Britain's entry into the European Community, contrasted the mainland European attitude towards language skill as part of their everyday equipment with the British attitude towards languages as 'school-based disciplines, unwillingly endured and promptly forgotten'.[11] If that attitude is to be altered, what happens in the middle years is of very great significance. Many of the possibilities which exist at the age of 8 have disappeared at 13 because of the nature of the experiences which have intervened. There is obviously much still to be learned about how to arrange linguistic experiences across the middle years so as to ensure that more children – boys as well as girls, and children from all backgrounds – find in modern languages not only justification for the somewhat arduous practice which the basic communication skills require but also those learning insights which come uniquely from the comparative approach to the study of culture. The argument based on practical value is powerful but not self-sufficient. What are described as 'general educational aims' are of significance too, and will grow in significance as the children move through the middle years from simple forms of learning to those more complex forms involving insight.

## Classical studies

A paper written for the project by a sub-committee nominated by the Schools Council Classics Committee makes a strong claim for the inclusion of classics (perhaps more accurately, classical studies) in the curriculum of the middle years. 'If the young are to see a true picture of their cultural environment, some understanding of Greco–Roman civilization is not merely relevant; it is indispensable.' There are two sides to the case. The study of classics provides not only greater insight into some of the essential values in our own culture but also, by providing experience of alternative cultures, adds another dimension for comparison with the familiar culture. Thus far the case for classical studies belongs to that part of the curriculum we have called empirical, but there is also a strong contribution in the aesthetic and moral content areas. The paper points out that 'the Greeks and Romans have left us a prodigious quantity of great literature and great literature is rare.' For some pupils this literature will be savoured in translation; other pupils will learn the languages. The paper discusses both non-linguistic and linguistic approaches to the study of classics in the middle years of schooling.

The growth, in recent years, in the number of schools offering non-linguistic courses in classical studies is associated in part with the Cambridge School Classics Project (1966–78),[12] which has produced a non-linguistic classical foundation course. The course is built round stories from the world of Ancient Greece, chosen because of their likely impact upon the imagination and for their universal appeal as examples of human experience. Using the discovery approach, the materials lead the children into finding out more about the ancient world. In this way they are brought into contact with some of the classical authors in translation or in adaptations. The work can lead on to writing of various kinds, drama and art. The non-linguistic approach to the classics may be particularly relevant to the problems of middle schools 'feeding' secondary schools with a strong classical side, and of secondary schools with reorganized lower school divisions where they wish to postpone the introduction of classical languages to 12 or 13. Some schools teaching middle-years children may wish to introduce classical studies before 11. Moreover, even though the subject may not be listed as such there can be few primary schools which do not provide some experience of people, places and things in the classical world.

204

Some schools may decide that for some pupils Greek and/or Latin should be provided. A background in classical studies will certainly ease the first steps towards reading the classical language. The paper prepared by the Schools Council Classics Committee comments on two types of linguistic course: firstly, the now common oral approach; and secondly, the Cambridge School Classics Project approach to language teaching, exemplified in its language course. In the oral approach, the aim is still to help pupils read literature fluently and with appreciation, but the approach is through speaking the language. Translation from Latin (or Greek) into English is held back though translation in the reverse direction is done in order to demonstrate and practise the use of the classical language as a means of communication. The paper further claims that by this method children are able to take the GCE O-level examination and obtain good results, sometimes after only three years of study. No doubt some schools will continue to start the teaching of classical languages at 11 or even earlier, but those which postpone it till 13, especially when it is preceded by a background course in classical studies, may still be able to keep open the door to specialization in the classics.

The second approach to the languages is that of the Cambridge School Classics Project. The aim in the language course has been to develop more quickly a reading competence in classical Latin and fuller understanding of Roman culture. Since fluent reading is the prime aim, composition and the formal presentation of grammar have been reduced. A central feature of the course is the recognition of patterns of expression – words strung together in phrases, clauses and sentences which provide broad areas of consecutive sense. The evidence from the pilot stage of this project was that

> this new approach to Latin generates the liveliest enthusiasm for the language alike in teachers and taught; that pupils in the top grade of ability, who start Latin at 10 or 11, are able to read Pliny, Catullus and Martial with profit and enjoyment after six terms; and that pupils of average ability attain a worth-while target of reading competence by the end of the middle years of schooling.

The case put forward by the Classics Committee may be summarized thus:

a    A non-linguistic classical foundation course is highly desirable for children in all schools between the ages of 10 and 13

b    Such a course might run from ages 10 to 12 or 11 to 13 according to local circumstances, but it should embrace the widest possible range of ability

**c**   Such a course is worth while in itself but has an additional function in preparing some children for a course in Latin or Greek language

**d**   A language course in Latin or Greek should be available at 12 or 13 (even earlier for gifted children) for all those judged to be able to profit from such a course.

This chapter has discussed the contribution which the study of the languages and cultures of other peoples may make to the education of middle-years children. The problem of fitting all that is judged to be worth while into the limited time available is particularly pressing in this area. There are, no doubt, some children capable of starting a first foreign language at 8 or even earlier, who will have a background in classical studies by 10 sufficient to ensure a rapid start to Latin at 11 and, despite picking up some German, Spanish or Italian from 13, will still wish to tackle Greek in time to achieve an O-level qualification in that subject. But such children are exceptional and so, too, are the schools able to provide this rich linguistic diet. Perhaps the most significant finding from the evaluation of the primary French programme is that enthusiasm on the part of heads and teachers is of great significance. Undoubtedly an enthusiastic classics or modern language teacher can provide a quality of learning which will enhance the child's interest in and enthusiasm for the subject. The same cannot be said of the less enthusiastic teacher. No school can do everything; as mentioned before, there are things that must be done, others that should be done and some which could be done. Schools may therefore wish to concentrate upon the things they can do well, but in teaching them should bear in mind that the neglected areas can, with modern methods, be explored to some extent from the periphery. The school which does little in the way of classical studies should on that account be all the more sure to provide for that grasp of the classical origins of so much in our culture which the classics if studied for their own sake would provide. The primary school which decides not to teach a foreign language should be all the more careful to ensure that the work in environmental studies includes a study of our European neighbours. When the curricular choices have been made there should be a review of all the arguments for doing that which is not going to be directly done, so that in planning the work the gaps can be compensated for by adjustments within the areas of what is going to be done. If each of the chosen subject areas is seen not so much as a part of the map of knowledge to be filled in but as a standpoint from which vistas of knowledge, skill and experience may be surveyed, the curricular choices which have to be made may come to be seen as less perplexing than they appear at first sight.

# References and notes

1. P. STREVENS, quoted in Department of Education and Science, 'Modern language teaching today', *Reports on Education* No. 75 (November 1972), p. 3.
2. Schools Council Working Paper No. 19, *Development of Modern Language Teaching in Secondary Schools* (HMSO, 1969), p. 3.
3. Department of Education and Science, 'Modern language teaching today', *Reports on Education* No. 75 (November 1972), p. 2.
4. Ibid., p. 4.
5. Ministry of Education, *Modern Languages*, Ministry of Education Pamphlet No. 29 (HMSO, 1956), p. 1.
6. Schools Council Working Paper No. 8, *French in the Primary School: the Joint Schools Council/Nuffield Foundation Pilot Scheme* (HMSO, 1966) p. 56.
7. C. BURSTALL, *French from Eight* (National Foundation for Educational Research, 1968); C. BURSTALL, *French in the Primary School* (NFER, 1970). See also, C. BURSTALL et al., *Primary French in the Balance* (NFER, 1974).
8. Department of Education and Science, 'Modern language teaching today', *Reports on Education* No. 75 (November 1972), p. 1.
9. The Schools Council Modern Languages Project (1967–75) was established to continue the work begun in 1963 by the Nuffield Foreign Languages Teaching Materials Project. The project is attached to the Language Teaching Centre of the University of York. Publisher: E. J. Arnold.
10. H. RÉE, 'A licence to learn languages', *Times Educational Supplement* (8 December 1972), 4.
11. Department of Education and Science, 'Modern language teaching today', *Reports on Education* No. 75 (November 1972), p. 1.
12. The Cambridge School Classics Project 11–16 (1966–78) is based at Cambridge University and directed by D. J. Morton. The project has recently been extended for three years (to 1978) to provide classical studies materials for pupils aged 13 to 16. This extension of the foundation course work will continue under the direction of Martin Forrest at St Matthias College, Bristol. Publisher: Cambridge University Press.

# XIII. Physical education

All discussion of curricular problems makes the assumption that each child's basic physical and psychological needs are met, that he feels wanted and secure, that he has sufficient food, clothing, exercise, air, heat and light, both at home and at school, and that he has adequate medical care. In other words the process of education, whether the term is used in a narrow or an all-embracing sense, cannot take place unless the organism is provided with what it needs to function adequately. 'Adequately' may not, however, be a strong enough word. Now that we have come to recognize that the quality of the nurturing environment affects significantly the level of future performances, it might be better to speak of the organism being given the opportunity of functioning as well as its nature allows. The case for physical education as an essential part of the middle-years curriculum may be regarded as starting at this level, but as we shall see, it extends very much further and is capable of making a contribution to every part of the whole curriculum. In addition it can provide unique forms of experience of some significance to all pupils, and of great significance to some.

It should be said at once that discussions about the place of physical education do not always provide that degree of consensus which the busy but non-expert teacher so often looks for as a guide to action. The specialist physical educationist will, as might be expected, see the subject differently from the non-specialist, particularly when that non-specialist is a specialist in something else; but in this respect the subject is little different from others. Within the specialist ranks there are differences of emphasis, sometimes marked by adherence to a particular approach, sometimes reflecting difference in sex. Teachers of physical education have been 'in the middle of a period of critical inquiry into the nature, status and aims of their subject.'[1] The project received comments from groups representing the full range of opinion, from those who thought that the subject's share of resources might be reduced to those who saw physical education as a subject requiring still further development in the curriculum. Though what follows is the view of the project team alone, we are glad to acknowledge the assistance and advice provided by the many people who commented on the place of physical education in the middle-years curriculum.

The Schools Council's Physical Education Subject Committee provided two papers: 'Physical education during the middle years of schooling', representing the considered view of that committee; and 'The place of physical education in the whole curriculum', a series of answers given by committee members to questions put by the Schools Council Working Party on the Whole Curriculum in the secondary school. Two publications are also worthy of note. Schools Council Working Paper 37, *Physical Education 8–13* (Evans/Methuen Educational, 1971) is a report of a conference organized by the Schools Council Physical Education Committee in January 1970. The papers are, of course, an expression of personal opinion by those invited to speak, but the conference ended with a series of recommendations, reproduced at the end of this chapter, which seem to have received a measure of support. The other publication is *Movement: Physical Education in the Primary Years* (HMSO, 1972) from the Department of Education and Science. This has a section on middle schools which is also reproduced below.

We have mentioned before the distinction between 'must', 'should' and 'could' in curriculum building. The answer, in terms of the 13-year-old, is different from what it might be in terms of the 8-year-old; the answer in one school (say, a middle school) will be different from what it would be in another (say, a preparatory school). It is important to start with what falls into the 'must' category, and in physical education it would be wrong to suggest that this refers only to those matters concerned with the basic functioning of the individual. In all subjects it is important to consider whether there are forms of worth-while experience readily accessible through that subject but more difficult to procure by other means. Physical educationists have a particular case to make here. There are many ways in which physical education can be shown to make a powerful contribution to areas normally approached in other ways, but there is also an area peculiarly its own, an area in which children can sample a unique form of experience. How far the child will be led along these paths will, of course, depend on curricular decisions, the allocation of resources and the availability of suitably trained staff, but it is clear that what may have begun with an initial concern with the functioning of the organism can be developed in the cognitive, psycho-motor, aesthetic and moral areas.

Something of this is apparent in the replies given to Dr J. E. Kane[2] when he asked 888 secondary-school physical education teachers to rank in order of importance the objectives of physical education teaching. The list was:

motor skills
self-realization
leisure
emotional stability
moral development
social competence
organic development

209

cognitive development
aesthetic appreciation

One of the replies to the questions set by the Schools Council Whole Curriculum Working Party summarized the broad objectives of secondary-school physical education as:

1    Development of motor skills – general body management and specific athletic and expressional skills
2    Organic fitness – the development of optimal physiological functioning
3    Cognitive development – the acquisition of knowledge and the development of concepts concerning motor skills and organic fitness – the special contribution to learning
4    Social competence – the development of desirable social attitudes such as co-operation, fair play, responsibility and fitness consciousness
5    Emotional development – through opportunities to develop, for example, self-control, self-realization and self-projection
6    Aesthetic appreciation.

These valuable formulations see the middle years from the secondary-school standpoint and should be put alongside the following passage from the DES publication, *Movement: Physical Education in the Primary Years*:

Physical education, using movement as its medium of learning and expression, is an integral part of the education process. The peculiar power and appeal of movement rest in its immediacy and directness. Expression and action are possible without dependence on words or written symbols, and most children's response is refreshingly uninhibited.

Movement provides a two-way channel of learning, being both a way of finding out and a form of accomplishment. It may result from other experiences and learning situations, or it may lead into them. As an expressive art, it shares and reinforces the contribution of music, drama and the visual arts. It has close links with literature, science and mathematics, and a teacher should constantly be on the lookout for opportunities for children to use movement in its many different roles and connections.[3]

When considering the content of the curriculum several preliminary points should be kept in mind. Firstly, to quote the Schools Council Subject Committee's paper on physical education in the middle years, 'the years from 8 to 13 are those in which the development of physical skills makes a very strong appeal.' Secondly, as in all middle-years work, an important overall aim is to provide experiences sufficiently rewarding to keep the possibilities open for a child who wishes voluntarily to go on with work in that area of the curriculum. Thirdly, sex differences and individual differences in the 8 to 13 period are large. A wide variety of physical activities should be available, limitations as well as achievements should be recognized, and work should in consequence be such as to invite rather than compel participation.

The Schools Council Physical Education Committee, in the paper on physical education in the middle years produced for the project, stated:

> A carefully constructed and well-presented programme which gives these children plenty of opportunities for exploration and finding out, which helps them to acquire games and swimming skills and to discover movement qualities in gymnastics and dance, can do much to help them live full and enjoyable lives.

The DES in *Movement: Physical Education in the Primary Years*, while resisting any attempt to compartmentalize the subject, divided its treatment of the content into:

gymnastics
dance
games
swimming
athletics
outdoor activities.

The Schools Council Physical Education Committee placed special emphasis upon swimming; all boys and girls who cannot already swim at 8 should learn to do so during the middle years. The Committee also felt that gymnastics and dance were particularly powerful ways of providing a balanced programme of physical activity which also included scope for creative and imaginative expression. While there 'should certainly be no system of options which enables a child to escape participation in a balanced programme of activities', the Committee envisaged the possibility of a measure of choice between activities in any one area. For example, older pupils might be allowed to choose between different games skills. Further views of the Committee are summarized in the appendix to this chapter.

The share of resources called for by a fully developed physical education programme may at first sight seem to be large. A period a day, a longer period for games, substantial (though not necessarily exclusive) use of a large space, some specialist staff, showers, and so forth. If, however, the wider objectives which take physical education into every corner of the curriculum are met, such an allocation of resources can be justified – especially when seen in the context of the educational aims which flow from considering the implications for the future of the curriculum of today. To return to the 'must', 'should' and 'could' categorization – the greater the resources allocated to the subject, the more activities in the 'could' category have to be taken up. The effectiveness of the programme (and the return on the investment of resources) appears in the lives and attitudes of the children. At the conference reported in *Physical Education 8–13*, the then Vice-Chairman of the Schools Council Physical Education Committee, closed with a remark which may fittingly end this chapter. 'If children of 13 and 14 want to contract out of physical education there must be something wrong with their physical education. I am sure that our task is to see that when boys and girls pass out of the middle years they do so as lively and enthusiastic devotees of a way of life rather than a subject.'[4]

### References and notes

1. P. RENSHAW, 'Physical education: the need for philosophical clarification', *Education for Teaching* (Spring 1972), 60.
2. J. E. KANE, *Physical Education in Secondary Schools*, Schools Council Research Studies (Macmillan Education, 1974), p. 35.
3. Department of Education and Science, *Movement: Physical Education in the Primary Years* (HMSO, 1972), p. 8.
4. P. C. MCINTOSH, in Schools Council Working Paper 37, *Physical Education 8–13* (Evans/Methuen Educational, 1971), p. 34.

**Appendix**  Three views on physical education in the middle years of schooling

**I**    In January 1970 the Schools Council Physical Education Committee held a three-day conference at Avery Hill College, London. The members of the conference produced the following recommendations after discussing the issues raised by the speakers. The conference is reported in Schools Council Working Paper 37, *Physical Education 8–13* (Evans/Methuen Educational, 1971).

THE CURRICULUM

**1**    Educational gymnastics and educational dance should be the basis of indoor work for boys and girls.

212

2   The development of games-skills leading to small-side team games, thence to minor games, thence perhaps to modified versions of major games, should be the basis of outdoor work. The major sports might be selected (depending upon local conditions) from soccer, rugby, hockey, cross-country, athletics, tennis, and cricket for boys, and netball, hockey, lacrosse, tennis, and athletics for girls.

3   Swimming is an essential part of the curriculum. There is a danger, however, of post-proficiency swimming being over-emphasized to the detriment of other aspects of the curriculum. Sub-aqua or synchronized swimming should not be undertaken.

4   There should be no system of options during the middle years. This is a vital time for the development of basic skills and if they are not mastered at this stage most pupils will never acquire them.

5   All pupils must be given adequate opportunity to experience some sense of achievement. This seldom comes unless enough time is given for the activity to become reasonably familiar and for the pupils to feel secure. For this reason it is undesirable to undertake more activities than those in which it will be possible to reach a fairly high level of attainment.

6   Inter-school and inter-class games should generally be club activities. When played within the curriculum it is essential that non-team members should receive good teaching.

7   There must be freedom within the curriculum for teachers to concentrate on their own particular interest and expertise provided that a balance is kept over the middle-years span.

8   Events such as the 'Five-Star Award in Athletics' are valuable for older children. The individual competes against himself and learns to be responsible in such matters as timing and measuring.

9   Outdoor pursuits should be undertaken whenever practicable. These might be linked with environmental studies or organized as an out-of-school activity.

TIME ALLOCATION

1   Schools should aim at one period of PE per day or its equivalent. The weekly allocation can be blocked if longer games periods are required.

2   Serious consideration should be given to the amount of time set aside for games, particularly where extensive travel is involved. The wide variation in skill and maturation found in children of the same age means that year-games may be inappropriate.

3   The timetable should be sufficiently flexible to allow variations of time in good or bad weather.

213

1 The staff of any school catering for children between the ages of 8 and 13 should include a PE specialist or a teacher with a special interest in PE. In a primary or a middle school the specialist should be a class teacher, but should help with the planning and organization of the subject throughout the school. He should undertake some specialist teaching of PE with the oldest children where it is felt to be necessary, and should advise, help, and inspire other members of staff.

2 It is an advantage for class teachers to teach PE to their own classes wherever possible. The teachers will know their own children and be aware of the abilities, needs, and difficulties of the individual. The problems involved in the changing and showering of a mixed class will be minimized and the school timetable made more flexible. Links with other aspects of the curriculum will be made more easily.

3 Specialists in secondary schools or senior high schools can help their colleagues in primary or middle schools – and be helped themselves in return. Advisers and organizers should try to foster these links.

MIXED CLASSES

1 In mixed schools there should normally be mixed classes for PE. There may, however, be occasions when the oldest boys and girls should be separated – e.g. for educational gymnastics or games involving hard bodily contact. The tradition of the school, the facilities, the atmosphere, the number of staff will all affect the school's practice.

2 There is a need, however, for carefully assessed experiments with mixed classes. But these should only be undertaken where there is strong support from the staff and after consultation with LEA advisers or organizers.

FACILITIES

1 Most children reach their peak in physical co-ordination during the middle years of schooling. This is the time when basic skills can be acquired most readily. This is therefore the time when they have most need of a self-contained, purpose-built gymnasium.

2 Such a gymnasium, not less than 16 ft high and 2400 sq. ft in area, should be standard provision for any school where there are children between the ages of 8 and 13. It should have a suitable floor surface, be heated, well-lit, and might well be faced with a natural brick surface. It should have not

214

less than 200 sq. ft of storage space and shower and changing rooms for boys and girls. Changing and showering space for staff are also essential.

3    Limited use of a general-purpose hall will also be needed for dance and dance drama.

4    A larger space, of sports hall design, not less than 6000 sq. ft, could be an alternative to the gymnasium provided that the installation of equipment and a resilient clean floor can be assured.

5    Three acres of grass and one of an artificial hard, porous surface, such as Redgra are the minimum areas required for outdoor games by a middle school. The grass area would permit one soccer pitch (100 yd × 70 yd), one hockey pitch (100 yd × 70 yd), one small-side soccer pitch (70 yd × 40 yd) and one small-side hockey pitch (70 yd × 40 yd). A suitably placed blank wall for PE activities would also be available.

II    The Department of Education and Science publication, *Movement: Physical Education in the Primary Years* (HMSO, 1972), included the following short section on middle schools.

The setting up of middle schools has brought into prominence the necessity for good and varied facilities for older children in the 8–13 age range. These years span a period when a child's accomplishment in movement reaches a peak. It is a time of almost insatiable hunger for wide-ranging physical activity and skill. Facilities need to be in line with children's growing powers. A gymnasium with separate changing-rooms and showers is desirable in middle schools, although in many cases it will only be possible to provide it as a dual-purpose gymnasium/ hall. Children of 10 and 11 outgrow the typical primary-school hall and much of the apparatus provided in it. They, too, would benefit from the sterner challenge of a space more suitably equipped for gymnastics and from the availability of changing-rooms and shower-baths.

For all children of 10 to 13 there should also be facilities that allow the development of football, cricket, hockey, netball and tennis. In purpose-built middle schools, wherever it is practicable in relation to the number to be accommodated, the gymnasium/hall should be supplemented by a smaller space suitable for music and drama and some forms of movement.

Whilst it is the general view that a class teacher should be responsible for the greater part of a child's work in the lower age-groups of a middle school, it is probable that some degree of more specialized subject teaching, or, at least, responsibility for planning and co-ordination, is necessary for the physical education of older pupils. There are several advantages if the more specialized staff can combine the teaching of physical education with teaching in another broad,

215

related area of the curriculum. Any combination of subjects that allowed a teacher to spend a high proportion of time with one or two classes would be an asset, and there might be special value in combining with subjects such as literature, drama, music and science that have a natural link with some aspects of physical education.

In the later years of the middle school, separation of boys and girls for certain aspects of physical education may be considered necessary. Boys' and girls' interests in games and athletics may run in different directions or, where they are similar, the increasing speed and strength of the boys may indicate a need for separate teaching. Problems may arise in connection with changing and taking showers, or from the supervision of older children by teachers of the opposite sex. The most effective organization can only be decided in relation to the circumstances and staff within individual schools, although there is much to be said in favour of continuing some activities in mixed groups.

**III** The following summary of conclusions is taken from the paper prepared by the Schools Council Physical Education Committee for the project.

GROWTH AND DEVELOPMENT

1    Variations in development will be small at 8 and large at 13. Programme, facilities and equipment should therefore be extremely varied and versatile throughout the age-range.
2    Separate facilities for changing and showering for boys and for girls must be provided.
3    Pupils' changing attitudes to physical education activities call for especially sympathetic teaching and careful planning of the programme.

CONTENT OF THE CURRICULUM

4    Educational gymnastics and dance should be the core of physical education because they permit every variation of physique and aptitude to be catered for.
5    Exposure to a variety of basic skills is needed for all the younger pupils.
6    Older boys and girls will be introduced to some traditional games and sports.
7    If boys and girls cannot swim by the age of 8, special efforts should be made to teach them during the middle years.
8    It is desirable that some time within the curriculum should be devoted to physical education every day. The length of the period will vary with the activity on the programme.

216

9   Boys and girls should be separated for activities involving hard bodily contact or for those revealing an extreme disparity of skill. For a number of activities they could probably work together but further experiments are needed.

## FACILITIES

10  A fully equipped gymnasium designed and equipped for physical education exclusively is essential. Use of a hall will also be needed.

11  The playground should be marked and equipped for the greatest variety of activity.

12  A playing field for boys' and girls' summer and winter games and for athletics is needed. A hard porous surface may be more serviceable than grass.

13  A swimming pool should be available, either at the school or in the neighbourhood.

## PROFESSIONAL NEEDS OF TEACHERS

14  All teachers should have had a basic professional course including a study of growth and the mechanisms involved in the acquisition of physical skills.

15  Teachers who have had a specialist's course in physical education will be needed in middle schools to do some of the teaching, to direct the programme and to co-ordinate the work of other teachers who will help with different aspects of the work.

## LINKS WITH OTHER SUBJECTS

16  Links with other subject areas in the arts, the humanities and the sciences should be forged.

# XIV. Integrated studies

Integrated studies is clearly a curriculum concept, but difficulties arise when we seek for a more precise definition. In the context of the middle years a variety of interpretations seems possible and the term is frequently associated with, or used as a synonym for, team teaching, interdisciplinary studies or the integrated day. Educationists outside the schools have offered a number of different definitions for each of these, while educationists within the schools seem likely to use one or other of the terms to describe identical or very similar activities.

If the actual words 'integrated' and 'studies' are taken to have their common meanings, the term can legitimately be applied to any amalgamation of the parts or elements of the curriculum which had previously been regarded as separate entities, or to any new element introduced into the curriculum which has the effect of reducing the emphasis which was previously placed on the study of specific subjects. Such an open-ended definition means that at the practical teaching level there can be no precise lines drawn between what is or what is not representative of integrated studies, for much will depend on what the observer has taken the parts or elements of the curriculum to be. The term is frequently applied to subject linkages which have recently taken place within a school, but not to amalgamations which took place at some more distant time in the past. Thus a school which establishes a new relationship between physics, chemistry and biology is likely to describe the new course as being 'an integrated science course'. Though at one time it was not uncommon to find that arithmetic, algebra and geometry were separately timetabled and taught to 11-year-old children, few teachers are likely to describe their mathematics teaching today as coming within the category of integrated studies. Nor is English so regarded, although that too was once frequently timetabled under a number of separate headings.

A brief review of some of the types of work which the project team observed might form a useful background for a consideration of the value of such studies in the middle years but, since there are marked differences in the way the terms are used at the primary and secondary level, it is necessary to discuss them separately to start with. The antithesis of integrated studies seems to be the curriculum offered in a 'formal' secondary school where the first- and second-year pupils meet a team of single-subject teachers who have undertaken little, if any, co-operation over the planning of their courses. Each subject has a place on the timetable and is taught by a specialist teacher whose syllabus has not been devised in conjunction with any other. Such a situation is unique to the secondary schools and cannot be paralleled in a formal primary school, although at first sight the timetable, the basic class textbooks and the detailed syllabus for each subject may appear to be very similar. What makes such a marked difference is that the primary curriculum is likely to be implemented by class teachers who work with the same group of children teaching them the whole range of subjects. Even in the few primary schools where a bell is still rung to mark the end of each period, there is unlikely to be a changeover of form rooms or teachers; the break between lessons is seldom sharply defined. In the formal primary schools observed by the project team, the class teachers were aware of the nature of the whole curriculum and, although separate subjects were in the main separately taught, there were still numerous instances of interdisciplinary relationships. Art and craft lessons, for example, were often based on work done earlier in history, geography or religious education, and written English frequently involved the children in writing based on work done in other subjects.

Some secondary schools have recognized a weakness in a completely fragmented curriculum and have linked together several subject courses which were previously completely autonomous. Where such associations have not been carried to the level of complete amalgamation, it would seem more accurate to describe the work as being 'interdisciplinary studies' rather than 'integrated studies', although many of the people to whom we talked treat the terms as being synonymous. One fairly common example of these close relationships can be seen where a school has appointed a member of staff to be the head of the design department, and whose task it is to co-ordinate the work in art, pottery, home economics, woodwork and metalwork, and frequently to introduce other crafts. Another example is where a head of social studies is in a position to plan a programme involving help from other specialist teachers, the most obvious being teachers involved in teaching history, geography, science and religious education. Here there is likely to be close curriculum planning between the specialists, and although the work may be implemented as a series of major projects, topics or themes, the separate subject aspects of these studies will still be developed and taught by specialist teachers. For example, an environmentally based study may involve the geographer in dealing with local geology, land usage, map work, simple surveying and so on, while the historian develops aspects of local history, and the scientist plans to use field studies and other local observations. The social scientist may act as co-ordinator of the programme and will probably develop his own aspect of the project. At times other specialists may be involved, but it seems that this often depends more on the willingness of department heads to become involved than on the actual nature of the studies being undertaken. Specialist teachers are likely to be 'written into the programme' because they are sympathetic to the idea of co-operative studies,

219

while other colleagues may remain sceptical or feel that they have enough to do to cover their own syllabus without being involved in 'studies which don't seem to lead anywhere in our established pattern of education', to quote one critic.

From the observations carried out in a number of secondary schools it appears that these interdisciplinary studies always involve teachers in some form of team planning, although the majority do not often adopt a team-teaching method when implementing the plan. Co-operation tends to be before and after teaching, rather than during teaching. Once the curriculum has been planned, individual teachers work with specific groups of children within the framework of the existing school timetable. Blocked timetables and team teaching might be regarded as optional extras and not basic requirements of this way of working. The project team has not visited a secondary school where this type of inter-disciplinary approach occupies more than a minor part of curriculum time, or where it involves more than a minority of the subjects taught. Almost invariably the specialist departments in the school have 'safeguarded' their subject interests and ensured that there is, in addition to the time devoted to the project or topic work, a degree of autonomy for their own subject. Opinion seems divided as to whether this work is best done with middle-years children in the first and second years, or whether it should be left as a special option for the early school-leavers at the top of the school. Some claim that it provided a valuable introduction to specialist teaching for children transferring from primary schools, while other teachers feel that there is a need to introduce them to specific subject studies before venturing into the more integrated curriculum.

A somewhat different approach has been observed in secondary schools where members of the teaching staff have questioned the value of the compart-mentalized curriculum and are attempting to replace it by new studies. These new studies may take two distinct forms, one being the complete amalgamation of two or more existing subjects into a new unity, the other – which will be dis-cussed later – involving the introduction of new material regarded as being 'subject free'. An example of the subject amalgamation was observed in a school where the mathematics and science staff combined forces to create a new work-shop-based course for first- and second-year pupils. They produced a series of work cards or assignment cards designed to develop certain concepts, skills and techniques in mathematics and science and to present children with some basic factual knowledge. The work is biased towards experimental and problem-solving situations and is based on practical activities rather than on textbook learning. The children work individually or in small groups. They are also able to some extent to work at their own pace, for the separate periods once allocated to either mathematics or science have now been amalgamated to form longer blocks of time. This kind of approach is more 'integrated' than in the earlier examples described, and the teachers tend to put forward rather broader objectives, such as the development of self-discipline, children's acceptance of responsibility for planning their own pattern of work, and other social and ethical objectives which go beyond those usually specified for individual subjects. Integrated studies of this kind are not revolutionary, for they have clearly evolved from the subject-based curriculum and the work can be seen to involve much subject learning. However, the teachers frequently stress the importance they attach to the achievement of their broader objectives and this is perhaps the chief difference between them and their colleagues who adopt a subject approach. They have not made the changes simply to achieve better teaching of 'their subject' – although they may claim that this is to be expected – but chiefly because the teaching of those subjects in isolation did not seem to offer them the scope to achieve other objectives which they regard as of paramount importance in the middle years of schooling. Not uncommon are comments such as the following. 'Not many of these children will go on to become mathematicians or scientists but what they are learning here we regard as being important for their whole future way of life.' 'Of course the work that they are doing in English and religious education is important but we think that this new combined course has achieved much more in changing their attitudes toward learning. We see the new work as being very similar to the discovery approach followed by some of our contributory primary schools and we seem to be keeping alive the youngsters' freshness and spontaneity toward learning.'

There is another type of integrated study which might be regarded as being at the other polarity from the subject-based curriculum. Here there is, at least in intention, a plan to change the balance of the timetable by introducing a new approach, rather than by attempting an amalgamation or integration of what already exists. This new content may take various forms but would seem most often to be concerned with helping children to develop a sound understanding of themselves and of contemporary society in a way that its supporters feel is not possible when children are offered a series of courses in a number of subjects. Sir Richard Acland in *A Move to the Integrated Curriculum*,[1] sees much that is wrong with the situation where 'subjects are taught in hermetically sealed compartments', and claims that 'it is not enough to offer adolescents an understanding of many, or even of most, of the separate parts of life in the contemporary world, if they are left almost clueless when they are confronted by life as a whole.' This holistic view of the curriculum 'allows us to confront the whole [world] situation more calmly and, with luck, more creatively. It shows us, under the superficial chaos of the on-going cavalcade of news headlines, that there is an underlying purpose, or at any rate a direction of events, which can be accepted as meaningful and worth while.' The effect of this type of

221

integration on the first two years of secondary education is at present very slight, and would appear to be more talked about and perhaps advocated than actually practised.

Individual schools have developed courses in social studies which seem to fit into this category, and some of the newer programmes in religious education have been developed by teachers with a concern to introduce pupils to a consideration of major social problems, but such tentative steps do not seem to go as far in the direction of curriculum revolution as the extreme advocates would wish. A fairly typical comment was made by one teacher who said, 'At the moment I am restricted to three periods a week with the first-year children to teach what I believe to be important. This sort of integrated learning should involve almost all my colleagues for a major part of the working week. Over half of what they are at present teaching is knowledge which we were all once taught in schools but have now forgotten because it was irrelevant. They are too concerned with giving the children a socially acceptable background to a dozen subjects and, as a result, there is no time left to help them understand life as it is today in the real world outside school. It is an education based on the world as it once might have been, not as it is.'

So far we have briefly mentioned four 'types' of integration at the secondary level:

1  Separate subject courses are planned by individual specialists with little or no co-operation and the whole curriculum is taken to be the sum of these individual parts.

2  Specialists co-operate and develop at least a part of their subject courses by means of projects, topics or themes of an interdisciplinary nature. This calls for some new content or a major reorganization of the old content; it may also involve changes in methodology. Nevertheless, the specialists still teach their own subject, and although their work may be modified by the project approach, the subjects still retain their own identities.

3  Two or more subject courses have been combined to form a new single course, but one which still involves the pupils in learning some of the elements of the original disciplines or areas of knowledge (maths + science; history + geography + social studies + religious education; art + craft + home economics + woodwork + metalwork, etc.).

4  A 'new' content, designed to restyle the curriculum so that it offers children studies judged to have a greater relevance to life.

It is hardly necessary to state that few schools fit neatly into one or other of these categories, or that the outlined typology is incomplete. At present it seems that integrated studies is not a completely 'neutral' term but is frequently

222

associated with a liberal or progressive view of education. As a result, teachers tend to be either for or against such studies, although their expressed attitudes may be no guide to the actual practices to be observed in the schools where they teach. Thus one headmaster strongly rejected the concept of integrated studies, claiming that his school offered 'No more, but no less, than a sound old-fashioned grammar-school education.' However, his lower school was offering pupils more integrated learning experiences than some of the schools visited which claimed to hold integrated studies in high esteem. The pupils were certainly following a range of subject courses in the first two years, but one afternoon each week was devoted to activities mainly of an interdisciplinary nature, although they were described on the timetable as being 'clubs and societies' – other schools might well have described the work the children were doing as 'projects'. The children took part in field studies which were only subject-isolated on the timetable, and there were extremely good and close relationships between art, music, drama and English.

Integrated studies at the secondary level is frequently associated with team teaching and many writers fail to distinguish between the two. Lovell describes team teaching as being 'a form of teaching organization in which two or more teachers have the responsibility, working together, for all the teaching of a given group of pupils in some specified area of the curriculum.'[2] This definition, he points out, is similar to that given by Justin T. Shaplin in *Team Teaching*.[3] Thus team teaching may be defined as an *organizational* concept, while integrated studies is a *curriculum* concept. In the middle years of schooling the two exist independently of each other as well as being found linked together. In the majority of primary schools, for example, integrated studies when taught are in the hands of the class teacher not a team of teachers. The project team also observed some examples of a specific subject being taught by a teaching team at the secondary level. One involved a team of teachers taking English and the humanities with a first-year intake, another was a team undertaking a new course in religious education under the direction of a team leader who took a series of core lessons, and in a third school some aspects of mathematics were taught by the head of department with his colleagues implementing the follow-up programme. One of the advantages claimed for team teaching is that it enables a school to make the maximum use of the key teachers and thus increase the efficiency of the teaching. The claims for integrated studies are somewhat different and lie in the direction of making the learning more relevant to the children's concerns and interests, more meaningful and less fragmented.

The pattern of integrated studies at the primary level is more varied and is also applied to a greater variety of practices. A primary class is likely to have certain facilities in limited supply – a single small cooker, for example, a limited

223

space where clay can be used, one carpenter's bench and a few tools, a painting area, a space for science and mathematics and a quiet reading area. It would be extremely difficult to provide sufficient facilities for whole primary classes to be able to work together on their cooking, carpentry and so on, even if this were thought to be desirable. The schools tend to make a virtue of the necessity and individuals or small groups are likely to be involved in a range of curriculum activities simultaneously, some painting, some reading, some model-making, some doing mathematics or writing stories. This simultaneous implementation of the whole (or most) of the curriculum is frequently described as integrated studies or the integrated day. Certainly a first impression of a class busily engaged on such a range of activities tends to support the claim, but a closer investigation often reveals that the bulk of the activities are quite capable of being classified under a traditional list of subject headings and the approach to the curriculum might more accurately be described as simultaneous group or individual activities covering the range of curriculum studies, carried out in the main without reference to time.

Some schools adopt a major project or theme which is followed by all the classes in the school. These may last for as short a period as one week or be extended for the length of a whole term. The project titles tend to be in the form of global headings such as 'Spaceship Earth', 'Our town past and present' or 'The sea'. The project is likely to be introduced to the whole school by the head, and teachers later discuss with their own class some of the ways in which the project might be developed. The amount of time spent on such activities varies from class to class, from project to project, and indeed from school to school. Occasionally several whole days may be devoted to a project as it nears a climax, but it is rare for such work to occupy a dominant place in the curriculum. Within each class there would also appear to be considerable differences in the degree of involvement shown by different children. The general aim seems to be to ensure that individuals and groups obtain as broad a concept of the scope of the project as possible and this generally means that their studies involve aspects of mathematics, English, history, geography, science, art, craft – in fact the range of normal curriculum studies. Projects tend to end with an exhibition, festival or other celebration to which guests are likely to be invited. In more recent times it would seem that this form of integrated study may be developing its own form of specialist teaching, for some schools have found that individual teachers have different interests and enthusiasms and children are offered the chance of joining a particular teacher who would develop a specific aspect of the project with them, perhaps through drama, history, art and craft, etc. This brings the work more in line with interdisciplinary studies than was originally the case. Other schools have recognized a weakness in a form of organization which expects one teacher

224

to keep abreast of developments across the whole range of the curriculum. They have adopted a form of year-grouping of teachers and three or four colleagues share the responsibility for the implementation of the curriculum. However integrated the work may be, the project team has not visited a school where, for example, physical education, games and swimming do not exist as clearly identifiable parts of the curriculum. The arts and crafts can be seen to exist, children will make music, undertake work in mathematics and certainly be encouraged to read for pleasure and information. It is not uncommon to find that they also participate in aspects of scientific inquiry and social or environmental studies, work which, outside the 'integrated ethos', would be regarded as geographical, historical or moral/ethical/religious studies.

It would seem that the general informal approach to education adopted by such schools tends to overshadow the degree to which children's learning does, nevertheless, fall predominantly into subject categories. The class is not likely to follow a set textbook in any specific subject, but they will almost certainly make reference to many books which cover a specialist topic. Furthermore, an examination of the projects undertaken by the children shows that few of them could really be regarded as completely subject-neutral. What does seem to be different is that their studies may range well beyond the scope of what has normally been regarded as the elementary junior curriculum in some aspects of their work but it may well not cover some of the traditional content. Also the methodology and organization of the school is likely to be quite different from the pattern of learning common to the formal, subject-based curriculum.

Although a precise definition of integrated studies appears impossible, it is somewhat easier to make positive statements about why some form of integration seems desirable in the middle years. Firstly such studies seem likely to be relevant, appealing and interesting to young children and more likely to demonstrate to them that education is a worth-while activity worthy of their full co-operation. Although specialization has intensified at an older level, the development of education with young children has been gradually towards forms of integration – set lessons for dictation, spelling, grammar, essay writing and so on are now almost universally subsumed under the more general teaching of English. The Plowden Report, *Children and their Primary Schools*,[4] stressed that 'children's learning does not fit into subject categories' and the Newsom Report, *Half Our Future*,[5] thought that 'for our least able pupils, subjects hardly come into the fields of possibility; for the better ones there is often no compelling reason why one should be chosen rather than another.' Subject teaching was obviously an efficient way of organizing the curriculum when educationists accepted a clearly defined body of knowledge which children needed to know. With the current emphasis on a multiplicity of objectives for middle-years education, it seems doubtful, to say the least, whether these are best achieved by means of a completely subject-based curriculum, although 'some objectives can readily be identified with the aims of certain aspects of the curriculum, or indeed more narrowly with those of "subjects". But many concepts, skills and attitudes can be fostered through several elements of the traditional curriculum.'[6] In an earlier reference, Sir Richard Acland was quoted as striving for a curriculum which showed an 'underlying purpose, or at any rate a direction of events, which can be accepted as meaningful and worth while.' J. M. Parry[7] claims that 'it is arguable that the fundamental malaise in the whole secondary programme lies deeper than the infelicities of any particular subject; it may arise because the pupils increasingly fail to see the relevance of much they are taught. Implicit in the curriculum of our secondary schools is the assumption that, for each pupil, out of the study of many subject disciplines there will gradually emerge a coherent unified view of human knowledge which will allow us to describe the pupil as developing into an "educated" or "cultured" human being . . . In fact, it requires an able and unusually independent-minded pupil to achieve this synthesis and this is done despite rather than because of early subject specialisation.' There is also a strong argument based on the observation of children. Any teacher who takes a group of youngsters to explore a pond or to visit an historic building knows full well that the learning cannot be compartmentalized; one is not pure nature study and the other unadulterated history. Now that teachers talk with children and not simply at them, there is a two-way flow of conversation and however subject-centred the teacher's approach may be, the children's discussion will soon cut across these boundaries – and not with the intentional 'red herrings' which adults may remember dragging across the path of unwary teachers in the past. It seems natural to suggest that children who have observed in the aquarium the *Ditiscus marginalis* rising backside upwards to breathe prior to making a feast of some of the other inhabitants might well find this more interesting to write about than some other arbitrarily set essay title. Life in the middle years of schooling is likely to offer an enormous range of similar everyday events from which, as Christian Schiller once said, 'children learn that which they knew not and grow to be that which they were not'. Such an approach to the curriculum carries no greater guarantee of success than any other. In the hands of an unskilled practitioner it might even prove to be more disjointed, random and haphazard than any compartmentalized curriculum of the past. However, in the control of a teacher who has established clear priorities, there is evidence in the schools to show that children will respond with enthusiasm. There is also sufficient evidence to show that such an approach is in no way linked with a decline in the basic standards of achievement.

## References and notes

1. SIR RICHARD ACLAND, *A Move to the Integrated Curriculum*, Themes in Education No. 7 (University of Exeter, Institute of Education, 1967).
2. K. LOVELL, 'Team teaching', *Trends in Education* No. 5 (January 1967), 26.
3. JUSTIN T. SHAPLIN and HENRY F. OLDS JR., *Team Teaching* (Harper & Row, 1964).
4. Advisory Council for Education (England), *Children and their Primary Schools* (HMSO, 1967), Vol. 1.
5. Advisory Council for Education (England), *Half Our Future* (HMSO, 1963).
6. Department of Education and Science, *Towards the Middle School*, Education Pamphlet No. 57 (HMSO, 1970), p. 12.
7. J. M. PARRY, 'Framework for the first form', *Trends in Education*, No. 11 (July 1968), 3–4.

# XV. The middle years of schooling

We end this report by reiterating a point we made at the start of our first report (Schools Council Working Paper 42, *Education in the Middle Years*, published by Evans/Methuen Educational in 1972). The Schools Council in sponsoring a project on the middle years of schooling did not thereby make any statement about the desirability or otherwise of developing a three-tier system of educational organization with a middle school as the second stage. Though the task of creating a curriculum for a middle school has undoubtedly presented many teachers with a special opportunity for thinking through a curriculum for children in the 8 to 13 age range, studies on the middle-years curriculum must be regarded as being as relevant to upper primary and lower secondary as to middle-school work. We have earlier made a plea for seeing the first two secondary years as part of a single span of the curriculum which springs out of the middle primary-school period and bridges the gap which too often separates the work of the primary school from that of the secondary school. Though there is a steadily increasing number of middle schools, for the majority of our children there will be a break at the age of 11. If the curriculum on either side of the divide is seen as a single phase it may perhaps be easier to avoid some of the problems of transfer already mentioned. To devise such a spanning curriculum teachers will be required to make much greater efforts than before to ensure that there is co-operation, discussion, agreement and understanding. It may be that such discussions will be more fruitful if held on the neutral ground of a teachers' centre but they are the prelude only to a more positive involvement in each other's work. There is really no substitute for the 'day-release' of the teacher from one school to work in another, and the greater number of supply teachers now available makes this a feasible undertaking. Children too must, where possible, interchange and the facilities of each school should be regarded as available to all so that the task of helping children 'to learn how to learn' can be carried through from 8 to 13 as a single undertaking. Where a middle-school system exists the same problems must be solved at 8 to 9 and 12 to 13, for there are now two transfer points not one. Since the Plowden Report, *Children and their Primary Schools* (HMSO, 1967), it has been legitimate to ask any school, 'What is your programme for ensuring positive contact with as many parents as possible especially those who are less likely to attend social functions?' It is now legitimate to say to all schools in any area, 'What is your programme of positive measures designed to procure the continuity of education of the children served

228

by your schools?' There could be few better starting points than discussion of the principles upon which the education of middle-years children might be based.

There is a further aspect of inter-school co-operation, which can be developed under the title 'diagnosis'. As presented in this report, and in Working Paper 42, the middle years are years in which children are encouraged to develop and to practise the skills of learning in order that these skills may be attached to the more precise (and possibly vocational) targets which appear next in the *curriculum vitae*. For the secondary school, the age of 16 is a turning-point; children leave with or without having taken a public examination and some decide to go further in the system of formal education. A three-year run-up to this turning-point is probably the shortest that most schools would find convenient. It follows that the middle years, while exploring the full range of skills, will have seen strengths, aptitudes and weaknesses appear. Clearly those responsible for the middle years must incorporate some element of diagnosis in the programme so that the grouping and setting which follows can be done on the basis, not of a single test or assessment, but of a record of the dynamic of a child's development through those formative middle years.

This study of the curriculum in the middle years has been conducted by going back to the principles which may today be regarded as informing an approach to education in keeping with the demands of the changed world about us. Similar questioning of the basis of our educational judgements appears also in the raising of the school-leaving age programme and in the report of the Schools Council's Working Party on the Whole Curriculum (published as Working Paper 53, *The Whole Curriculum 13–16* by Evans/Methuen Educational, 1975). These are only probes which will lead in due course to a reformulation of the aims of our educational system. Meanwhile the pace of development will be necessarily uneven from sector to sector and place to place, and there is the risk of a degree of discontinuity and a lack of coherence. For example, some of the approaches discussed in this report do not lead smoothly into a traditional O-level course. It is nevertheless an important principle that teachers should assess what they decide to teach instead of teaching what they think will be assessed, and if the changes now occurring in middle-years education are seen to be valid and apt for their purpose then it is the assessment which should be altered. Fortunately work is also being done on examinations at 16+ and present discontinuities may not therefore persist. Meanwhile the compromises and adjustments designed to ensure that children continue to progress are possible and teachers will, as always, find ways of ensuring that change, when judged to be necessary, can occur without damaging the prospects of the children. This is not to say that there will be no problems or tensions. These are perhaps seen

229

most clearly in the case of middle schools created from existing schools. Staff appointed to do one kind of job are asked to undertake another. Hard-won skills are declared redundant and acccumulated practical knowledge is found to be superfluous. New skills and new approaches are required and what might be called the pedagogical life-style is changed almost overnight. Obviously such alterations can be eased if there is adequate preparation in the form of in-service education and careful planning of career development, in the sense of seeking as far as possible to ensure that somewhere in the teaching service of an employing authority a place can be found to suit the skills of a particular teacher. Professional associations may be relied on to ensure that all their members are properly protected when reorganizations or substantial changes of direction take place. It is clear, however, that the teacher has to fit the pattern of learning judged to be best suited to the children's learning and not vice versa. Readers of these reports will already be sensitized to the overtones of the word 'judged' and will immediately ask who makes the judgement. Increasingly curricular judgements of this kind are shared and though the head is ultimately responsible and must make the decisions, in practice a small advisory group assists him. It may be that employing authorities should take more care about the precise wording used in letters of appointments; protection of status and emoluments must never imply that curricular development can be frustrated by firm adherence to a job description later judged to be outmoded. It should perhaps be added that the points raised here are largely the authors' comment on questions repeatedly raised at meetings with teachers. They do not represent the view of the Schools Council and are mentioned here because, though peripheral to the main focus of the project, they do undoubtedly enter into the minds of those who have to plan the curriculum for middle-years children.

Another issue – teacher training – which is at first sight peripheral does undoubtedly affect the shaping of the curriculum. The staff available at any one time represent a finite number of skills and possible curriculum content. In the matter of skills there is perhaps too great a contrast at the moment between the typical primary-school skills and those we associate with secondary schools. No doubt a more or less distinctive middle-years style will emerge in due course and will in turn have its impact upon the world of teacher training. A training aimed at a middle-years approach will be particularly useful since it will put its fortunate possessor in the position of being able to move one way or the other. In terms of content the problems are rather greater because of the bias in our school and higher-education system towards single-subject specialization. In middle-years education, the call for 'semi-specialists' is really for generalists with several semi-specialist strings to their teaching bow. Some colleges are beginning to produce courses designed to meet this need. There are courses in which the

230

traditional main and subsidiary subjects have been replaced by an applied education course consisting of six modules drawn from a list comprising all the main teaching subjects in primary and middle schools. A middle-years teacher offering a semi-specialism must certainly know more of the subject than is assumed in the so-called 'curriculum' courses. There must be a sufficient grasp of the structure of the subject to enable the teacher to see the relationship of the work being done at the age of 8, at 10 and at 12, to the subject as it is presented at age 14, at 16 and at 18. If personal performance in the subject can be taken to the 18-years-old level, and if at the same time the pedagogical aspects are developed, there is no reason to assume that the work cannot be intellectually demanding, personally satisfying and at the same time professionally relevant.

There is one further peripheral consideration. Much of what has been written in these reports has implications with regard to resources, human and material. The approach through a carefully ordered sequence of prepared learning materials undoubtedly increases the demands being made upon teachers. These increases in responsibility and work-load must be met in part by providing a support system (including sub-professional personnel) many times more expensive than anything so far provided. Team teaching may not be required (though co-operative teaching will certainly emerge) but much of the infrastructure of team teaching (resource centres, clerical assistance, reprographic services, etc.) is undoubtedly needed. It would not be appropriate to develop this point further here but it is one which constantly recurs in discussions on education in the middle years.

The traditional hierarchies of school systems may not fit institutions which emphasize the process rather than the content of learning and which take as their goal breadth rather than specialization. The usual pattern of above-scale posts is not particularly apt for middle-school organization, and in secondary schools which have set up heads of lower school or similar co-ordinating tutors the relationship between these and subject heads is not always clear. These decisions can rarely be taken without consideration of other factors, but if the problem were limited to what would be best for middle-years children the balance would lie in favour of giving the higher priority to the teacher charged with the overview. This is a reflection of the point of view put forward here that the subject is to be seen in terms of the contribution it is able to make rather than in terms of what the child can do for and with the subject. Year-group leaders are one form of co-ordinating tutors though not all schools would wish to divide the children into year groups. Another is to appoint tutors with an overview of an area of the curriculum – for example, aesthetics, the moral area, the basic skills, and so on. These teachers would have a particular expertise in one part of the area but would also have the duty of assisting the other members of the group to

231

co-ordinate their activities and perhaps to develop a form of team teaching. The advice of such teachers would be on offer rather than proffered, though there would nevertheless be a measure of responsibility to the head to keep the area under review, to be active in developments in the area and to assist the members of that team to develop themselves professionally.

When the curricular choices have been made, the resources mustered and the curriculum deployed, there remains the task of evaluation, review and recycling. In some areas precise measuring instruments are available. So important is the skill of reading, for example, that it would be irresponsible not to carry out systematic checks on the ability to read and to comprehend. Obviously the question to be asked is not 'Can they or can't they?' but 'What is their quotient: (a) in relation to the norm for their age; (b) in relation to their previous scores?' The advancement of skill, the development of attitudes and sensitivities, the maturing of behaviours is to be looked for. If the work being done at age 12 cannot be distinguished from that being done at 8 or at 10, the school has failed to make sure that the middle years are also the growing years. Even though – for example, in developing the imagination and sensitivities to language – it is not possible to have bench marks of the kind provided by reading quotients, scores on concept development tests and other objective measures, the evaluation should always seek for indications of that advancement in learning which the wise and caring teacher will look for in these years.

The review of progress should also look at the results of earlier curricular decisions. If, for example, the school has decided in the empirical area to use the approach through home economics rather than social studies, it is legitimate to ask how far the objectives which would have been set for a course in social studies have been met in the home economics course. How far has the approach through the family, typical of work in home economics, broadened out to include some treatment of those larger macro-sociological ideas (such as class, race, demography) which would have formed the centrepieces of a social studies approach? If, to take another example, history has not been included but social studies has, how far has the historical heritage been 'picked up' in literature, social studies, art and other studies? The chosen subject is being looked at here less for what it offers in itself and more for the extent to which it provides experience in subjects not directly tackled in the curriculum.

Reviews of this kind should look forward as well as back. What has been the effect of the curricular decisions taken previously? What evidence is there in the work of the older pupils that they have progressed in the way intended? Should the programme be altered? What new objectives can be set? How have the children fared in their next school? Teachers have always thought about, and from time to time discussed, questions such as these. It may perhaps be appro-

232

priate to formalize such discussions and there is a case for regarding day conferences of the teaching staff of a school as a normal part of the school year.

We end as we began. There are many things that could be done and the teacher owes it to herself as a professional person and to the children whose lives are being shaped to consider carefully the criteria by which one activity is chosen and another rejected. It is also necessary to repeat the exercise from time to time as ever-changing patterns of living alter the criteria. And if the problem seems to be unduly difficult it may be remembered that Aristotle too (*Politics*, viii, 2, 4–5) found it far from straightforward: 'There is no doubt that such useful subjects as are really necessary ought to be taught [to children]. But this does not mean the inclusion of every useful subject.'

# Appendix

Checklist of Schools Council projects
concerned with the middle years of schooling*

**English**

English in the Middle Years of Schooling (8–13)
Director, Bernard Newsome, Goldsmiths' College,
University of London
1970–72

Language Development in the Primary School (5–11)
Director, Connie Rosen, Goldsmiths' College,
University of London
1969–71

Extending Beginning Reading (7–9)
Director, Vera Southgate Booth, School of Education,
University of Manchester
1973–76

English for Immigrant Children (5–16)
Organizer, June Derrick, Institute of Education,
University of Leeds
1966–71

Teaching English to West Indian Children (7–9)
Directors, James White (1967–72) and F. J. Worsley (1972–73),
School of Education,
University of Birmingham
1967–73

Question and Response by Children in School (8–16)
Director, Dr W. P. Robinson, Department of Psychology,
University of Southampton
1968–73

* Up-to-date information on the work and output of all Schools Council projects is
available from the Schools Council Project Information Centre, 160 Great Portland
Street, London W1N 6LL.

Children's Reading Habits (10–16)
Director, F. S. Whitehead, Institute of Education,
University of Sheffield
1969–74

The Effective Use of Reading (10–14)
Directors, Professor E. A. Lunzer and W. K. Gardner, School of Education,
University of Nottingham
1973–76

## Humanities

Religious Education in the Primary School (5–11)
Director, Clifford M. Jones, Institute of Education,
University of Leeds
1969–71

Religious Education in Primary Schools: Development Project (5–11)
Director, Professor Ninian Smart; Deputy Director, Donald Horder,
Department of Religious Studies,
University of Lancaster
1973–76

Environmental Studies (5–13)
Director, Melville Harris, Cartrefle College of Education,
Wrexham, Denbighshire
1967–71

Social Studies 8–13
Director, Dr Denis Lawton, Institute of Education,
University of London
1968–70

Project Environment (8–18)
Director, R. W. Colton; Deputy Director, R. F. Morgan,
Department of Education,
The University, Newcastle upon Tyne
1970–73

History, Geography and Social Science 8–13
Honorary Director, Professor W. A. L. Blyth; Associate Director, R. Derricott,
School of Education,
University of Liverpool
1971–75

Moral Education 8–13
Director, Peter McPhail; Deputy Director, J. Ungoed-Thomas,
Hughes Hall, University of Cambridge
1972–76

Integrated Studies Project (11–15)
Director, David Bolam; Deputy Director, D. Jenkins,
Institute of Education, University of Keele
1968–72

Religious Education in Secondary Schools (11–16)
Director, Professor Ninian Smart; Deputy Director, Donald Horder,
Department of Religious Studies,
University of Lancaster
1969–73

## Languages

Evaluation of the French Pilot Scheme (8–16)
Senior Research Officer, Clare Burstall,
National Foundation for Educational Research,
Slough, Berks
1964–74

Cambridge School Classics Project (11–16)
Director, D. J. Morton, Cambridge University
1966–78
(See page 207, note 12)

Modern Languages Project (8–16)
Director, D. Rix (from January 1973),
University of York
1963–75

## Creative studies

Art and Craft Education 8–13
Directors, Audrey Martin, Dr Renée Marcousé and Michael Laxton,
Goldsmiths' College,
University of London
1969–72

Music Education for Young Children (3–11)
Director, Dr A. Bentley; Deputy Director, Iain Kendell,
School of Education, University of Reading
1970–76


**Science**

Science 5–13
Director, L. F. Ennever, School of Education,
University of Bristol
1967–74

Progress in Learning Science (5–13)
Director, Dr Wynne Harlen, School of Education,
University of Reading
1973–76

Development of Scientific and Mathematical Concepts (7–12)
Director, Dr J. Rogers; Adviser, E. Rothwell Hughes,
University College of North Wales, Bangor
1968–73

Nuffield Combined Science (11–13)
Director, M. J. Elwell, City of Birmingham College of Education
1965–69


**Mathematics**

Nuffield Mathematics (5–13)
Organizer, Professor G. Matthews,
Nuffield Foundation
1964–71

Nuffield Mathematics: Development of Individual Assessment Tests (5–13)
Director, Dr L. Pauli, Institut des Sciences de l'Education,
Geneva
1966–70

Primary School Mathematics: Evaluation Studies (5–11)
Director, Professor J. Wrigley, Schools Council
1972–75

## Interrelated studies

Education for a Multiracial Society (5–13)
Director, June Derrick, National Foundation for Educational Research,
Slough, Berks
1972–76

Health Education 5–13
Director, Trefor Williams, St Osyth's College of Education,
Clacton-on-Sea, Essex
1973–76

Home Economics in the Middle Years (8–13)
Director, V. G. Hutchinson, F. L. Calder College of Education,
Liverpool
1975–78

## Special education

Language Development for Deaf Pupils (8–12)
Director, Dr D. C. Wollman, HMI, Centre for Educational Technology,
University of Sussex, Brighton
1973–76

## Welsh

Science and Mathematics in Welsh Medium Schools (5–12)
Director, M. Griffiths, Faculty of Education,
University College of Wales, Aberystwyth
1969–72

The Teaching and Learning of English in Wales (8–13)
Director, D. W. H. Sharp, Department of Education,
University College of Swansea
1973–76

## Organization

Resource Centres (9–18)
Research Officer, Norman Beswick, Institute of Education Library,
University of London
1970–73

238

# Project team and consultative committee

## Project team

Professor Alec M. Ross
(Director)

A. G. Razzell
(Senior Project Officer)
1969–72

E. H. Badcock
1969–72

D. B. Daniels
1969–71

Miss Irene Farmer
1968–69

J. Islip
1970–73

## Consultative committee

| | |
|---|---|
| Sir Lincoln Ralphs (Chairman) | Chief Education Officer, Norfolk*; Chairman, Schools Council 1972–75 |
| Miss M. F. M. Bailey | Headmistress, Skerton Girls' County Secondary School, Lancaster;* formerly member of the Plowden Committee |
| J. W. G. Boucher | Headmaster, Thames Primary School, Blackpool; formerly member of the Nuffield Primary Mathematics Project |
| Miss C. H. Braund | Bournemouth School for Girls (Schools Council Steering Committee A) |
| J. Coe | Senior Adviser to Schools, Oxfordshire; formerly County Council Inspector, West Riding of Yorkshire |
| L. J. Cowee | Inspector of Primary Schools, Surrey Education Committee |
| Miss S. M. C. Duncan | HM Inspectorate,* formerly member of the Plowden Committee |

* Now retired.

| | |
|---|---|
| Dr J. Garner (until August 1972) | Department of Educational Research, University of Lancaster |
| J. S. Nicholson | Headmaster, Delf Hill Middle School, Bradford* |
| J. C. D. Rainbow | Deputy Education Officer, Lancashire County Council† |
| R. Selby | County Council Inspector, West Riding of Yorkshire |
| T. A. Sparrow | Headmaster, Bethune School, Kingston upon Hull (Schools Council Steering Committee A) |
| N. Thomas (co-opted November 1969) | HM Inspectorate |

* Now retired.
† Chief Education Officer from April 1974.

## Acknowledgements

Extracts from *Geography in Primary Schools* (Geographical Association, 1970) are reproduced by permission of the Geographical Association; and from the Department of Education and Science, *Movement: Physical Education in the Primary Years* (HMSO, 1972) by permission of the Controller of HM Stationery Office.